TWAYNE'S WORLD AUTHORS SERIES

A Survey of the World's Literature

Sylvia E. Bowman, Indiana University

GENERAL EDITOR

JAPAN

Roy E. Teele, Southwestern University

EDITOR

Natsume Soseki

(*TWAS 99*)

TWAYNE'S WORLD AUTHORS SERIES (TWAS)

*The purpose of TWAS is to survey the major writers
—novelists, dramatists, historians, poets, philosophers,
and critics—of the nations of the world. Among the
national literatures covered are those of Australia,
Canada, China, Eastern Europe, France, Germany,
Greece, India, Italy, Japan, Latin America, New Zea-
land, Poland, Russia, Scandinavia, Spain, and the
African nations, as well as Hebrew, Yiddish, and
Latin Classical literatures. This survey is comple-
mented by Twayne's United States Authors Series
and English Authors Series.*

*The intent of each volume in these series is to present
a critical-analytical study of the works of the writer;
to include biographical and historical material that
may be necessary for understanding, appreciation,
and critical appraisal of the writer; and to present all
material in clear, concise English—but not to vitiate
the scholarly content of the work by doing so.*

Natsume Soseki

By BEONGCHEON YU

Wayne State University

Twayne Publishers, Inc.   ::   New York

895.6
N279Y

Preface

ASK the Japanese whom they regard as a novelist representative of modern Japanese literature. Nine out of ten will name Natsume Soseki (1867–1916), regardless of their personal biases. If it is difficult to discuss Soseki separately from modern Japanese literature, it would be inconceivable to deal with the history of Japanese literature as a whole without referring to him. Indeed, Soseki is generally accepted not only as one of the most important writers of modern Japan, but as one of her truly "national" writers. Although his works are regarded as modern classics in Japan, his name and works are known outside Japan only to a handful of specialists. True, some of his works have been translated into various Western languages, but they have as yet failed to find either a significant number of readers or any appreciable response from critics. Considering his unquestionably high status in his own country, this is certainly a strange phenomenon, especially when more recent Japanese writers enjoy both a wide circle of readers and critical acclaim outside their native land. Is this because Soseki is, as often suggested, the kind of writer who loses much in translation?

I refuse to accept this theory as true. Soseki, rightly understood, should be able to claim his place in the literature of the world. To many readers a straight biography would seem the logical approach. Under the present circumstances, however, I have adopted a somewhat different one. There are in Japan, already many, perhaps too many biographical studies, including Professor Komiya's three-volume definitive study, to which all Soseki students must constantly refer, either for agreement or for disagreement. At least to me, to write just another biography seems altogether meaningless. But this is not my only reason; a supporting consideration lies in the fact that Soseki the artist was a late starter, all of his works being produced during the last decade of his fifty-year career. Professor Komiya's treatment of Soseki's art does not even begin until the middle of the second volume. Addressing a Western audience familiar with neither Soseki nor the complex situation of modern Japanese literature, I can take nothing for granted. After much deliberation I have set the following course: in the introductory chapter I shall give an account of both Meiji literature and Soseki's career up to his debut as a novelist, so that the reader may attain some notion of the intellectual and cultural milieu in which Soseki lived. The next five chapters are, in the main, chronologically ordered, grouping works, when necessary, according to their thematic and structural development. Within each group I shall deal with individual works, first relating them to their predecessors, summarizing their plots, and then discussing their themes and techniques. In the concluding chapter I shall relate Soseki's art to his life, consider the significance of his achievement, and attempt to determine his position in Japanese and world literature.

In modern Japanese literature, no other writer has been written about as much as Soseki. Already there is a library of books about him, and every year sees new additions. One reason lies in Soseki's many-sidedness: besides being a novelist, he was a writer of short stories and sketches, of many letters, and of diaries and fragments; he was a conversationalist of wide repute and a gifted lecturer. Moreover, he was an essayist, a critic, a *haiku* poet, a painter, and a brilliant scholar. (The complete works of Soseki in the recent Iwanami edition consist of thirty-four volumes.) The present study treats Soseki exclusively as a novelist both because this is the way Soseki personally wished to be considered and because as a novelist, Soseki was able to integrate all his gifts, without succumbing to their separate lures. As my general plan should indicate, I am in this study primarily concerned with a critical examination of his novels, first individually, secondly in groups, and finally in their entirety.

At the same time I shall stress three other points which scholars have not sufficiently explored. First is the significance of Soseki's belated debut as the first professional novelist in modern Japan— after the tortuous beginnings which might have led to almost any other career: he could have been a *haiku* poet of high quality, or an eminent scholar, or even a great dilettante, if he had wished. In spite of such choices, even in spite of his personal tastes, he chose the hardest, but nevertheless one of the most rewarding, of them: the career of a professional novelist in Meiji Japan. Second is the significance of his contribution to the development of Japanese literature. It was Soseki who helped elevate Japanese fiction as art and who gave intellectual substance to it. Third is the significance of Soseki as an exemplary case of the impact of Western literature on the creative spirit of modern Japan and the Orient. Soseki was, as Professor Saito said, "probably the greatest student of English literature" of Japan when he forsook the known rewards of an academic career for the uncertainties of a novelist's at that particular time in Japanese literary history. Although some critics seem to regret Soseki's decision, it must be pointed out that he was able to make the most of his scholarship to enrich his own art. He once described his brain as half-Japanese and half-Western, producing an art symbolic of the fertile union of the West and Japan (and the East in general), as Okazaki Yoshie pointed out in his *Japanese Literature in the Meiji Era.* But for his background in Western literature, Soseki's art would have been vastly different from what it is. On the other hand, Professor Keene recently observed: "Natsume's works still delight Japanese, largely because of his beautiful style, but a Western reader may find the oriental calm achieved by Natsume to be at times insufficiently engrossing." Remembering Okazaki's verdict along with Professor Keene's warning, I wish to examine Soseki's art in terms of world literature, and explore the means of facilitating the Western reader's reponse to his works, hoping thereby that my study may make a valid contribution to the existing body of Soseki studies.

In the last few decades Japan has come to occupy an eminent place in the growing understanding between East and West. Popular and scholarly studies have done much toward introducing many aspects of Japanese culture. Japan has certainly turned out to be an inexhaustible hunting ground for social scientists, but somehow or other, her literature has not yet attracted this universal favor. Although our market is just beginning to be flooded by translations of some more recent Japanese writers, it will obviously be some considerable time before even the most glaring deficiencies can be remedied. Literature must come out of the hands of those few specialists; it must not be treated as an exotic landscape, because any national literature, by its own nature, tends to be part of the world at large. And it must, first of all, be treated as an art which knows no racial, national, or cultural boundary. Although such a stage is still too far off, I hope for the time being that this study will in some way help make Soseki part of the world of letters. Toward the end of his career, Soseki replied to one of his friends who sought to bring out an American edition of his work: "Sorry. There is none of my works I wish to be read by Americans." By this study, I hope to prove that Soseki was wrong.

An Explanatory Note

The text for the present study is the Iwanami edition of 1956–59, *Soseki Zenshu* (*The Complete Works of Soseki*), 34 vols., edited by Komiya Toyotaka. All translations cited are my own.

Japanese names appear in the Japanese order, family name first. For instance, Natsume Kinnosuke, rather than Kinnosuke Natsume.

Throughout this study, various types of diacritical marks are omitted since they are unnecessary for those who know Japanese and are of no special help to those who do not.

To spare the reader confusion, English titles are used wherever possible, and the works most frequently cited are listed below in chronological order in both Japanese and English:

"Eibungaku Keishikiron"	"The General Concept of Literature"
"Bungakuron"	*On Literature*
"Bungaku Hyoron"	*Eighteenth-Century English Literature*
Wagahai wa Neko de Aru	*I Am a Cat*
Yokyoshu	*Seven Stories*
"Rondon To"	"The Tower of London"
"Kairairu Hakubutsukan"	"The Carlyle Museum"
"Genei no Tate"	"The Phantom Shield"
"Koto no Sorane"	"The False Sound of the Lute"
"Ichiya"	"One Night"
"Kairoko"	"The Song of Evanescence"
"Shumi no Iden"	"The Legacy of Love"
Uzurakago	*Three Stories*
"Botchan"	"Botchan"
"Kusamakura"	"The Grass Pillow"
"Nihyakutoka"	"The 'Storm Day'"

"Nowaki"	"The Wintry Blast"
Gubijinso	*The Poppy*
Kofu	*The Miner*
Sanshiro	*Sanshiro*
"Yume Juya"	"Ten Nights' Dreams"
"Eijitsu Shohin"	*Spring Miscellanies*
Sorekara	*And Then*
"Mankan Tokoro Dokoro"	*A Passage through Manchuria and Korea*
Mon	*The Gate*
"Omoidasu Kotonado"	*Random Recollections*
Higan Sugi Made	*Until After the Spring Equinox*
Kojin	*Kojin*
Kokoro	*Kokoro*
"Garasudo no Naka"	*Within the Sash-Door*
Michikusa	*Loitering*
"Tentoroku"	"New Year's Thoughts"
Meian	*Light and Darkness*

Contents

Preface

An Explanatory Note

Chronology

1. Introduction: The Heritage   15
2. The Frustrated Years (1903–1907)   29
3. The Moment of Decision (1907–1908)   53
4. The First Trilogy (1908–1910)   72
5. The Second Trilogy (1910–1914)   99
6. Another Vista: Last Years (1915–1916)   135
7. Conclusion: An Assessment   163

Notes and References   179

Selected Bibliography   184

Index   189

Acknowledgments

In the process of preparing the present study I have consulted various Soseki studies, especially those by Ara, Eto, Komiya, Masamune, McClellan, Morita, Shiotani, Viglielmo, and also special Soseki issues of *Meiji Taisho Bungaku Kenkyu* (Nos. 6 and 7).

I wish to thank Mr. Maurice Schneps, Editor of *Orient/West*, for permission to reprint here my article on *Kokoro* which appeared in its issue for March–April 1964; and Dr. Harold A. Basilius, Director of Wayne State University Press, for permission to use my introduction to *The Wayfarer* (1967). My thanks are also due to my old friend Atsushi Takata for showing unfailing interest in my research; Professor Roy E. Teele, Japanese Editor of the Series, for assisting me with insight in revising the manuscript; Mr. Frank Kirk of Twayne for not sparing his professional care in preparing it for the printer; and Miss Minori Tachibana, of Iwanami Shoten, for providing a list of Soseki's works in European languages. And lastly, I am grateful to the Wayne State University Graduate Faculty Research Committee, whose financial assistance enabled me to undertake and complete this project.

B. Y.

Chronology

1867 Natsume Kinnosuke—better known by his pen name Soseki —born February 9, Edo (Tokyo), Japan. Soon put out to nurse.

1868 Adopted into the Shiobara family.

1874– Attends primary schools in Tokyo.
1878

1876 Returns home with stepmother after divorce from her husband, but retains the name of Shiobara.

1878– Attends secondary schools in Tokyo; studies Chinese classics and English.
1884

1881 Mother dies.

1884– Attends the First Higher School, majoring in English.
1890

1888 Regains the name of Natsume.

1889 For the first time uses the pen name Soseki.

1890– Attends the Imperial University of Tokyo, majoring in English literature.
1893

1892 Writes on Laotzu; joins the editorial staff of *Tetsugaku Zasshi;* writes on Whitman.

1893 Reads a paper on the concept of nature in English poetry; enters the Graduate School of the University; appointed a lecturer of the Tokyo Higher Normal School.

1894– Stays for several weeks at a Zen temple in Kamakura.
1895

1895 Accepts a position with the secondary school in Matsuyama; composes *haiku* poetry.

1896– Teaches at the Fifth Higher School in Kumamoto.
1900

1896 Marries Nakane Kyoko.

1900– Sent to England to study English; stays in London.
1902

1903　Returns to Japan; appointed a lecturer at both the First Higher School and the Imperial University of Tokyo; in the latter, begins a series of lectures on English literature.

1905　*I Am a Cat* begins to appear in *Hototogisu.*

1906　Publishes his first collection, *Seven Stories;* completes *I Am a Cat;* at his home, holds the first of the Thursday gatherings; declines the *Yomiuri* offer.

1907　Publishes his second collection, *Three Stories;* accepts the *Asahi* offer to serialize his work; resigns from the university; delivers "The Philosophical Basis of Literary Art"; *The Poppy,* the first serial novel.

1908　*The Miner;* delivers "The Novelist's Attitude"; *Sanshiro.*

1909　*Spring Miscellanies,* a series of personal essays; *And Then;* declines the gold cup for the highest vote in the *Taiyo's* contemporary artist popularity poll; journeys through Manchuria and Korea; agrees to take charge of the *Asahi* literary columns.

1910　*The Gate;* suffers a serious attack of ulcers at Shuzenji; begins *Random Recollections.*

1911　Declines the government's Doctor of Letters degree; on lecturing tours, suffers an attack of ulcers; treated for hemorrhoids; his fifth daughter, Hinako, dies.

1912　*Until After the Spring Equinox;* treated again for hemorrhoids; tries water-color painting; complains of loneliness; begins *Kojin.*

1913　After an interruption, completes *Kojin;* delivers "Imitation and Independence."

1914　*Kokoro;* suffers the fourth attack of ulcers; delivers "My Individualism."

1915　*Within the Sash-Door;* journeys to Kyoto, where he suffers another attack of ulcers; *Loitering.*

1916　Treated for diabetes; *Light and Darkness;* following his last attack of ulcers, dies December 9; buried in Zoshigaya Cemetery, Tokyo.

CHAPTER 1

Introduction: The Heritage

I *Meiji Japan*

IF it is true that no man is an island, it is equally true that no nation can be an island forever. Commodore Perry's arrival in 1853 off the shore of Japan reminds us of this truth. But to say this from history's comfortable distance is one thing, and to experience this old truth is quite another. To learn, or to be forced to learn the truth, individually or collectively, is always painful even if it does promise an eventual *élan vital*. Such was the case with the pre-Meiji Japanese who had since the seventeenth century enjoyed relative peace under the rigid Tokugawa feudalism. To those who had for some time sensed that this vast feudal machinery, through depreciation and exhaustion, was coming to a breaking point, and who had now witnessed its feeble capitulation to Perry's firm ultimatum, backed by his fleet of black ships, this meant not a period of self-pity or inert despair, but a period of action. Their course of action divided them into two camps, the Shogunate and the Royalist, depending on whether they favored traditional isolationism or an open-door policy. Facing this dilemma they could still heed their instinct of self-preservation. Both camps, whatever their political rivalry, agreed on the necessity of uniting their divided forces.

This accounts for the fact that the Meiji Restoration of 1868 was accomplished with little bloodshed, a rare phenomenon in a large-scale political revolution. The nation rallied around youthful Emperor Meiji, whose vision and courage during his reign of nearly half a century, proved to be instrumental in creating a modern state out of the Old Japan. As the first step in this magnificent enterprise, he moved the seat of government from Kyoto, capital for a millennium, symbol of the Old Japan, to Edo, formerly the headquarters of the Shogunate. He renamed the city Tokyo. And then, as his master plan for New Japan, the Emperor announced the five-point program: that the feudal system would be abolished; that his subjects would enjoy the freedom of occupation, and the freedom of beliefs and opinions; that the nation would pursue an open-door policy and, as a member of world community, establish free intercourse with other nations; and that the new government would promote education as a surer means of creating a civilized society. Under pressure of foreign encroachments, and guided by Imperial directives, Japan launched into one of the most dramatic chapters in her long history, declaring her determination to reorganize herself as a modern state, using Western powers as political, social, and cultural models. Thus to Meiji Japan, modernization meant Westernization, and vice versa.

Indeed, hers was a mass reorientation, on every level and in every direction, unmatched in recent history. In the political sphere the central government, despite its tendency toward clan politics, was quick to assume control over this once feudal nation. There was, of course, a series of local rebellions by some ex-samurai, malcontent with the new regime, which finally culminated in the Seinan Uprising (1877). But their attempts proved to be futile in the face of the new regime's modernized superior military force, which was composed mainly of non-professional conscripts. With this victory, which renewed confidence in its cause, the Meiji government continued to strive for national unity; now, sure of its own political hegemony and in keeping with its original promise, it was ready to hold a popular election for the Diet. To meet the popular demand for a democratic government, such political organizations as Itagaki's Liberal Party and Okuma's Progressive Party were formed. And with the creation of the Imperial Diet in 1890, Meiji Japan at last emerged as a constitutional monarchy. It was as the first constitutional monarchy in the Far East that Japan defeated China in 1894–95 and then Russia in 1904–5, thereby asserting itself as a major Eastern power. Her victory in both instances signified the first joint venture of three factors vital to the triumph of modern efficiency: bureaucracy, militarism, and capitalism, which, when carried to extremes, was destined to develop into Japanese Imperialism.

In the sociocultural sphere, this modernization-Westernization, under the slogan of enlightenment, reached its peak during the period of 1883–91. The universal craze for anything Western was probably due in part to what might be called the imitative genius of the Japanese, but more was involved than this; it was equally a part of the government leaders' conscious scheme to meet the immediate political necessity of shaking off as a national disgrace such unfair treaties as those involving extraterritorial jurisdiction which Japan had signed, under pressure, with Western powers. Since the foreign powers' resistance to this attempt was based on their assertion that the native ways of living, manners, and the like were too odd to be acceptable, the leaders, such as Ito, Inouye, and Mori, recognized the urgency of modeling at least the ruling class on Western lines, in addition to the modernization already begun in the educational system, in transportation, and in communication.

The era came to be called the Rokumeikan Era, named after the social center where leaders gave concerts of Western music, held cultural and social parties, and staged masquerades. So complete was their adoption of the Western style of social life that their wives and daughters were fully integrated into their programs and they felt confident enough to invite foreign diplomats to witness their successful Westernization. They were not the only ones to carry the banners; the general public also caught this universal fashion. There were pathetic endeavors to adopt formally the Latin alphabet, encourage marriage with Westerners, and substitute English for Japanese. Modernization carried to such extremes was bound to encounter a nationalistic reaction by those who believed otherwise. The assassination of Mori, Minister of Education, on the day of the Promulgation of the new Constitution, heralded the tide of nationalism or Nipponism, which was tremendously boosted by the swift victories in the wars with China and Russia. This gave rise to a more mature form of cosmopolitanism, an attitude of mind that neither of these two extremes should be the proper course for Japan to follow, and that in all possible fields Japan ought to contribute her share to world society by cultivating what was unique with her.

II *New Voices in Literature*

Literature, by its very nature, can not be forced from without or handed down from above, like politics; it is a sphere where progress becomes possible only with the spontaneous or conscious collaboration of tradition and individual talents. This may account for the fact that Meiji literature as *belles-lettres* followed rather than preceded the over-all political and social re-orientation by decades. Yet no vacuum was allowed to exist in this world where everything old had to make place for the new. In this sense it is still possible to designate the literature of the Meiji era as part of the larger scheme of modernization-Westernization, in short, universal enlightenment. Meiji literature evolved through a succession of two characteristic periods: Japanization of Western literature, and Westernization of Japanese literature. As a result of collective efforts to achieve in less than a half century what had taken the West several centuries, Meiji literature was a field swept with confused alarms of struggle and flight. It was a chaos darkling under multicolored banners and slogans: enlightenment, classicism, romanticism, realism, naturalism, neo-romanticism, neo-idealism—all overlapping in their invasion of this island, so that none took full, deep root in the soil.

The first half of the Meiji period is generally called a period of translations and adaptations, the period devoted to the Japanization of Western literature. Led by Nakamura Keiu's translations of Samuel Smiles's *Self-Help* and Mill's *On Liberty*, Nakae Chomin's translation of Rousseau's *Social Contract,* and Fukuzawa Yukichi's popular pamphlets, the enlightenment helped bring journalism and literature closer. Translations made from such writers as Disraeli, Lytton, Scott, and Hugo, and further adapted into Japanese settings, totaled a hundred. The predominant genre was, as might be expected, the political novel, a fact which reveals the pervasive political orientation of the period. But devoid of genuinely artistic works, it was a period of transition, a step toward creating literature as *belles-lettres*.

The Westernization of Japanese literature, first of all, demanded a new literature which would completely sever itself from the still lingering Edo literature, which was entertainment rather than serious in character and which had proved notoriously unable to satisfy the age. On the one hand a mere rehash of the urbane elegance of Saikaku's world of the gay quarters, and on the other, the Chinese orientation of Bakin's chivalric romances, it was not suited to the taste of the new reading public. The age now belonged to the writers of a new generation, all in their twenties, who departed radically from tradition in subject matter, in literary style, and above all, in attitude toward life and literature. It was an age for young literary aspirants educated under the new system—all Japanese counterparts of the Elizabethan University Wits.

New voices began to be heard in all fields of poetry, drama, and fiction; but the age was predominantly an age of fiction, since the two other genres, because of their peculiar conventions and traditions, were longer in changing. The pulse of new fiction was felt first in Tsubouchi Shoyo's two works, *The Essence of the Novel* and *Modern Student Temper*, both in 1885. Shocking as it was that a university graduate should turn to fiction writing, a trade long practiced only by social and cultural inferiors, Shoyo, in practice as well as in theory, dictated the course of Meiji fiction in the direction of realism. In the former, the first Japanese theoretical treatise based on Western realism, Shoyo argued that in fiction human sentiment must be primary, and social manners and customs secondary; that in expressing humanity, psychological consideration not be sacrificed for the sake of plot; and that fiction be freed from didacticism, whether in the form of stereotyped ethical sentimentalism common to Edo literature, or utilitarian propaganda typical of the current political literature. And in the latter, Shoyo humorously and vividly depicted scenes from university student life of around 1882 as he and his friends experienced it.

Modern Student Temper was evidently meant to embody *The Essence of the Novel*, but the truth was that Shoyo did not quite succeed in practicing what he preached. In plot his novel lacked real progression toward its denouement. As a series of social comments it possessed much interest, but was not free of that predilection for didacticism to which he had objected. Moreover, his style being still somewhat old-fashioned could not be called a new medium of expression. In all these Futabatei Shimei (pen name of Hasegawa Tatsunosuke), Shoyo's disciple, went beyond his master. In *The Drifting Cloud* (1887) Futabatei was far more thoroughgoing in his realistic handling of material, and his bold use of colloquial Japanese. His success was partly due to his background as a student of Russian realistic masters.

This new voice of realism was not left unheard. Its impetus was felt in various quarters. The first to rise to the challenge was Yamada Bimyo, Futabatei's childhood friend, who, when barely twenty years of age, established himself as one of the leading writers, especially in his insistence on the use of colloquial Japa-

nese. At almost the same time the Kenyusha came into prominence, a group of young aspirants around Ozaki Koyo. Under his
dominance it virtually ruled the literary world during the period
from 1885 to 1903. The group objected to the fashionable genre of
political novels, reacted against Shoyo and Futabatei's importation of Western literary methods, and in competing with Yamada,
took as its preoccupation the creation of a new literary style in
Saikaku's tradition. By contrast with Shoyo and his school, the
Kenyusha thus grew into a traditional school with a flavor of romantic estheticism. Even in a cursory glance at Meiji literature, it
would be a mistake to omit Mori Ogai, who, together with Shoyo-
Futabatei's realism and Ozaki's Kenyusha school, represented
the midpoint of Meiji literature. A German-trained army surgeon,
Ogai began to draw increasing attention to his translations, critical essays, and his first novel, *The Dancing Girl* (1890). While in
Germany, he had read widely in Goethe, Schiller, and Hartmann,
and had become an idealist. The first Japanese writer to become
familiar at first hand with European literature, he was making
significant contributions toward the modernization of Meiji literature. In this and other respects he was later compared with Soseki.

The Kenyusha school which dominated the literary world for
more than a decade came to an end in 1903 with the death of
Koyo at the age of thirty-seven. His death signified a new era for
those who had failed to produce the Kenyusha type of fiction, or
refused to do so, being critical of the school's romantic sentimentalism, ethical naïveté, and escapist estheticism. Shimazaki Toson,
Tokuda Shusei, Kunikida Doppo, and Tayama Katai, later joined
by Aoyama Seika and Masamune Hakucho, were among those
who welcomed this new era—all indebted to the French naturalist
tradition of Zola, Flaubert, Maupassant, and the Russian realistic
tradition of Turgenev, Dostoevsky, and Tolstoy. These writers,
despite their individual differences, were sufficiently unified in
outlook to constitute a literary movement, especially when Toson's *Transgression* (1906), and Katai's *Quilt* (1907), were hailed
as a declaration of the naturalistic spirit by Shimamura Hogetsu,
who had recently returned from abroad and taken over the editorship of *Waseda Bungaku*. The first decade of the twentieth
century thus came to be called by literary historians the heyday of
the Meiji naturalist movement.

Toson's *Transgression*, which Soseki lauded as perhaps the

greatest masterpiece of Meiji literature, posed a daring challenge to the rigid social caste system by depicting an educated youth who, in trying to be honest with himself, transgressed his father's injunction that his origin as a social outcast be kept secret, and departed for America, a symbol of freedom. Katai's *Quilt*, on the other hand, was a frankly autobiographical confession, the pathetic account of a middle-aged novelist who, unable to make up his mind about his own woman disciple, had to be content with only the quilt she had left. Because of its frankness the work was condemned as a *pièce de scandale*. Nevertheless, it could not but impress many young writers, who were confusing art with life. If there is one thing in common between these two works it is that both urged the necessity of self-discovery or at least self-honesty. Yet their difference is precisely that between self-discovery and self-honesty, and that is also the difference between Toson and Katai.

Toson and Katai represented the polar ends of the naturalistic movement in Meiji literature. The mediocrity of Meiji naturalists can be explained by the fact that young writers, through choice or temptation, followed Katai rather than Toson. It was certainly an easy way out, artistically speaking, but perpetuated the Japanese tradition of the confessional pseudo-novel. In this respect, Katai's *Quilt* betrays the fundamental weakness inherent in Japanese naturalism. Often indulging in a narrow range of personal trivialities, it lacked a broader view of society; being addicted to naïve emotionalism and sentimentalism, it also lacked the spirit of ruthless drives; and above all, it lacked any intellectual foundation, the kind of philosophical and scientific basis which made European naturalism such a significant force in the evolution of modern literature. Hence there were no Japanese naturalists comparable in stature to Zola, Flaubert, and Maupassant; and consequently few masterpieces from this movement.

All this was perhaps inevitable in an age which forced writers to desert their native traditions, skim hurriedly over new ground, and exhaust new materials without fully digesting them. All in all, Meiji naturalism was a literary fashion without any profound intellectual resources. Yet the result of the movement was not wholly negative; there was a positive aspect also. It widened subject matter beyond comparison; it urged the artist to have a serious attitude toward life and art; and last of all, it settled the problem of the choice of language as an artistic vehicle, leaving little doubt about the essential superiority of colloquial speech for the creation of literature. In other words, the movement helped pave the way for a new literature. Ground-breaking was over, and the literature to come must draw its vitality from writers able to provide the age with intellectual energy. This was the moment when Soseki made his literary debut. He instinctively knew what the demands of the age were and, moreover, he had the ability to satisfy them.

III *Soseki's Early Years*

Meiji Japan, in its radical departure from the feudal tradition, was as profoundly romantic as Renaissance England, a comparison which has often been suggested by historians. Few artists could escape its pervading romantic spirit in their zealous pursuit of life and art. But set within this context, Soseki, at first glance, seems a strange exception, for few artists' lives have been so unromantic, unexciting, and prosaic as his. Except for his last dozen years, which were charged with a sudden, explosive creative energy, his life would command little attention. He was neither an *enfant terrible* nor a *poète maudit*. Outwardly at least, Soseki was decidedly no citizen of Bohemia.

But Soseki was a true child of Meiji Japan. Natsume Kinnosuke, better known by his pen name Soseki, was born of a once well-to-do family of Edo (Tokyo), in 1867, on the eve of the Meiji Restoration. Born the fifth, last, and unwelcomed child of aging parents, he was immediately put out to nurse, and then soon adopted by a married couple whose transparently selfish love the child rejected instinctively. Although his stay was short because of the foster parents' marital discord, his legal status was not settled until he was well into early manhood. As he recalled later, his was not a life meant for domestic happiness.

Whether or not this wound really affected Soseki's life as a man and as an artist is a matter of speculation. Whether the wound was healed or merely concealed, one thing is certain: it did not cripple Soseki's spirit. On the contrary, he had an abundant zest for life, as evident in his youthful declaration: "to live is the sole end of man." Incomparably more important to us, as to him, is the fact that his birth coincided with the most crucial juncture of modern Japanese history, and that he made the most of it. By birth,

Soseki was naturally an heir to the popular Edo culture which, during the two preceding centuries, evolved into something comparable to that of Paris in its refinement and sophistication. By early training he had access to the Chinese classics, which further fostered his sense of tradition, a tradition far older than that of Edo. Then, by choice he became a student of English literature, the field which undoubtedly promised to his generation a new world, a new order, and a new vision.

But a triple tradition, such as this, does not necessarily make an artist. Rather there is every indication that with such a background Soseki might have become a refined dilettante or at most a gentleman-scholar, instead of a novelist. Intelligent and perceptive as he was, Soseki's ambition was disappointingly vague in his early years and very slow in forming. At one time he thought of distinguishing himself in Chinese—a dream feeble enough to be discarded without much regret at his elders' advice. His friendship with Masaoka Shiki, later leader of the new *haiku* movement, lured him in the direction of *haiku* poetry, rather than fiction, at least at this stage. Then at another, he thought of becoming an architect as a compromise of his oddity, his taste, and his practicality; this idea came to nothing when a friend reminded him that no Japanese architect could possibly create a work as ambitious as St. Paul's cathedral. Then he decided, or rather was made to decide, to pursue English literature as his undergraduate major. While doing so he had to abandon yet another dream, that of accomplishing something significant in English, for he realized it was nearly impossible. Still uncertain, he confided to Shiki his wavering: "Perhaps it is better to be a champion of Japanese than a champion of Western learning." This is all we know of his youthful ambitions, unfixed and oscillating. Since he had to earn a living, specializing in English literature seemed to be the surest path to follow. Soseki proved to be a brilliant student, writing criticism of Laotzu's transcendental mysticism, praise of Whitman's democratic poetry, and an analysis of the tradition of English nature poets. Finally in 1893 Soseki graduated from the Imperial University of Tokyo, holding its new bachelor of arts in English. Both his academic performance and his B.A. degree seemed to assure his future career as a professor of English, a career which was considered by no means humble at the time.

Soseki had no difficulty in securing a lectureship at Tokyo

Higher Normal School. He later said he was made a teacher of
English without having really mastered anything to his satisfaction. Despite his glittering academic degree, a sense of emptiness
was growing within him. Soseki soon fell victim to a vague,
though real, anxiety when he discovered an insuperable gap between his life and his profession. Now aware that teaching was
not meant to be his vocation, he could not yet be certain what
should be. Perhaps it was frustration which drove him to a Zen
master for a time, and then to Matsuyama as a high school
teacher, a decision shocking to everyone except Soseki himself. In
Matsuyama, where he said he had gone to "bury himself alive," he
saw three alternatives: study, debauchery, or marriage. But that
he could not gamble his life for the last two was evident in his
active interest in *haiku* poetry and even in his passing complaint
that his chances to save money for study abroad were dwindling.
After one year in Matsuyama, Soseki went farther west, this time
as a lecturer at the Fifth Higher School in Kumamoto. Staying
there for four years, he continued to grope for something to gratify his innermost longings. He became involved with the local
haiku circle in response to Shiki's new *haiku* movement then
spreading all over the country. He wrote articles on such works as
Sterne's *Tristram Shandy*. By now he was a husband and also a
father. Despite the seeming fullness of his life in Kumamoto, Soseki was not content. Even though he was a success as an educa-
tor, he expressed his desire to change his profession, so that he
might be able to devote himself to a literary life; he wished to
have a life of leisure which would allow him to read and express
what was dear to his heart. Then in 1900 came an interruption to
this period of seven-year wandering when he was sent to England, ironically, for a study of his special field. Of this wandering
period, Soseki later wrote:

Since my early years I was fond of Chinese classics. My acquaintance with them, though by no means long standing, naturally led me
to form a concept—even if vague—of what literature is. I had the
feeling that it would apply to English literature, and, if so, I could not
possibly regret devoting my life to it. This reasoning, altogether child-
ish and simple, prompted me to major in English literature at the
university. Through my three years there, I was tortured by Latin,

German, and even by French; none of which I could master, and which allowed me little time for my own field. And when I at last graduated with that honored bachelor's degree, deep down I could not but have a feeling of emptiness.

Still the future was ahead of me with enough time for my own study. My only regret was that though I had studied, I had never mastered the heart of things. Thus upon graduation I somehow suspected that I had been cheated by English literature. With this suspicion heavy on my mind I headed westward to Matsuyama; and a year later, farther west to Kumamoto, where I stayed for several years, and even before that suspicion could be allayed, I had to proceed to London.

IV *The London Years*

His stay in England, little more than two years (1900–1902), proved to be a very trying experience, which he never cared to repeat. For one who had reached the age of thirty-four, who was already the father of a child and another on the way, and who had to live alone on a meager government allowance, life in London was desolate and very difficult to adjust to. An almost indigent stranger lost in that indifferent metropolis, Soseki was homesick; in fact, a report was even sent to the home government that Soseki was on the verge of insanity. He was then suffering from his first attack of nervous strain which, along with his later chronic ulcers, was to afflict him for the rest of his life. But his was far from the sentimental desperation of a sensitive mind exposed to the harshness of reality. Soseki was at that time going through a personal crisis; his agony was that of an honest soul coming to grips with itself.

The crisis had been long in coming since his flight to Matsuyama and then to Kumamoto; when it finally came the blow was staggering. Upon arrival in England, Soseki had chosen London over Cambridge and Oxford for financial reasons, and over Scotland and Ireland for the obvious reason that it seemed the most logical place for him to study English. He had registered as an auditor at the University of London, but soon found the lectures falling short of his expectations and stopped attending them; now his academic contact was only with his tutor, Dr. Craig, a Shakespearean scholar, but not an especially stimulating personality. In the meantime he had attempted to read as many books in his special field as he could, in particular those standard works whose names he had only heard but never read. After a year, Soseki realized that the attempt had not allayed the suspicion he had held since graduation. He had in fact been moving further and further away from his problem rather than confronting it. The time had at last come for him to plunge headlong into it. The moment was indeed the dark night of Soseki's soul.

Soseki now resolved to seek a new definition of literature, a definition fundamental and universal enough to reconcile the differences between the Oriental and Western concepts of literature. This would justify his choice of literature as a vocation. Doubting literature itself, Soseki would let nothing go unexamined. He must grapple with literature on his own terms and clarify to his personal satisfaction its *raison d'être*.

An impetus came from a certain acquaintance with whom Soseki daily in his London lodging discussed everything—literature, philosophy, and religion—well into the night. It was an eye-opening experience to re-examine literature on the most fundamental level. Only in this light can we understand Soseki when he confided on several occasions: "Lately it seems to me ridiculous to try to be a scholar of English literature. I wonder vaguely what good I can do for others and for our country. Well, maybe there are many people like me." "If you want to do research of some kind, it had better be of a cosmopolitan kind. . . . I strongly urge you to do something big in your special field of physics." "Lately I have developed a dislike for literary works and am reading books about science. While here I am trying to gather material to write a book when I return. But how can I trust myself? Just now in the book I'm reading I have come across exactly the same idea as mine. Hang it!"

A dozen years afterward, Soseki described this crucial turning point:

Thereafter, in order to solidify my ground in relation to literature, or rather to build it afresh, I began to read books which had no immediate bearing on literature. In a word, I had finally hit on the four words, "on my own terms," and trying to prove them, plunged into scientific studies, philosophical reasonings. . . . Having thus grasped in my hands these four words, on my own terms, I for the first time felt secure. Now I had the courage to defy the world. Indeed, it is these four words, on my own terms, that rescued me from the state of despair and directed me where to stand firm and in what direction to proceed. . . . At that moment the sense of insecurity left me altogether. With a lightened heart I looked around that gloomy London. To use a figure of speech, I felt as though I had finally struck a vein of ore after those many years of frustration. To repeat, I felt like one who, having been long lost in a thick fog, was shown his way clear in a certain, particular direction.

It was no longer the despairing Soseki, but a reoriented Soseki, determined to commit himself to the pursuit of literature as the dictate of his existence. Jettisoning his fragmentary knowledge of literature, he launched on an enormously ambitious project which he called his ten-year plan. He locked himself up in his room and set out to read everything possible, devouring books not only about literature but those related to the most fundamental branches of human knowledge—philosophy, psychology, sociology, ethics, and other sciences—determined to examine the meaning of literature in human society. Touching on this, Soseki wrote to his father-in-law in March 1902:

Since my arrival here last August or September, I have made up my mind to write a book, and to this end reading, taking notes, and jotting down my own thoughts are my daily chores. Since I am going to write a book, I intend not to make it an imitation of Western books, but something I can show others with pride. But the problem being of such a vast nature, I fear it may end only in miscarriage. Even if not, I do not think it will be completed in two or three years. Although to advertise a book yet to be written seems as foolish as to make a fuss about the name for an unborn baby, I'll give you some idea about it anyway. First, it starts with the question, how to view the world; moves on to the next, how to look at life, along with the meaning and purpose of life, and the development of its vitality; and then goes on to define civilization, analyze its constituting factors, and discuss its impact on the evolution of literature. The task, on such a grand scale, should of necessity touch philosophy, history, politics, psychology, biology, and also evolutionism. Although I myself am amazed at the boldness of the scheme, I intend to pursue it to the bitter end. My only desire now is for time and money. My worry is there won't be any leisure for thinking and reading when I return home and am dragged back to teaching English. Now and then I lapse into a dream in which I pick up a hundred thousand *yen,* therewith build a library, and there do my own writing.

And again later in his preface to *On Literature,* Soseki wrote, recalling those days in London: "I stored all my belletristic works away in my trunk, for I had come to realize that to study literature by reading these books would be as futile as to cleanse blood with blood. I was resolved to enquire psychologically by what necessity literature came into being, by what process it has evolved, and for what reason it has decayed. Again, I was resolved to investigate sociologically by what necessity literature came into existence, by what process it ripened, and for what causes it has declined." In a word, this was to be his version of the rise and decline of literature that would justify his vocation. And when his notebooks, "filled with letters as tiny as flies' heads," reached the thickness of five or six inches, Soseki returned to Japan. It was the first month of 1903.

CHAPTER 2

The Frustrated Years (1903–1907)

ONCE back in Tokyo, Soseki found himself lecturing on English literature at the First Higher School and the Imperial University, each his alma mater—to his relief as well as to his disappointment. In a way, it meant a realization of his personal wish to stay in Tokyo, the center of literary activities, instead of returning to Kumamoto; but it also meant an interruption to his fresh determination to devote himself, if possible, to what he had called his ten-year plan. But there seemed to be no choice since he had to support his growing family. Especially at the university, where he was to lecture for the next four years, his position as the first Japanese successor to Lafcadio Hearn was understandably delicate and difficult—under the circumstances surrounding his famous predecessor's resignation; and his dry and analytical approach to literature was in marked contrast to Hearn's intuitive, interpretative approach, and his poetic eloquence. Moreover, the students were not prepared for his kind of lecture.

Soseki's lectures, delivered over a period of four years, consisted of "The General Concept of Literature" (April–June 1903), "On Literature" (September 1903–June 1905), and "Eighteenth-Century English Literature" (September 1905–March 1907). There is little doubt that all of these lectures, especially the first two series, drew on the copious notes Soseki took while in London, with a view to probing into the secret of literature and thereby clarifying the confusion in contemporary Japanese literary circles.

I *"The General Concept of Literature"*

These two points Soseki restates when he opens his first series, "The General Concept of Literature." Having surveyed mutually conflicting definitions of literature from Aristotle to Tolstoy, from Arnold to Buckle, Soseki pauses to make the following statement: "I shall be content if only I can convey to you some of my ideas

concerning literature. Furthermore, I do not believe that literature, like science, either ought to be or can be defined. In this
series I shall merely attempt to consider by what process and from
what angle we Japanese should approach Western literature, and
thereby determine to what extent we Japanese can comprehend it.
In attempting this, I shall take one Natsume as representative of
the Japanese with the average background of Western, especially
English, literature." A writer's attitude toward literature will govern his definition, and he may display a natural tendency to overstress certain aspects. As a result, such an approach usually leads
nowhere. Recalling this, Soseki himself prefers to divide literature
into two parts, form and substance, granting the difficulty of
doing so. Then he lays down the general plan of his lectures:
"First, we shall discuss the problem of form by detailing its limits,
and then proceed to the problem of substance in like manner, by
setting its limits and examining its factors, its variety, etc. Thus
gaining a clear picture of form and substance, we shall discuss
their relationship, and trace the differentiation of substance that
comes about contingent on the passage of time. And further we
shall see the effect of literature on man, together with the general
rules that bring forth the effects, and lastly deal with both the
pleasure the artist experiences while creating, and the pleasure
the reader experiences while reading."

In dealing with the problem of form, Soseki does not follow the
familiar procedure of setting up divisions by genres, but comes
straight to the question of taste. Like Brooke, he observes that the
form of a literary work should appeal to the reader's taste, taste in
the sense of liking or disliking it, not a complex philosophical
sense. This differs from the fashionable eighteenth- and nineteenth-century critical term "taste." What appeals to the reader's
taste, Soseki points out, varies according to the individual, subjec-
tively; and according to the thing, objectively. The latter is the
issue, the valid ground of discussion. Then he proceeds to classify
what he terms the objective condition of literary form. Indeed, by
means of examples and illustrations, throughout his discussion Soseki tries to sift the universal from the local, the general from the
accidental, all necessarily mixed in every literary form. Once we
are capable of making such fine distinctions, Soseki implies, we
can take a more appreciative attitude toward the various forms of
Western literature. Thus it is clear that in these lectures Soseki

attempts to set forth certain objective criteria by which a given literary work succeeds or fails to appeal to the reader's taste.

II *"On Literature"*

"The General Concept of Literature" served as an introduction to his second series, "On Literature." The first deals with the question of form; the other deals with substance. In this series, which Soseki later disparaged as "the carcass of a deformed child," rather than a memorial of his now abandoned ten-year plan, it is not difficult to detect Soseki's characteristics: a highly analytical attitude toward a certain objectivity; a competent handling of materials which would illuminate his chosen issues; adroit references to scores of authorities, past and present, with whom he freely disagrees; an original insight, coupled with his astute observations from literary and non-literary standpoints; suggestive comparisons of Eastern and Western literature; and above all, an eagerness to come to the basic principles governing literature itself, not just English literature, which to him is only a particular manifestation of it. By virtue of these characteristics, "On Literature" becomes one of the most significant treatises on the subject ever formulated by a Japanese student of literature.

Every literary substance can be reduced to the basic formula $(F + f)$, F signifying the focal impression or idea, and f, its accompanying emotion; in other words, all literary substance is the combination of cognitive F and emotional f factors. F, which occupies the apex of the continuum of consciousness, therefore, can appear not only as the F of consciousness at every instant, but as the F of a certain period in an individual's lifetime, and further as the F of a certain period in the course of social evolution. Starting from the psychological basis, F extends as far as society. Accordingly, this series falls into five sections: classification of literary substance; quantitative change of literary substance; essence of literary substance; interrelationship of literary substance; and collective F.

In the first section Soseki classifies literary substance, thereby clarifying the scope of literature, which is far wider than generally held by both those who take it solely as intellectual pleasure and those who deny it any moral aspect. All human experience—impressions and ideas—is of three kinds: one which contains only F, such as our concept of a triangle; one which contains both F and

f, such as our concept of flowers and stars; and one which contains only f, such as our fear for no particular reason. And of these three kinds of human experience, the second alone can be literary substance, in which sense it combines F and f. The basic sensory elements that come into literature are usually six (touch, temperature, taste, smell, hearing, sight). Following Ribot's classification, Soseki says that the psychological or emotional elements in literature are of two kinds: the first, relatively simple emotions, such as fear, anger, sympathy, ego-feeling, sexual instinct or love; and the second, more complex emotions, such as jealousy, loyalty, supernatural feelings, generalized truths. If Soseki goes into elaborate illustrations, it is because he holds that emotion is the touchstone of literature; in other words, it is with emotion that literature begins and ends. Any human experience, if only it creates f, can be used for literature. Then, all that can be literary substance, or can be transferred to the fundamental formula $(F + f)$, falls into four classes: sensory F, human F, supernatural F, and intellectual or ideological F. The first points mainly to the natural world; the second to the human drama which mirrors good and evil, joy and grief, and pain and pleasure; the third to the supernatural or religious realm; and the fourth to the philosophical and ideational notions about human problems. And of all the four F's, it is the intellectual F which is the least effective as literary substance, for the reason that the more concrete the literary substance is, the more likely it is to create emotion.

But Soseki here does not indulge in classification for its own sake. What he tries to demonstrate is the fact that literature, thus tabulated, covers much wider ground than it seems to those who seek only intellectual pleasure or exclude from it any moral element. Along with this Soseki also dwells on certain peculiarities of Western literature, such as its passionate interest in sexual instinct or love, and the predominance of supernatural F, namely God. And lastly, on the basis of the above classification Soseki warns that life is not literature, or at least, it is not romantic literature, for while literature does begin and end with emotion, life is and should be wider than emotions.

In the second section, in order to examine the principles which effect changes (increase or decrease) to these four classes of $(F + f)$, Soseki begins with F. There is no doubt that F on the whole increases constantly in proportion to the development of our cognitive power and its range, and this applies not only on the individual but on the collective level. The increase of F entails that of f under three major principles: transference, expansion, and fixation. Then turning to the nature of f itself, Soseki at length discusses two kinds of f, one as a direct experience and the other as an indirect experience, or if we use our own critical terms, the natural and the esthetic emotion, their difference being both quantitative and qualitative. His discussion of how the artist transmutes one into the other (thus the question of his sincerity is largely that of his sincerity about his method) is as detailed as that of how the reader responds to it by eliminating or suspending certain elements. The same holds true for the tragic f, or the esthetic emotion a tragedy creates, which is in Soseki's opinion the highest form of indirect emotion, an effect which depends on the artist's ability to create the most intense indirect experience, as well as on the reader's to eliminate all his ego-feelings and ideas. Tragedy can be regarded as an actor's disguised or feigned pain which develops in a certain direction. To this type of pain are drawn those who can love stimulation, desire adventures, and shed what Soseki calls the tears of luxury. And here is the *raison d'être* of tragedy, which meets the basic needs of human life.

The discussion naturally leads to the question of artistic truth. The nature of artistic truth (or the artist's F) becomes clear especially when compared with scientific truth (or the scientist's F). In general, science exists only in time, since its primary function is to describe "how," the process by which things develop, whereas literature not only does this but deals in addition with the timeless dimension of life. Also, science is always analytical, ready to reduce its object to an intangible concept, whereas art is synthetic, always viewing its parts in terms of the organic whole, alert to represent life in tangible action. There are frequent conflicts between literary and scientific truths, and the artist has every right to sacrifice scientific truth for the sake of his literary truth, and should not hesitate to exercise this right. For this purpose the artist uses various methods, such as exaggeration, omission, selection, and combination. Soseki points out the most important of all his methods to achieve this kind of truth is association of one kind or another. He finds traditional and popular rhetoric of no particular use in this case. This method of association includes projection (e.g., personification), comparison with things other than self,

comic effects (humor, puns, wit), harmony (e.g., the use of nature in Oriental literature), contrast (comic relief, intensification,
irony), realism (either profound or commonplace), and temporal
and spatial distance (e.g., the use of the historical present, manip-
ulation of the point of view).

At the outset of this series Soseki declares that F signifies the
focal point of consciousness, not only individual but also collective. Having examined basic problems concerning literary substance itself, he now discusses the collective F, its kinds, its
evolution, and its vicissitudes, thereby clarifying those general
principles which effect the rise and decline of literature, the differentiation of literary schools, and the fate of literary movements.
The discussion, he points out, which necessarily involves society as
a whole, can not be thorough. With this preliminary warning, Soseki proceeds with three major classes of collective F on the basis
of form rather than substance: the consciousness of mass imitation
(imitation per se, tradition), talent (which gets ahead of its
time), and genius (which has its own nucleus, and its own wave
of consciousness). The difference between the first and the third
depends on the speed of sensing F, and that between the second
and the third is that talent always makes a success in this world,
while genius, far rarer, is honored by persecution rather than by
success. Soseki analyzes some aspects of the general law governing the change of collective consciousness, such as suggestion, and
shows the variety of their application. In the appendix he dwells
on the varieties of suggestion (economic, scientific, political,
moral) which affect literature. All these factors come into play,
determining the life of a given artistic work, but as usual in this
world, they are complex rather than pure. Indeed, Soseki points
out again that only in an ideal world does the intrinsic merit of a
work of art determine its life.

III *"Eighteenth-Century English Literature"*

If these two series are Soseki's search for objectivity in literature, the last of the series, "Eighteenth-Century English Literature," is then his application of the previously discussed principles
to eighteenth-century English literature. In spite of his apology
for being not well prepared for the lectures, Soseki, in his lengthy
introduction, touches on some vitally necessary preliminary problems: First, the general practice of period division is really con-

trary to the fact that time is a continuum; divisions are necessary
only for our convenience. Second, although literature differs from
science, neither literary criticism nor literary history can avoid the
method of science. They are at least in part scientific, for they
presuppose the objectivity of taste. We like or dislike, not the materials used in literature, but their arrangement or composition,
the interrelationships of these materials being eminently organic
and objective. Only in this sense does our literary history combine
subjectivism and objectivism, for it is an attempt to explain scien-
tifically a work of art on the basis of one's taste. Furthermore,
there are three attitudes toward literature: appreciative or subjective, critical or objective, and their combination, critical-apprecia-
tive. And the last of these three attitudes, Soseki believes to be the
one he is going to adopt in his lectures. Regarding foreign literature there are also two attitudes; to rely entirely on his personal,
independent response, or to present an informative and descrip-
tive picture, commonplace but not necessarily worthless. In this
series Soseki combines them. In a literary history there are again
two approaches: to treat literature as a part of or isolated from
society, both approaches having strong as well as weak points.
Here likewise Soseki prefers to combine them.

Having set forth his general method, Soseki first surveys the
over-all situation in eighteenth-century England, such as philosophy, politics, arts, social manners and fads, London and its inhabitants, its principal entertainments, the social position of contemporary artists, and the non-metropolitan area. After this Soseki
discusses five major makers of English neoclassical literature:
Addison and Steele, Swift, Pope, and Defoe. In dealing with each
of these major writers of the period Soseki performs at least two
of the primary functions of a literary critic: to grasp the unique-
ness of an individual artist and also the basic principles which
govern his art. This accounts for Soseki's discriminating, varied
approach to each writer, focusing on the relationship of an artist's
personality to his time. So he emphasizes the common-sense quality of the writing of Addison and Steele in relation to an audience
which prized clarity above suggestion, entertained a sense of self-
complacency about the achievement of their age, and, above all,
cherished the virtue of moderation. On the other hand, Pope's
poetry, under the pressures of his age, tended toward excessive
artificiality. English authorities may rate Pope as a great master

but Soseki feels that his art falls far short of the level of poetic genius. Regarding the abundance of intellectual *F* in Pope's poetry—mostly practical and popular—Soseki poses the question whether this is the expression of the poet's own personality or the result of the impact of his age upon him. In view of Pope's demonstrated ability to deal with human *F*, Soseki suspects that Pope's poetic talent, if left alone to follow its course, could have developed quite differently.

Obviously dissatisfied with Pope, Soseki is enthusiastic about Swift—understandably so, for he himself was then exceedingly popular as a rising satirist. Probably he also felt a certain temperamental affinity with the "Satirical Jupiter." Hence, he gives us a masterful essay which leaves little to be desired in its exploration of the nature of Swift's satirical art. In Soseki's view, the biographical approach in explaining the secret of Swift's satire is fallacious. By examining certain biographical facts about Swift, Soseki exposes obvious contradictions between these facts and literary historians' assertions. All considerations lead him to the conclusion that satire is Swift's nature; in other words, "Swift is the kind of person whose vision, applied to the world or to man, is completely satirical; and his satire is not based on a temporary attitude but the deeply rooted, ineradicable nature he was born with." Swift as a moralist realized that the Enlightenment was indispensable and yet it failed to satisfy men; but he was more than a moralist in that his "cold cynicism" often extended beyond moral concern. This is not to say that from the start Swift was a master satirist; the artistic difference between *A Tale of a Tub* and *Gulliver's Travels* makes this clear. Defining Swift's attitude in the last book of *Gulliver's Travels* as indifference, not callousness, Soseki states: "From start to finish Swift, maintaining a solemn countenance, pours out his satire—mechanically. His composure and his transcendence are such that the reader may have difficulty in deciding whether Swift is satirizing others or whether he himself is the object of his own satire. His is not the kind of raillery which is charged with heat and fury; instead it is cold, below zero. Like the Jupiter of the realm of satire, he stands cold but quiet atop Mt. Olympus, looking down on the far-off human world and describing it without sympathy, a totally different world."

Nowhere is Soseki's intention of "expressing his own view of literature through his chosen writers" more evident than in his discussion of Defoe. Here he no longer dwells on the relationship between Defoe and his age which surely lacked a sense of sublimity. Instead, Soseki focuses his attention on the secret of Defoe's fiction, an attitude natural for one who had by now learned something of this trade, and was soon to forsake his academic career for fiction writing. Where do we get our impression that all of Defoe's novels are overlong, asks Soseki. It comes not from our failure to appreciate his kind of fiction, but rather from Defoe's own lack of genuine artistry. In his novels he almost invariably gives us all available information about his characters—from birth to death, that is, their life-history. An endless list of facts, thus mechanically given, may create an external unity, but not the kind of inner or organic unity which is the essence of all art, including fiction. This confusion on Defoe's part between art and a mechanical listing of life-facts constitutes the worst defect of his works, as for example in *Robinson Crusoe* and *Moll Flanders.*

What, then, is the secret of making long stories appear short? It is what we call interest, composed of three things in fiction: character, incident, and scene. And the closer the second draws to the first, the more intense the degree of necessity; and the closer the second swings to the third, the more importance is given to chance. Most novels, being complex, contain all three in varying amounts. But all successful novels must achieve unity. And this unity of the three kinds of "interest" can be achieved through acceleration, development, and change. Out of this unity emerges the theme of a work. Defoe fails to recognize the necessity for this interest. His characters, like Robinson Crusoe, constantly wrestle with nature, but instead of acceleration, proceed mechanically with little inner change and development. *Moll Flanders* is still worse. To modern taste, such novels are hopelessly dated. Soseki then compares Defoe's method with Stevenson's in using for instance a storm scene for their backdrop. This comparison clearly shows the difference of interest between the two artists: Defoe's interest is always in facts, while Stevenson's is in the process itself. Defoe can never grasp his characters in dramatic action; he simply explains them by way of his favorite, never changing catalogue of facts and items. His novels have no inner or organic drama which assures his characters necessary development. In this sense Defoe is not even a master of realism, although this label is accepted by many critics as the best epithet for his art. To

Soseki he is not a novelist even, merely a master of accurate reportage; and reportage, no matter how good, is not art. This term realism, Soseki suggests, should be reserved for a worthier cause.

It is mainly these three series that made Saito eulogize Soseki as "probably the greatest student of English literature" Japan ever produced.[1] Referring to the last, which appeared in book form in 1909 under the title *Bungaku Hyoron*, Masamune, who does not think much of Soseki as an artist, said: "As a Japanese view of Western literature, it is thoroughgoing and without equal. Personally I would be more grateful had Soseki left more of this kind of criticism dealing with various periods of English literature instead of turning to fiction."[2] With some reservations, Ara said of *On Literature* (published in 1907): "On a psychological premise Soseki in this book created a unique aesthetics such as his predecessors had not even dreamed of. To such a contribution we should give full recognition. Our respect is due also to his quality of tenacious and logical vigor, rarely found in Japanese writers."[3] Of course there is also a minority opinion: Eto says of *On Literature* that it is "nothing but a child with an unheard of deformity, neither a scholarly treatise nor a piece of literary criticism," and that the only value of this "dishonorable" fruit of labor lies in Soseki's skepticism about literature itself.[4] But even taken at Soseki's own estimate, "the carcass of a deformed child" of his ambitious ten-year plan, these lectures have intrinsic value as one Japanese critic's serious confrontation with the basic problems of Western literature.

IV *Dissatisfaction with Lecturing*

Besides these three series of lectures which were delivered consecutively for four years, three hours a week at the University, Soseki on occasion gave extra reading courses. Throughout this period he also taught at both the First Higher School and Meiji University, in order to defray his increasing family expenditures. Altogether he spent thirty hours a week on teaching alone. In spite of these heavy commitments, he still had time to write such scholarly articles as "On the Ghost in *Macbeth*." These alone were sufficient to insure him a brilliant academic career as one of the most gifted professors of English literature in Meiji Japan. Yet Soseki was not satisfied with his life or with himself. It was this dissatisfaction that drove him, despite his recurring nervous strain, to a wide range of non-academic activities: water-color painting, and such writings as "My Bicycle Diary," his London reminiscences, a dozen poems in English, poems of varying length in Japanese, translations, and so forth. Soseki wrote these pieces not because he had leisure, but because he wanted to—had to —write. Indeed, these writings did not help allay Soseki's dissatisfaction, but rather helped lure him away from his teaching into a creative career. Finally in the last month of 1904, his creative energy exploded; from his never ceasing pen came *I Am a Cat, Yokyoshu,* a collection of seven short stories, and then *Uzurakago,* another collection of stories, sometimes simultaneously, sometimes one trailing on the heels of another. And all that while he was teaching some thirty hours a week. It was an almost superhuman feat, a feat which could be accomplished at a moment of "madness," or thanks to his madness, as Soseki himself duly noted in his preface to *On Literature:*

The Englishmen called mine a case of nervous breakdown. A certain Japanese, I understand, sent home a report that I was insane. I presume that these sagacious gentlemen cannot be accused of falsehood. My only regret is that due to my dullness of nature I am incapable of expressing my gratitude for their kind opinion.

Even after my return home I have been said to be a victim of nervous strain and insanity. Since even my own relatives confirm this view, I realize that there is no room for my plea of innocence. However, when I consider that I owe to this nervous breakdown and insanity, *I Am a Cat, Yokyoshu,* and *Uzurakago,* I think it quite proper to acknowledge my indebtedness to my condition.

As long as there is no change in my personal situation, this condition of nervous breakdown and insanity will continue—the rest of my life. And since, as long as they last, it is my hope to produce many an *I Am a Cat,* many a *Yokyoshu,* and many an *Uzurakago,* I only pray that nervous breakdown and insanity may never desert me.

Only because this nervous breakdown and insanity ruthlessly drive me into creative activity, is it possible that I shall have no more leisure to indulge in an academician's theorizing—such as *On Literature.*

V I Am a Cat

The first chapter of *I Am a Cat,* which begins, "I am a cat. Haven't gotten my name yet," appeared in *Hototogisu,* January 1905. It was followed immediately by the second chapter. The remaining nine were written intermittently, and the work was finally completed with the eleventh chapter which appeared in the same magazine in August 1906. Thus the work became the first major outlet for Soseki's dark personal spleen and his pent-up creative urge. Also it first established Soseki, then nearing the age of forty, as a new writer of Meiji literature. It had been Shiki, his old friend, who first lured him to the path of writing by publishing such pieces as "A Letter from London"; now it was Takahama Kyoshi, editor of the same *Hototogisu* after Shiki's death in 1902, who invited Soseki to write the first chapter of *I Am a Cat* and encouraged him to add another. And it was the enthusiastic public that drove Soseki to write nine more chapters. The work owed its genesis to a series of fortunate accidents which Soseki was able to make the most of. Due to the peculiar circumstances surrounding its birth, *I Am a Cat,* as Soseki himself was later to warn, has no formal, fully developed plot; "nor does it have any particular set design, structure, uncertain of its head and tail." In spite of Soseki's own warning, in spite of our first impressions, the novel, shows a sense of plot as it progresses. In fact, the last two-thirds of the work is less episodic, less digressive than the first third, revealing its spontaneous unity, as is often the case with a novel written under such circumstances.

It is, as the title suggests, a life-story of an unnamed feline hero who also serves as a learned, quizzical, and satirical narrator. Saved from starvation by a certain English teacher's family, he introduces us to the master's immediate circle: Master Kushami (Sneeze), who dabbles in anything, if impractical, from *haiku* poetry, new poetry, archery, *utai,* drawing, to violin playing, who always eats more than his poor stomach can tolerate, and who retires to his study only to doze over difficult English books; this gentleman has a wife, three carefree mischief-loving daughters, and a maid. Then our circle of acquaintances widens and we get to know Kushami's friends: harried philosopher Dokusen (Lonely Hermit); esthetician Meitei (Maze); and his former students, physicist Kangetsu (Cold Moon) and a poet Tofu (Vernal Breeze). All seem to have nothing to do and rattle away in a happy-go-lucky manner on various subjects such as suicide, nervous breakdowns, dynamics of hanging, stability of nuts, womanhood, noses, East-West culture, and human civilization. And this pitiable tribe of humanity, our feline hero dubs peace mongers.

The feline hero, of course, experiences his first and last love, for a tortoise-shell cat, a lovely neighbor treated regally at a music teacher's establishment. At a ricksha man's, he also has an unpleasant encounter with another male cat, who constantly boasts of his strong muscle. But these are interludes. The pace of the story begins to quicken when Kushami's world of everlasting peace is jolted by the intrusion of an unexpected enemy, the Kanedas (Gold Fields), a newly rich neighboring family. They demand Kangetsu, a valued member of the Kushami party, as a match for their lovesick daughter. This confrontation of the two parties, with the poor physicist in between, sets the second half of the story in motion. Neither party is willing to give in. The Kushami group naturally warns Kangetsu against the potential danger of the offer, whereas the Kanedas make it a condition that he first secure his doctoral degree, whatever that may be. The tug of war between the two parties reaches its climax when the Kanedas, aided by the music teacher and the ricksha man, bribe some reckless high school students to annoy Kushami at every turn. Two of Kushami's old acquaintances, one his university friend and the other a former student, both aspiring to reach the Kanedas' social status, are bribed to persuade Kushami to cease his futile opposition. When the aspiring businessman announces his engagement to the Kanedas' daughter, Kushami and his party toast him with beer. After the beer party, everyone feels a sense of emptiness. The feline hero belatedly joins in by dipping into the leftover beer. One glass intoxicates him, and being momentarily tipsy, he unluckily falls into a cistern and drowns.

In *I Am a Cat*, plot is the least important element; the charm lies elsewhere. What made the book an instantaneous and sensational success? And what is it that makes it still a popular work despite the passage of time? When it came out the public immediately recognized that it belonged neither to the tradition of lovers' romances nor to the half-baked naturalistic genre; it was as new and fresh as they were worn out. Equally novel was Soseki's use of a nameless cat as his narrator, able to look at man and society whimsically and with detachment, from a non-human dimension. This alone was refreshing in contemporary literature. Futhermore, it was a delightful satire. And the work provided Soseki opportunities to plunge into intellectual discussions which were speculative but stimulating, extreme but unique; it was, in fact, a vehi-

cle for a dazzling display of wit and humor, which hit the reader
when he least expected it. If these are some of the reasons for the
work's phenomenal success when it came out, they are still valid
for today's readers.

It has been pointed out that *I Am a Cat* echoes Meredith's
comic laughter, Sterne's rambling digressions, Swift's savage in-
dictment, and Hoffmann's famous feline hero. There is a trace of
the Popean mock-heroic tradition when Kushami tries to strike
back at his enemies, the swarming troops of high school students,
and also when the narrator-hero pursues a malicious mouse in the
manner of Achilles hounding Hector. The case for Swift's Yahoo-
Houyhnhnms as the probable source of Soseki's inspiration cannot
be taken too literally, in spite of Soseki's glowing eulogy of Swift's
cold cynicism. The narrator-cat says of Kushami and his entou-
rage as representative of the human race in general: "Man is
really good for nothing except to move his mouth—just to kill
time, work himself into laughter—about unfunny things, and in
general get himself worked up—over nothing at all." This is as far
as Soseki's satirical sword can penetrate the human mind. The
effect is rather that of tickling than that of biting. All is gay, because everyone gets the same satirical treatment, which is more or
less never fatal in any sense. Everyone gets even with everyone
else. It is as gay as it is satirical. Soseki once said of the essence of
comic literature: "The artist must be able to elicit sympathy amid
laughter." Judging by this standard, *I Am a Cat* is no doubt a
success, although it falls far short of the greatness of *Gulliver's
Travels*.

Fine but never great—this verdict Soseki would be willing to
accept. It is this complete absence of pretension on the part of
Soseki that makes the work still delightful to read. Because of its
quite accidental birth, the work seems to progress with as much
freedom as the progenitor himself. Since there is no immediate
end in view, the story seems eternally on the way—at least until
the author exhausts his vehicle. In fact, the cat-hero makes a sudden exit when Soseki reaches the technical limitations of the form.
There are simply moments to enjoy, incidents to survey, moods to
attune ourselves to, characters to smile at, and movements to keep
pace with. This rambling pace, with its many pauses, Soseki probably borrowed from the so-called *shaseibun* (sketch writing),[5] of
Kyoshi and his *haiku* group. Soseki took their stylistic motto and

wrote the first section of his book solely for their enjoyment. But only in the sense that Soseki carried this style as far as he could can we agree to Soseki's statement that the novel is "realism at its best." Soseki was surely wrong when later he wished the style of *I Am a Cat* less expansive and loose, for it is one of the primary reasons why the modern reader still finds this such a delightful satire.

Soseki's colloquial style, due to its sensitive vibration between the elliptical *haiku* and the high-flown Chinese style, is, perhaps, untranslatable into any different language. But we can still translate the conflict between the Kushamis and the Kanedas into our own terms. As the story moves along, the narrator-hero gradually loses his feline nature, coming to resemble his human creator more and more closely. Soseki maintains the feline mask, but behind that mask the reader cannot fail to notice Soseki's two different profiles: trifling amusement and telling seriousness, often vying for supremacy. This is the point where something like an elemental plot emerges from the story, tension between the two masks develops into conflict, and the central theme is suggested. This is the serious implication beneath the half-satirical, half-gay surface, an implication with twofold significance.

First, the conflict between the moneyed philistines and the defensive intelligentsia is symptomatic of the reality of a rising new bourgeois society in Meiji Japan. Although in the novel they maintain a precarious balance, or more properly, the cat beats his sudden retreat from our view before that balance is broken, we have an inkling that the stalemate between the two forces, non-communication and non-capitulation, cannot be the solution to society's problems. Soseki's failure to press the issue to the extreme was perhaps due to the limitations inherent in his technique. Nevertheless, it was a major source of annoyance to contemporary naturalists as it is to many serious-minded readers today. Second, the narrator-cat has his own weakness, the weakness which is also his creator's. The delightfulness of this work as a satire is that no one is left unwounded by the sharp edge of Soseki's satire; yet it is unmistakable that the cat is instinctively and irresistibly partial to his own master Kushami and his ilk. For an erudite and sophisticated domestic animal it is natural perhaps to feel closer to the world of the Kushamis than to that of the Kanedas. *I Am a Cat,* is, then, Soseki's own objectification of his

private world. Using his feline agent he can view the world of the
Kushamis with considerable, if not complete, detachment. But it
is a world that seems to be more and more overshadowed by the
rising philistines. Time seems to be running out for him to play
about under the mask of a cat; life is becoming a more serious
business.

VI   Seven Stories

"The Tower of London," "The Carlyle Museum," "The Phantom
Shield," "The False Sound of the Lute," "One Night," "The Song
of Evanescence" and "The Legacy of Love"—these seven short
stories which constitute Soseki's first collection, are brain children
of the creator of *I Am a Cat,* yet they are so different that one may
at first glance doubt their common paternity. Their simultaneous
creation is sufficient evidence that *I Am a Cat* could neither entirely satisfy Soseki nor express the whole of his artistic personality. Favored by accident, Soseki poured out *I Am a Cat,* giving
vent to his spleen and frustration; these seven stories he consciously willed to write, as much to convince himself as others of
his virtuosity, his ability to create something different.

Both *I Am a Cat* and *Seven Stories* are the crystallization of the
author's scholarly erudition, artistic taste, and creative imagination. In the first, his imagination, owing to the self-imposed feline
mask, is earthbound, crawling around immediate human affairs;
in the latter, his imagination is on the wing, a thirst for exotics and
fantastics. The one thrives on realism, the other on romanticism;
the one is prose in spirit, the other poetry; the one reality, the
other dreams; and in their combination alone does life find its
fullness.

These seven stories are in the nature of *études,* created rather
than born; indeed they were consciously and elaborately shaped
and etched in Soseki's mind. Now timid, now daring, Soseki's poetic touch creates a variety of little worlds remote and near. "The
Tower of London" and "The Carlyle Museum" may resemble
some of Irving's pieces in *The Sketch Book,* but they are really
drawn from Soseki's own experiences in London. The delicate
balance between the present and the past, between fact and
memory, often tips in favor of the latter. Consequently we are
borne into the misty remote medieval England of "The Phantom
Shield" and "The Song of Evanescence." Inspired by the Arthu-

rian cycle, and couched in highly ornate language, both poetically re-create the bygone world of valor, honor, and love. The one weaves a knight's faith in the shield, his family heirloom, and his devotion to his ladylove together into the rich symbolic texture of courtly love, whereas the other distils Malory's somewhat "vulgar" treatment of Lancelot and Guinevere into the purest pattern of sexual passion which encompasses heaven and hell. Love, which is the poetic essence of these two exotics, also maintains its ultimate mystery in "The False Sound of the Lute" and "The Legacy of Love," both set in mundane modern-day Japan, and are written in a prosaic style. The one relates an agonizing experience of a certain bachelor of law who, though skeptical of his friend-psychologist's interest in ghosts and contemptuous of his old housemaid's belief in omens, begins to worry almost to death over the well-being of his fiancée. If this sounds like a case history, the other is—par excellence: the narrator discovers that the love at first sight between a friend and a certain girl is really the result of their ancestors' unfulfilled love, a case history of hereditary love. As case histories, both stories are perhaps successes, but as stories neither succeeds; Soseki is timid and evidently uncertain how to weld the fantastic with the mundane. But such defects are absent from "One Night," a story undoubtedly set in this world but still successful as a story of the other world. There are only three characters sitting immobile in one room; they are unnamed and are described merely as a bearded one, a beardless one, and a woman. It is a success because Soseki is intent only on creating an atmosphere charged with the electricity of spiritual correspondence, and the characters are there only to serve as a tripod sustaining that intangible world of poetry. If it is true that *haiku* poetry is not intended to have any verbal meaning, "One Night" meets this basic requisite of good *haiku* poetry. Though written in prose, the story is a poem in spirit.

These seven story-*études*, interestingly enough, coincide with the introduction of symbolism into Japan. From this fact alone, one must not conclude that Soseki simply capitalized on this new literary movement. In view of his rather unkind opinion of symbolism, such a judgment would be a gross error. That these stories were meant to meet the deeply felt needs of Soseki's being is plain once juxtaposed with *I Am a Cat.* Their antithetical relationship has been made much of in the recent years by various critics—as the eloquent manifestation of Soseki's mental polarity, the polarity of realism and romanticism, reality and dream. Yet in schematizing the contrast between *I Am a Cat* and *Seven Stories*, one must not overlook the significant pattern within the collection itself. In it Soseki, judging from the result, seems to oscillate between two types of symbolism, Western and Eastern. For example, if we put "The Phantom Shield" and "The Song of Evanescence" at one end of the line, and "One Night" at the other, then "The Tower of London" and "The Carlyle Museum" group together near the center point facing "The False Sound of the Lute" and "The Legacy of Love." Where these two types of symbolism, Western and Eastern, intersect, we can locate *I Am a Cat*, that is, precisely at the zero point. This seems to be what Soseki meant when he said: " 'The Shield' is my ceremonial dress; 'The Tower' my formal attire; and *Cat* my plain clothes." At this stage, Soseki is still free to don at will whatever dress he needs. To put it another way, he still has not succeeded in finding what he could really be satisfied with.

VII   *"Botchan"*

"The Legacy of Love" appeared in *Teikoku Bungaku* for January 1906, when Soseki had only three more chapters to write of *I Am a Cat*. During this period Soseki also finished three stories, "Botchan," "The Grass Pillow," and "The 'Storm Day,' " later collected in *Three Stories*. The three stories here combine the characteristics of both *I Am a Cat* and the earlier collection, in relation to his four series of university lectures. "Botchan" inherits the comic spirit of *I Am a Cat;* "The Grass Pillow" perfects the poetic vision of the Kushamis, and especially the poetic world of "One Night"; whereas "The 'Storm Day' " compresses to the point of near violence the social consciousness implicit in *I Am a Cat*. Thus Soseki still embraces the polarity of the literature of detachment—"The Grass Pillow"—and the literature of commitment—"The 'Storm Day.' "

Together with *I Am a Cat*, "Botchan" is one of Soseki's most popular works and the most frequently anthologized. This fact is sufficient to tempt many readers to identify the hero with his creator. The temptation, though dangerous, contains some measure of truth, not because it is supposedly based on Soseki's own experience as a teacher at the high school in Matsuyama, nor because it is first person narrative. Rather it is because the hero reveals some aspects of Soseki at this stage, not the Soseki who went to Matsuyama to "bury himself alive," but the Soseki who, on the way home from London, resolved to fight against the world rather than retreat from it.

"Because of the recklessness I inherited from my parents, I have been a loser ever since my childhood." This opening sentence sets the mood, pace and direction of "Botchan," for it focuses on the Edo-born hero's brief but eventful stay at a local high school, at the climax of which he makes a triumphant exit as a loser, but as a willing loser after a head-on clash with the pettiness of his students, colleagues, and superiors. "Botchan" is a sort of extension of *I Am a Cat*, or *I Am a Cat* somewhat melodramatized. Now that Soseki drops his feline mask and stands behind this Japanese Candide, the social contrast in *I Am a Cat*, the contrast between the moneyed philistines and the defensive intelligentsia, becomes the direct clash between the conventional majority and the unconventional minority, and between the so-called leaders of society and the rebels. And in Soseki's world where the division between the good and the bad is neat, characters remain as distinct social types, suggested by their nicknames: Old Badger, the school principal who is experienced in the way of the world; Red Shirt, head teacher who has an effeminate, oily personality and who delights in maneuvering the situation to his advantage; Nodaiko, a sycophant who always knows which way the wind blows. As these align themselves on one side, on the other stands only Porcupine, who combines forces with the hero. The "good" and "bad" clash over Gourd, a good-natured but feeble colleague who loses his fiancée to Red Shirt and falls prey to his intrigue. But the most typical of all, needless to say, is Botchan (an untranslatable Japanese word which has been inadequately rendered "Master Darling"), a diamond in the rough who loves justice but has no gift for playing the games of the world. Since he speaks in a direct and natural style in this first-person narrative, the story moves rapidly toward its denouement without digressions, and "Botchan" makes delightful reading for those not seeking profundity of thought or subtlety of feeling.

The central situation leads to a final exposure of the nature of those respectable hypocrites whose types can be found everywhere in our society, which must establish conventions in order to survive. To this extent "Botchan" is a satire, but no more. The hero is only vaguely aware of his own position. It is not his consciousness but his personality that dictates his line of action. This quality adds more spice to the comic tenor of the story. If *I Am a Cat* turns the serious into a jest, the hero here has no sense of the comic; he is serious through and through, though always only according to his bent. It is this comic character and situation that saves "Botchan" from degenerating into a flat melodrama which would leave no room for the hero's triumphant exit as a willing loser. To dismiss "Botchan" by hastily identifying the hero with his creator, and thereby criticizing Soseki's ethical naïveté, is to make a serious misjudgment, for Soseki cannot be identified with the hero of "Botchan"; the most that can be said is that "Botchan" reveals one aspect of Soseki, even at this stage. The qualities which make this story delightful and ever fresh are many, but the ultimate one is Soseki's comic touch, which stirs up in everyone's heart a nostalgia for the natural, wild innocence he has lost, willingly or not, as a citizen of the world. The theme of the story, then, should be the conflict between the natural and the artificial, whose potential tragedy Soseki is not quite ready to face.

Emotion, to Soseki, is the foundation of literature; moral sentiment, being one kind of emotion, has its vital place in literature. In ignoring this indisputable truth, the devotees of art for art's sake have committed an unpardonable sin; their opponents, on the other hand, have failed to realize the truth that moral sentiment is but a part of literature, no matter how vital. On the basis of this reasoning, Soseki pointed out in *On Literature* that willing suspension or elimination of the moral idea of good and evil is an indispensable prerequisite for our appreciation of a certain area of literature; it is the kind of literature which transcends our moral sentiment—a sort of non-human literature, as exemplified in some poems by Li Po, Tu Fu, Cowper, Lover, and others. This is true of many poems dealing with nature; Eastern literature, especially, has cultivated this tradition to a great extent, and to it belongs "The Grass Pillow." Already in "One Night," Soseki had ventured in this direction, and in "The Grass Pillow" he sought to more fully approximate the esthetic moment of those cultured idlers of the Kushamis and the poetic spirit of "The Tower of London," "The Phantom Shield," and "The Song of Evanescence"—in the eternal nowness of nature.

VIII   "*The Grass Pillow*"

At the midpoint of life, a painter, weary of the humdrum world, sets out on a poetic journey along the mountain path on a vernal day, the season when the least romantic creature becomes neglectful of its allotted daily activities; he is completely oblivious to the canvas and easel he carries. When the journey terminates at a tasteful hot-spring inn and he happens to meet the daughter of his host, something like a story develops. To fall in love with this woman, who is all the more alluring because of the shadow of her unexplained past, is out of the question. Instead, as a detached artist he wants to gaze at her as if she were a work of art. Yet her person lacks something—something that leaves her less than a complete picture. Gradually he realizes what that something is; it is a sentiment called *aware,* which connotes in Japanese more than either pity or tenderness. It means more even than the "ahness of things," a translation recently concocted. It is the human sentiment unknown and yet most akin to God. The moment this *aware* crosses her beautiful but somewhat too wilful brow, his vision of her will be completed, so the painter says to himself. The moment arrives at last, when they go to the station to see her cousin off to war, and her eyes happen to meet those of her former husband on the departing train. Soon his face vanishes, and her eyes absently follow the train. It is in her absent-mindedness, unexpectedly, that the painter for the first time discovers that "something"—the sentiment of *aware* which completes his vision of her.

With this finishing touch the vision, the journey, and the story—everything completes itself in evanescence, leaving us only with the sentiment of *aware,* that immaterial but exquisite fragrance of beauty. In order to arrest this sense of esthetic beauty, Soseki eliminates from his story virtually everything that makes a novel. On the other hand, in order to conjure up, not explain or describe, that esthetic moment, he exhausts every means, every device, all the knowledge at his disposal—in the incense of pure art. As a result, we are constantly dazzled by an endless tapestry of poetry, Eastern and Western, which he creates in a deliberate but often witty style. Thus, "The Grass Pillow" becomes an art novel, or an artist's novel about art, artists, and the artistic vision of life. Translated into English, the story might bear the title, "A Poetic Journey." Yet it is very different from the so-called art novel, a special genre in modern literature. In an interview following the appearance of "The Grass Pillow," Soseki explained it as an attempt to go in the opposite direction from our ordinary fiction, as a sort of *haiku* novel whose essence is beauty, and defended it as the kind of literature that would make a man oblivious to the pain of life, thereby offering solace. He suggested that it might blaze a trail for a new movement in the world of literature. On another occasion he restated this view and added that, if not a masterpiece, the story nevertheless has no precedent.

The narrator who records his poetic journey is a painter because Soseki feels that of all arts, painting is the most detached from things human, or that painting could best bear man into the transcendental realm. Being freed from the toothed wheel of time, the painter in the story can ramble around the woman, who is, no doubt, the mobile symbol of nature. His sort of rambling has no place in an ordinary novel, where everything is related to and supports everything else, but it is supremely important in "The Grass Pillow," where every moment exists for itself. Indeed, his poetic journey itself is a rambling. What good does that do us? This question itself may sound too mundane, but it is a question that must be answered. The painter in the story says: "If the twentieth century needs sleep, it also needs this sort of unworldly, transcendental poetic spirit. Nowadays, I say with regret, makers and readers of poetry are all so Westernized that they no longer are interested in the upstream journey toward this valley of paradise. Not a professional poet, I am not a reformer zealously propagating the poetic world of Wang Wei and T'ao Yüan-ming in our present age. For me, however, this poetic spirit seems far more valuable than a concert or a ball, more gratifying than *Faust* or *Hamlet*. For this reason alone I am following the vernal mountain path, carrying my paint box and easel. I simply wish to inhale directly from nature the poetic spirit of Wang and T'ao, roaming the realm of non-humanity. It is just for sheer fun." Is he an escapist? The poet asks what is wrong with it, if that makes you a cosmic bohemian rather than a social bohemian? It is an escape into a larger world. Is it possible only for the artist? Our painter thinks otherwise, for every man is potentially an artist. Take a traveler: while on the road he is an ordinary weary man, but when he reminisces about his travel, he is already a poet. That is, if one can rub

off one corner of this square world of common sense, and live
within that triangle, he is then an artist.

IX   *"The 'Storm Day'" and "The Wintry Blast"*

In his preface to Kyoshi's *The Amaranthe,* Soseki divided modern fiction into two kinds, detachment and commitment, com-
menting on their relative merits. In contrast to the latter (which
we might call *littérature engagée*), characteristic of modern, especially Western fiction, the former is typically Eastern with three
major traits: detached objectivity, leisurely irony, and antifictional
fiction. To this category belong most of Soseki's works that have
so far appeared—notably *I Am a Cat* and "The Grass Pillow." Yet
of the former, Soseki emphatically stated that the views of life
there expressed belong to the characters not to him, and of the
latter that it conveys only a part of his view of life and art. And in
"The 'Storm Day'" and "The Wintry Blast" we find still another
aspect of Soseki, the man who described himself as "a socialist of
one sort."

"The 'Storm Day'" presents two main characters ready to scale
a volcano called Mount Aso; one is committed, the other detached; one is a fighting and the other a transcendental type. Only
at the close of the story does the theme come through: "The principal purpose of our existence in the world," says the fighter, "is to
destroy the evil elements of civilization and give some peace to
the common people who have neither money nor power. Isn't that
so?" They agree and, just before the "storm day," set out toward
the volcano which is "emitting a century of complaints into the
infinite blue." Of his characters, Soseki said that they suggest two
different directions for present-day youth to follow.

"The Wintry Blast," which appeared two months later, develops
this theme to its ideological limit. The dubious friendship between
two young literary aspirants, one who already enjoys money and
fame, and the other who must struggle for survival, constitutes an
underplot of this novella, preparing the reader for the appearance
of its hero, a former teacher who is now working on a provocative
essay on human character. While his ununderstanding wife and
his philistine brother conspire to destroy the manuscript, the hero
makes a speech, "An Address to the Modern Youth," a title which
Soseki once considered using for the story itself. At the climax of

the story, the hero urges the young intellectuals of the Meiji era to uphold their ideals and exercise their leadership, in order to wrest the world from the corrupting force of both the titled and the moneyed. The story ends in an anticlimax when the destitute youth buys the manuscript with the money his successful friend offered him so that he might complete this ambitious work. This he does as atonement for an old injustice to the hero, whom he and other classmates had thrown out of the school.

"The Wintry Blast" intensifies the clash between the Kushamis and the Kanedas, the difference being that here the intellectual leaders do not combine their forces to challenge the moneyed philistines. As for the hero of the story, he is a Botchan, not as the unconscious lover of rough justice, but an intellectual fully committed to the cause of social justice. In this he resembles Ibsen's heroes, especially Dr. Stockmann. (Soseki designated the literature of commitment as Ibsenesque.) Soseki is wholly serious about the hero's indignation over the increasing social injustice, and also in insisting on the intellectuals' awakening to their own obligations. If his hero seems quixotic as does Ibsen's, it is not this aspect that damages the story; nor is it the emphasis on what Soseki calls the intellectual F, the weakest of the four F's in literature. The story fails because the case is generalized instead of being dramatized. Soseki once said that the artist who has intellectual breadth should be able to embrace the polar extremities of life at once. In "The Wintry Blast," Soseki tried to grasp only one of them. Moreover, the story does not go beyond the level of experimentation, remaining one of the author's most outspoken and therefore least successful *Tendenz* novels.

CHAPTER 3

The Moment of Decision (1907–1908)

I The "Miser of Time"

ALTHOUGH teaching thirty hours a week and preparing three lecture series was more than one man's work, Soseki at the same time produced *I Am a Cat,* along with a dozen stories. Furthermore, he wrote a variety of poems, critical articles, translations, and made himself available for two dozen magazine interviews. As his fame extended beyond the academic grove, he found himself surrounded by his former and present students, now his most enthusiastic admirers, such as Terada Torahiko, Morita Sohei, Suzuki Miekichi, Nogami Toyoichiro, Komiya Toyotaka, Matsune Toyojo, and Sakamoto Setsucho—lately joined by Abe Nozei, Abe Jiro—all serious students of arts and ideas. This circle of disciples, admirers, and acquaintances widened with such rapidity that late in 1906 every Thursday had to be set aside for them. From then on the Thursday circle as a sort of literary *salon* began to exercise a significant impact on the contemporary literary world, often rivaling the Ryudokai, another group consisting chiefly of naturalistic writers. Throughout these crowded years Soseki had also learned to live with ever recurring nervous strain, as well as his known marital tension.

All this new distinction would have satisfied Soseki if he had remained the old Soseki of Kumamoto who vaguely wished to have a literary life, so that he might be able to read, speak, and write as freely as he pleased. But now he was no longer the old Soseki; he felt that what he had hoped would be a dilettante's ease and leisure had become instead the rush and intensity of a literary whirl. In December 1904, just after he finished the first part of *I Am a Cat* and was working on "The Tower of London," Soseki wrote half in jest: "From now on, living on a mild diet and mastering deep breathing, I am going to become a great literary artist." To one nursing such an ambition, time must have been priceless. Later, in *Loitering,* the novel generally regarded as an accurate account of the author during this period, Soseki described his hero as "a man constantly driven by time," and called him "a miser of time." Time is in any case a cruel master, not allowing his slave any prolonged compromise. Time now made Soseki see this. He began to realize that he had to choose either teaching or writing, because time always demands his slave's wholehearted devotion. Teaching was bringing him less and less satisfaction, whereas writing was now absorbing his real interest and had ceased to be a mere pastime.

Perhaps the most eloquent record of his dilemma is Soseki's correspondence throughout this period. In April 1905 he wrote: "Presently preparing my university lectures and simply hate this. I wish I could quit school altogether. I should rather write even the *Cat* stuff than the school lectures." In May he mentioned the pleasure of thanking one of his admirers: "This sort of pleasure far outweighs the pleasure of drawing a Manila sweepstake, or being called a great savant, or offered a professorship or a doctoral degree." In July he wrote: "While teaching full time at both the University and the Higher School and part-time at Meiji University, I am trying to write full time, too. What folly! Impossible unless I can persuade our Lord Sun to stretch 365 days into 10,-000. After giving much thought to this matter, I even decided that I would quit teaching for a newspaper job if they would pay me 10 *yen* for a column." In August: "So little time for a mountain of work to do. Really impossible unless I become two Sosekis, or one day stretches to 48 hours." In September: "Worst of all, school is to start soon. Well, my psychological makeup is not meant for school, I guess." A few days later in the same month: "Far from being greedy, I would be just as happy as could be if only I could write a couple of works that satisfy me. But in order to do that I have to eat beef and eggs—some such stuff. So now I am in a mess, losing myself in something that gripes my soul. What could be worse? (Do I sound a bit comical?) At any rate, teaching is what I must get rid of; writing is really my heart's desire. If only I could devote myself just to writing, for that's the only reason I am fulfilling obligations to heaven and others—including myself." Still in the same month: "Though frustrated and anxious, I haven't accomplished anything. Thoroughly disgusted with myself. That quitting teaching would mean becoming a writer—maybe just wishful thinking."

This sense of frustration increased in the following year. His old sense of humor gave way to a new tone of seriousness. The more confident he grew about his own worth the more intimately involved were his feelings about the contemporary literary scene, not as a detached observer, but as a warrior intent on surveying the morrow's battlefield which might turn into his monument or his grave. In January he wrote: "We must try to cultivate our critical eye—impartial enough not to hurt an author's virtue. As for others' works, I would merely like to enjoy them. Willingness to read their works comes first. But on reading, I discover there aren't too many that really impress me. More often I am impressed with foreign works. This is not because I am blindly worshipping them. Far from it." Now he lamented the distorted genius of Izumi Kyoka, and now he was completely impressed with Toson's *Transgression,* so much so that he did not hesitate to recommend it as a masterpiece of Meiji literature and admitted that he had not accomplished anything as great as Toson's. In October he wrote: "Meiji literature is just beginning. So far, it's just born. Young people from universities are going to make it a great one. Now we are facing a period of rich promise. Since I am fortunate enough to be living in such a wonderful time, I am prepared to work myself to death to clear the way for you young people and set a great stage for many a genius to unfold. It may yet get dark while we are undecided. We must hurry. We must work with might and main. Let our people realize that literature is a nobler and more useful affair than what those cabinet members are doing. Let those good for nothing millionaires bow to artists, instead of to ministers." In the same month he wrote to a dejected disciple: "In a hundred years hundreds of Ph.D.'s will turn into clay; so will thousands of professors. My ambition is to leave my art to a hundred generations to come."

II *University of Kyoto Offer*

It was about this time Soseki was approached by his old friend to join the faculty of the Imperial University of Kyoto. In his two long answering letters, Soseki divulged what was then on his mind: If he were the same old Soseki, the Soseki who fled Tokyo to Matsuyama, from there on to Kumamoto, he would gladly have gone to Kyoto as a professor of English literature. But he was no longer the same old Soseki. He was a child, only three or four

years old, in the sense that he was reborn with his resolution made
on return from abroad. If he could accomplish something of
worth, all that would belong to the future. So he would refuse to
repeat the mistake of ten years ago. He would stay in Tokyo for
life or death:

So far, I have had no opportunity to test my own worth. Nor have I
ever once trusted myself. All along I have relied on my friends' sympathy, my superiors' charity, and my fellowmen's goodwill. But from
now on I'll never rely on that sort of thing—not even on my wife,
children or relatives. I must go alone as far as I can until I collapse.
Otherwise, I feel I shall never find the real meaning of life, neither
the challenge to live nor the certainty whether I am alive or dead.
Since life to me is a gift from heaven, I would be sorry if I didn't
personally experience the meaning of life.

In the same vein Soseki wrote to one of his disciples:

To live in neatness and beauty, that is, to live poetically—I do not
know what portion of life's worth poetical life occupies, but I think its
portion must be very small indeed. One mustn't be like the hero of
"The Grass Pillow." That may be all right, but in order to exist in
this world of ours, and develop what he has to the fullest, one must
venture out as positively as Ibsen's heroes. From this point of view,
the literature that is only beautiful is but idle words; ancient scholars
rightly scorned it. And the *haiku* spirit means only delight in roaming
this world of idle words. So long as one loafs in the small world, the
great world can not be shoved forward an inch. Furthermore, on all
sides there are formidable foes who will not be trifled with. Anyone
who regards literature as his life cannot be satisfied with the beautiful
alone. He must be as determined as those royalist samurai of the
Meiji Restoration to stand hardships, I should think. Indeed, to be an
artist, he must take everything in stride, nervous breakdown, insanity,
and even prison. . . . As for me, I should like to appreciate *haiku*
literature, and at the same time pursue literature with the same passion
as those samurai of the Restoration, risking my own neck.

True, it is not only war that demands heroism and creates a
hero; literature also demands its own heroism and creates its own
heroes, for literature is a war of peace, as Soseki called it. When
asked of the literary situation after the Russo-Japanese War, Soseki stated that Japan had "won the war but lost the peace," im-

plying that Meiji literature had still to declare its independence from Western literature. But he also hoped that this military victory might lead to a new creative age comparable to the English Renaissance. It seemed to herald the day when Japan would boldly declare her literary independence. Yet the age awaited those fully qualified to sign the declaration. Soseki was one of those riding the tide of time, and he became more and more conscious of the significance of the moment. As a free man of Meiji Japan he wanted something greater, more genuine, and more lasting than a military victory; he wanted a cultural victory; he wanted a complete victory. In fact, for the two previous years Soseki had been waging his own version of the Russo-Japanese War within himself. The moment had now arrived to test whether he was capable of an act of heroism leading to such a victory.

III *Newspaper Offers*

In February 1907, a feeler came to Soseki from the *Asahi*, then the largest daily in the country, whether he would write exclusively for their readers. This was not Soseki's first offer; only a few months earlier he had been offered the chair of English literature at the University of Kyoto; he had turned it down without much hesitation, for it meant not only continuing the same sort of academic career, but also a retreat from Tokyo, his literary battleground. Then a little later he had also received an offer from the *Yomiuri*, an influential Tokyo daily, to take charge of its literary columns, and, after much soul-searching, decided not to make any move. In the offer, though tempting to one eager to quit teaching, Soseki still could not see any security, only the possibility of some foreseeable and some unforeseeable entanglements, such as literary partisanship and favoritism and jealousy and rivalry among his new colleagues. Above all, he wanted to do his own writing— creative, not critical. But the *Asahi* offer seemed different from either, since it would enable him to leave teaching and devote himself to what he wanted to do.

IV *The Decision*

Yet he could not readily jump to the offer; no longer a reckless youth, he had his large family to think of—his wife, his three children, and a fourth on the way; nor was he in any position to have to seek a job elsewhere. At almost the same time it became clear

that he could, if he wanted, occupy the chair of English literature
at the University of Tokyo. Knowing that the moment of decision
had at last arrived, he was all the more cautious about the whole
matter. Soseki knew better than anyone else that to resign his academic position meant forsaking a career of relative security and
social prestige for an unknown future. The negotiations thus extended into the following month. He wanted to clarify all possible
points with the other party. For instance, he wanted to remind
them of their own risk. "I want you to consider," wrote Soseki in
one of his letters, "the fact that my kind of work is not suitable for
today's newspaper. Of course, it may be all right in ten years. By
then Soseki may no longer be as popular as now. Have you taken
this into account?" Surely in this matter the risk of the *Asahi* was
equal to Soseki's own, though the offer was motivated not just by
Soseki's reputation as a new writer, but by their confidence in his
promise, his talent, and above all his integrity. In mid-March the
deal was successfully closed with the agreement of both parties on
the following major points: (1) monthly salary of 200 *yen,* with
regular fringe benefits; (2) no dismissal without reason; (3) all
literary works to be published in the *Asahi,* but the amount, kind,
time left to Soseki; (4) non-literary writings and scholarly and
miscellaneous writings to be at his own disposal; (5) absolutely
no interference from the management with his work, even though
not in the current fashion; (6) Soseki to retain the copyright to all
his publications in the *Asahi.*

Today we are suspicious of such an alliance between literature
and journalism which has so often proved to be disastrous or de-
moralizing to one party or the other. Yet to see in Soseki's decision
indications of a compromising nature, to interpret his compromise
as symptomatic of the artist's willing capitulation to the new tyranny of journalism, and to dismiss the whole case as a sort of
artistic and intellectual prostitution is too categorical. The fact is
that it is a rare exception to the *mésalliance* of literature and journalism, in that both parties not only agreed on these points but
carried them out without bending their principles and sacrificing
their integrity. Thus the Soseki-*Asahi* alliance marked a rare moment in the fruitful cooperation between literature and journalism
—at least in Meiji Japan, and furthermore set the direction of
Soseki's artistic career as a popular writer, and eventually as a
national writer.

All this, we can say from the vantage point of history, however. At the time, Soseki's decision came as a shock to his contemporaries, to his admirers as well as to his critics. Although it is true that the *Asahi,* like many other newspapers in Meiji Japan, as one of the most effective vehicles of enlightenment, addressed in the main the intellectual class, Soseki's decision to leave the academic grove for the "vulgar" world of journalism was something his contemporaries were not ready to accept. In their tradition-bound eyes this impossible exchange of the Imperial University of Tokyo for a private enterprise like the *Asahi* was beneath the dignity of his professional status. But this was not the only shocking aspect. Soseki's decision seemed to them degeneration from scholar to story writer, a madman's behavior indeed. It was contrary to the pattern set by other writers, such as Tsubouchi Shoyo, who abandoned his creative career to return to the academic world, and Futabatei Shimei, who, in doing the same, seemed to declare that literature after all is not worth dedicating one's whole life to. Soseki's own first announcement in the paper clearly suggests what was in the air at the time. With his characteristic forthrightness, Soseki stated that there should be no difference between an academy and a newspaper. For him, in fact, the latter had the advantage that he could "devote himself entirely to creative work which he regarded as his life," not as a leisure-time hobby. "Nowadays," he said, "Soseki does not feel alive unless he is writing something." Then he concluded: "Heart is won by heart, as an old saying goes. For the *Asahi,* which accepts an oddball like me, I shall certainly do as much as an oddball can do, and I consider it my pleasant obligation."

The significance of Soseki's decision cannot be overestimated, for it signaled at one and the same time the birth of the Soseki legend, and of the professional artist in modern Japan. Cutting himself off from the rising bureaucracy, he declared his individual right to exercise a newly acquired freedom, the freedom of shaping his own destiny as a non-aligned artist.

As soon as he made up his mind to accept the *Asahi* offer, Soseki tendered his resignation to the University authorities, and visited Kyoto for two weeks. In April the arrangement was made formal. In the same month, while a plan for his first novel was still on his mind, he gave a speech at the Literary Association of the Tokyo Academy of Fine Arts under the title of "The Philosophical

Basis of Literary Art." Revised and expanded, it appeared in the
Asahi, as Soseki felt it proper to express his views of literature.
This lecture is a kind of afterthought on *On Literature*, but certain
points stand out: based on the evolutionary concept of universal
individuation and integration, Soseki first points out that man's innermost desire for the continuity of consciousness which is existence itself, creates in due course of time four kinds of ideals: the
beautiful, the true, the good, and the sublime; each corresponding
with his four major mental faculties. The ideal artist, in his opinion, should be able to realize all these four ideals in his work, but
this is so only in theory. In actual practice, artists necessarily tend
to stress one or two of these ideals. Naturalism, for example, is a
case in point. As a literary movement it does have its rightful
place in the domain of literature; however, the true, which is its
professed ideal, is but a part of the whole. Clearly it errs in insisting that its truth is the one and only truth, thereby limiting the
scope of literature itself. As a corrective to this lamentable situation, Soseki suggests the necessity of cultivating character and
technique. Literature is, after all, art in the original sense, and
genuine literature comes into existence only when art is completed by its maker, especially his character. Only then can the
artist exercise his right in modern society, and his work continues
to exercise its impact on the future of the human race. The lecture
is Soseki's defense of literature at large, and it reveals in what
spirit he was then facing his first assignment.

V The Poppy

Late in May when the *Asahi* announced Soseki's forthcoming
serial, *The Poppy*, the sensation was instantaneous and conta-
gious; metropolitan department stores were quick to catch the alluring connotations of the title which Soseki said he had thought
up casually, and started special sales of "Gubijinso" robes, "Gubijinso" rings, and the like. Even without such enthusiastic response
from his prospective readers, Soseki could not but be tense for the
challenge. Like his readers, Soseki was conscious that this was
going to be his virgin work as a professional writer. Aside from
the tenseness common to all artists in similar situations, Soseki
also knew that as a novel it could not be the same as any of his
previous works: they were all either like *I Am a Cat*—though
long, usually loosely linked—or short stories of varying length like

those in his two collections. This time, however, he had to write a novel, and he was going to do just that. The result was a novel overdone in almost every respect. Indeed, the charms, as well as the flaws, of *The Poppy* stem from this source.

Although written in highly ornate language, the story follows its logical course to the end. The beginning seems leisurely, alternating between two locales and simultaneous incidents: on the one hand, the Kyoto trip of Kono, a philosopher, and Munachika, an aspiring diplomat; and on the other, the Tokyo scene, bringing together Fujio, Kono's half-sister who is virtually engaged to Munachika, and Ono, a university classmate who has received an Imperial gift watch. These two parallel lines, further complicated by some minor characters, finally cross each other at the Ueno Exhibition, accelerating the tempo of the drama. Ono is torn between his obligations to his old teacher and his daughter Sayoko, who have just arrived from Kyoto, and his desire for Fujio, a symbol of beauty, sophistication, and wealth; on the other hand Itoko, Munachika's sister, despite her affection for Kono, willingly follows the way of resignation. Along with these contrasting sets, the supporting characters likewise reveal their own makeup: Fujio's devoted but intriguing mother; Munachika's unconventional but understanding father; and the practical Asai, who, unprincipled and unscrupulous, volunteers to convey to the already bewildered father and daughter Ono's intent to break off their engagement. For a while everything goes wrong, then the drama suddenly takes a turn in favor of the just sufferers. With candor Munichika makes the weak-kneed Ono see the right path to follow, and face Fujio in the presence of everyone. Fujio, realizing her defeat, turns to Munachika only to suffer another defeat. The shock and shame are sufficient to fell the proud heroine.

As this brief summary should suggest, *The Poppy* is a novel, not a story, in that it owes its dramatic force to the interplay of structure and character, though they are not always fully integrated. As the novel starts, the two circular movements, Kyoto and Tokyo, appear to be too loose and slow moving to be very promising; yet, the moment both gather forces, they fuse into a single whirl which, at each stage of acceleration, draws all the characters toward its center. At the center stands Fujio; on the immediately adjacent concentric circle stand Ono, Munachika, and Kono; on another, Itoko and Sayoko; and on the outermost, Fujio's mother,

Ono's teacher, Munachika's father, and Asai. This structural paral-
lelism, which throughout the story echoes the mechanical regular-
ity of two symbolic watches (one being Ono's Imperial gift and
the other, Fujio's which, by her father's promise, should belong to
Munachika, but which she wishes to offer Ono instead), is perhaps too artificial, but may make some readers admire Soseki's
structural exercise, for it is something not to be found in his previous works.

Soseki's original intention, as he explained it, was not to make
love the sole interest of the novel, but to present two or three
interests which, after a series of fluctuations, come to the final
point of explosion. By two or three interests Soseki might have
meant those familiar motifs: friendship, scheming stepmother,
blood is thicker than water, three varieties of love, the conflict of
generations, character contrast. Whatever his original design, the
dominant person of the novel is Fujio, who carries the story forward and fascinates the reader. Soseki himself was well aware of
her potentially tragic personality and was, in fact, intent on ex-
ploiting it. Thus, she becomes the most completely delineated
character. What most interested Soseki about this character (as he
confided while working out the denouement) is her egotism, so
peculiar to an emancipated modern female, all the more enhanced
by her pampered upbringing. The title of the novel seems admi-
rably suited for her regal pride and pose, now like Cleopatra (to
whom Soseki likened his heroine more than once) and now like
Yang Kuei-fei, the Chinese imperial concubine whose beauty is
said to have ruined the T'ang Dynasty. Although her destructive-
ness might easily have affected those around her, as much as herself, Soseki preferred to rescue everyone else from destruction. He
said of Fujio, while still working on the climax: "I have grown
tired of *The Poppy;* I want to kill her off soon." Soseki was apparently wrestling with his own creature, for he also remarked:
"Every day I work on *The Poppy.* Don't be so sympathetic about
Fujio. I do not like her. Certainly romantic but never gentle, in a
word she is a female devoid of moral sentiment. To kill her off is
the theme of the novel. If I cannot kill her off nicely, I'll let her go
as she is. But in that case Fujio will become more and more depraved. I'll tack a philosophy onto the conclusion, the kind of theory which I'm writing this novel to prove. So don't be kindly dis-

posed to her ilk. Sayoko, on the other hand, deserves more pity."
At the same time, Soseki admitted that he could not go against the
laws of nature; he could not kill off Fujio any more than he could
the novel itself.

As a novel, *The Poppy* has too many obvious flaws; even his
admirers cannot possibly gloss over them. Its highly ornate style,
while singularly becoming the heroine, is out of place in fiction; its
structure, though complicated, is not free of the traces of Soseki's
mathematical design; its characterization is not subtle enough;
and all his characters except Fujio are too generalized and consist-
ent, tending to become pure, unmixed types. All in all, the work is
a promising failure, not because Soseki went against the laws of
nature or stopped short of them, but ironically because in his eagerness he often went beyond them.

There is too much of Soseki in the novel. Either out of his excessive concern with his characters or out of kindness to his audience,
he cannot detachedly let the story run its own course or allow the
characters to act out their own assigned roles. Following the story
and its actors through all stages, he constantly makes comments in
a stylized manner. This is not to say that he tries to change the
course of the story or the basic traits of his characters in order to
prove his theory. For example, both Ono's last-moment change of
heart and Fujio's downfall may disturb some readers because of
their seeming abruptness. Despite this feeling, the changes are in
keeping with Ono's and Fujio's personalities. Yet, on the whole,
the author interferes excessively with the natural, organic interplay between plot and character; this habit becomes most con-
spicuous at the denouement, where he feels obliged to bring plot
and character forcibly together and theorize on their implications.
Soseki follows Meredith's method in closing the novel with Kono's
diary entry and Munachika's cryptic remark on London, so that
his own philosophy may be stated unequivocally. The point is actually neither what Kono observes ("All human comedy ends in
tragedy") nor what Munachika remarks ("In this part of the
world, only comedy is in fashion"), nor their combination, but
rather Soseki's failure to have his theory of life emerge out of the
situation itself. Soseki may be free to impose his concept of life on
the world of his characters, but the readers know better, that tragedy here is clearly out of place because their world is not even

comedy, but melodrama. All human comedy, as Soseki implies, may sooner or later end in tragedy, but no melodrama can end in tragedy.

Soseki himself said in 1909 that any work should be called a failure to the extent that it betrays the author's intention. This is the case with *The Poppy*. Later, in 1913, he labeled it an artistic failure and wished it were out of print. Yet *The Poppy* is an important landmark in Soseki's career as a novelist, not merely in a negative, but in a positive sense. Even though it is an artistic failure, it is the first novel attempted by Soseki. In it Soseki displayed his ability to construct plot, develop situation, and create a variety of characters (though they were still types). Besides his technical dexterity, there was much intellectual substance, whose lack Soseki deplored as one of the most serious weaknesses of Japanese literature in general. He had something interesting and important to say through his new medium. Moreover, in these sets of male and female characters he unconsciously suggested the whole range of his heroes and heroines—between Kono and Ono, between Sayoko and Fujio, and even the conflict of the sexes. And there was his discovery that tragedy is greater than comedy because it alone takes life seriously. In *The Poppy* the problem has been touched on lightly, and to explore it in depth becomes the major concern of his later novels.

VI   The Miner

Turning from *The Poppy* to Soseki's next work, *The Miner*, we suddenly find ourselves in a world entirely different from that of *The Poppy*. Here is a story written in a down-to-earth and matter-of-fact style, with an un-hero-like hero and a minimal number of characters; but without any obvious intimacy, without any plot, and therefore without any human drama of interest. *The Miner* is a novel devoid of every conceivable element of fiction. It would be no exaggeration to call it a sort of antinovel. In the whole cycle of Soseki's works that followed, *The Miner* is an exception, with no thematic relationship to the rest of his works.

By Soseki's own account, it drew upon the material he had recently been forced to buy from a certain youth. What made Soseki write this novel, based on another person's experience? One possible theory is that he lacked other material just when he received an unexpected request from the Osaka office of the *Asahi* (both the Tokyo and Osaka editions were to carry Soseki's serials) to write a story for the New Year. Another theory is that Soseki wanted to try something different from *The Poppy*, that he was wearied of its artificiality. And perhaps there are many more theories. The matter here is: what possibilities did he see in another person's experience as the material for his novel—since being an artist, not a reporter, he could have chosen something quite different? What in fact were Soseki's own intentions?

This novel, which has little story interest, is told by the narrator as a reminiscence of his youthful experience. But we come to realize this only when we finish the entire story. Nor does Soseki at the outset provide us with the necessary background information that this youth from a respectable family, with a decent education, has run away from Tokyo, disgusted with his inability to decide between a girl of his own choice and a girl of his family's. The story is related throughout in the present tense. Without any preliminaries we meet the youth in action, who, though weary, must walk on along the highway as if pursued, thinking of the extreme lengths to which he can go with his own life. In this state of mind he is suddenly lured away by a fellow in padded clothing, who is really a swindler who recruits innocent prospects for work in a mine. With this dubious guide, the youth takes a night train to a certain destination and from there follows the dark mountain path—joined by another victim; after spending the night in an equally dubious mountain shack, they arrive at a mining town. Although a sympathetic foreman offers to send him back home, the youth goes through ordeals: a crowd of inhumane miners drags a half-dying friend out to witness a dead miner's funeral procession; his own first night is often interrupted by crawling bugs. The following morning he is taken down by a guide through the mazelike pit, or more appropriately, a damp and slippery "hell," now jeered at by a group of miners, now scared by bottomless ore holes, now shocked by exploding dynamite, now cheered by a warmhearted miner with a dark past who also advises him not to make the same mistake he had made, but to return to the world before it is too late. The story comes to an abrupt end when the youth is found by a doctor to be unfit for work, but somehow makes himself useful as a white-collar worker for five months until he returns to Tokyo.

The Miner follows very closely Soseki's long outline, presum-

ably a faithful record of the original experience. Moreover, Soseki's handling seems so matter-of-fact, so unassuming that we
may be tempted to dismiss the novel as reportage. But on further
inspection we realize that Soseki is shying away from any method
that might make good reportage. Why does he constantly translate the specifics (including the identity of the mine itself) into
the general? (In fact, his original outline is full of those necessary
specifics.) And why does he also consistently adopt the present
tense? More likely it is that, far from writing reportage, Soseki is
experimenting on certain vital points of fictional art, and this is
precisely the case, as is evident in his interview which appeared
immediately following the novel. There Soseki refers to his intellectual narrator, so unlike a miner, as the creation of his own imagination, and discusses the advantages of his narrative method.
While the first-person narrative helps maintain the immediacy of
atmosphere and experience, there are also several specific reasons
why Soseki chose to have it narrated as a reminiscence. First, in
this way the narrator could be fair to his own experience, viewing
good and evil equally; second, by virtue of the distance it gains,
Soseki could take off the sharp edge of sensationalism; third, this
general method enabled Soseki to attempt something unpopular
in contemporary Japanese fiction and yet very dear to his heart,
namely a detailed analysis of human behavioral motifs. As he explains, his primary interest lies not so much in following the progression of a certain event, or its underlying continuity of cause
and effect, as in rambling around those various factors which constitute the event itself. Hence his use of the present tense throughout the novel as the best way of "grasping the nowness of things."
Soseki is applying his much used rambling method so that the
chemistry of human conduct may be investigated. Soseki concedes
frankly that to those readers with little intellectual curiosity, his
novel will appear to be only "dragging on" and "rambling around
and around one spot to no good purpose." Of course, such an
approach, Soseki stresses, is dictated not by his principle, but
rather by the necessity inherent in this particular case.

From this it becomes clear that *The Miner* is the result of deliberate choice of artistic method; it is certainly not meant to be
reportage, nor does it fall into that category. It clearly intends to
be a work of art, the kind of novel which purports to explore the
boundary of fiction as art. Soseki's findings from this experiment

are many, scattered through the novel, and they are voiced through his narrator, of which some points stand out conspicuously. First of all, many human affairs in real life refuse to be neatly arranged in fiction, thus appearing to be a sort of miscarried novel. As fiction a novel may be "interesting," but life as fact is always more "mysterious." The implication is that *The Miner* is closer to the latter than to the former. Next, this empirical discrepancy between fiction and life becomes most evident in the truth of character in both realms. In life, character is basically formless and inconsistent; whereas in fiction character itself is fiction. "No novelist can possibly put down truths on paper; and if he could, it would not be a novel. A real person, a man of flesh and blood defies any easy formulation,—a creature even God finds it difficult to handle." Third, life consists of a series of chances, on which basis man is capable of choice. Since fiction constantly seeks to eliminate chance, it deprives a character of a capacity for choice. Fourth, human behavior is far more complex than fiction pretends to reveal on its mechanical principle of cause and effect, for life is full of unknown factors which make it mysterious. This, the narrator tries to point out by referring to some psychological phenomena, his desire for life, and his wish for death—both of which come over him almost simultaneously. In like manner, the narrator is tossed back and forth between the two incongruous extremes of human nature. The moment he becomes convinced of the animal nature of the miners, he confronts something that forces him to revise his categorical view of human nature. One such example is a fellow in the dark pit who, symbolically, leads the lost narrator back to the outside world. So he realizes the truth of an old saying: "Even in a depraved hell you may run into a Buddha."

While following this depraved but Buddha-natured man, the narrator cannot but pose this question: Which is at fault, the man who has taken refuge in hell or the society which does not stop hounding him? The question can also apply to the miners in general and to their wretched condition. Yet Soseki refuses to pursue, to explore the opposite direction, though the novel could easily have developed along the line of the symbolic *rite de passage*. As the guide remarks, "Now this is the gate to hell. Have you got the guts to go in?" The novel can well be the youthful narrator's ordeal in initiating himself into the maze of human nature. But as it is, *The Miner* is only potentially so. Instead, Soseki seems intent on writing an antinovel in every sense, obvious in his refusing to develop the story in either direction, not gratifying the reader's sense of suspense which he himself has built up, and finally leaving the novel in a complete anticlimax. The novel ends thus: "— This is my whole experience as a miner, and everything I have said is a fact,—the best proof being that it is anything but a novel."

If Soseki's experimental antinovel seems to voice a strongly antinaturalistic position, it is because of the historical fact that contemporary fiction was so deeply imbedded in the tradition of naturalism, prior to the fructifying invasion of both new psychology and anthropology. *The Miner* is Soseki's challenge to naturalistic fiction; Soseki was correct in demonstrating the naïveté of the naturalist's truth which was based on the mechanistic concept of causality, remaining blind to the vast, rich, and complex reality of human life. *The Miner* is Soseki's experimental demonstration in this direction; the second half of the above-mentioned interview, and his long essay of 1908, "The Novelist's Attitude" constitute Soseki's theoretical analysis of the same issue. These two discussions show beyond doubt how seriously Soseki, in order to fortify his own independent position, wrestled with naturalism and other related matters and settled them to his satisfaction.

In Soseki's opinion, there is a great deal of confusion about naturalism; this is especially true with Japanese literature, for in this case naturalism in direct contrast to romanticism is always considered from the historical point of view; and such historicism is bound to lead into various fallacies, dogmatic categorization, confusion between historical facts and artistic truths, ultimate denial of the individuality of an artist and his works. In order for Japanese literature to go beyond such a confused state, Soseki suggests, one must realize the most basic fact that the decisive quality of a literary work has nothing to do with historical labels. Once lifted out of their respective historical context and viewed from the psychological standpoint, naturalism and romanticism merely signify two polar human attitudes, objective and subjective, always oscillating over the middle point, classicism, where both meet. While claiming its pursuit of truth, naturalism comes to deny free will because by logical necessity it applies its naïve law of cause and effect; it is precisely here that romanticism can and should demand a place for itself in literature, by virtue of its contrary view of human will. Despite his objection to literary labels, genre, antinaturalism, anti-ism, and historicism itself, Soseki does not deny to naturalism its salutary aspect, especially objectivism, since this is the very quality vital to reinvigorating traditional Japanese literature: not only in characterization which needs depth, but in psychological analysis which can reveal the conflict-filled complexity of human behavior. This is perfectly possible because history moves not in mere alternation of romanticism and naturalism, but in their dialectical synthesis. Only then will Japanese literature come to have its own independence by creating neo-idealism as a synthesis of both.

Viewed in this light, Soseki's intentions in *The Miner* become very clear; so does its significance. After writing a novel-like novel, *The Poppy*, Soseki had to make another attempt in the opposite direction, a kind of antinovel. By encompassing the two poles represented by these works, Soseki could find the basis for his future art which has been called neo-romanticism or neo-idealism in modern Japanese literature. Soseki's exploration of the borderland between art and life, fiction and fact, and naturalism and romanticism—this primary concern, to the regret of those who nevertheless prefer a novel, prevented Soseki from developing in *The Miner* another potential theme of a descent to hell. But something similar to this, Soseki does in his next work, "Ten Nights' Dreams."

VII "*Ten Nights' Dreams*"

"Ten Nights' Dreams" is further evidence that *The Miner* is an experimental novel. In this collection of ten night dreams Soseki becomes far more direct and subjective. These ten short pieces, like those in *Seven Stories*, reveal somthing of Soseki's romantic fantasy; yet unlike their predecessors which are in essence literary probings of the mystery of love, these dream pieces explore from various angles the psyche which our dreams alone can channel. Somewhat similar to those prose fantasies by Poe, Baudelaire, and Hearn, they are Soseki's fantastics and grotesques—charged with psychic symbols.

With a clear, precise, and controlled style, Soseki evokes the essence of each of these ten formless night dreams, some easy to disentangle, some not. This realm where anything can happen eludes our clumsy prosaic handling. The first dream is about a man's waiting a century for the return of his dead beloved in the form of a white lily. If this is the bliss of awaiting finally fulfilled, the fifth dream is the agony of a captive warrior about to die, waiting for his beloved who, together with her galloping horse, falls over the cliff. While the intense desperation of this dream is carried into the second piece about a samurai anxious to gain spiritual enlightenment so that he may kill his insolent Zen master, the irony is even greater in the ninth dream, where a wife, with her child on her back, is praying for the safe return of her samurai husband who has already been killed. The sixth is still a dream, but the painful one of a Meiji artist who emulates in vain an ancient master by carving out the image of a Deva king hidden in a tree trunk. The seventh dream is obviously based on Soseki's early experience as a voyager; weary of his never ending westward voyage, or its meaninglessness, he plunges into the ocean. With the ship disappearing he is still sinking "with an endless regret and horror."

The eighth dream injects weirdness into a common experience at a barber's. The woman early seen in the mirror counting bills and bills, is nowhere to be found, but instead he notices an immobile vendor of goldfish. All seems to depend on one's angle of vision, and the difference of angle is all that matters here. This weirdness strikes home in the fourth dream about an old stranger who walks into the river and never appears again while the dreamer and children are anxiously expecting a snake to come out of the stranger's box. This sense of weirdness completes the tenth dream, which is about a neighborhood dandy's experience. A week has passed since he disappeared with a basket full of fruit accompanying a beautiful woman. When he returns from nowhere, he tells his baffled listeners about his adventure: When they—the woman and he—reached the edge of a cliff, he was told either to jump off the cliff or to be licked by pigs. Much as he disliked pigs, he chose the latter. Then for a week, day and night he had to continuously strike them down the cliff with his stick— one after another—until he was exhausted and, as he had chosen, was licked by thousands and thousands of pigs swarming all over the field. Equally unforgettable is the third dream: the dreamer is carrying on his back a child—certainly his own who, though blind, talks like an adult and seems to know everything. He decides to desert the child. "For some time it has been raining. The road is growing dark. I am scarcely myself. This little creature clinging to my back shines like a mirror from which nothing can escape, my past, my present, and my future. Worse still, he is my own child, and blind at that. It is unbearable." They soon come into the dark woods. When the child says, pointing to the roots of a cedar tree: "Dad, wasn't it exactly a hundred years ago you killed me?" Then the old memory flashes back in his mind, how exactly a hundred years ago he killed a blind man at this very same spot on such a dark night. "The moment I remembered I was a murderer, the child turned suddenly heavy, as heavy as a stone *Jizo.*" To some critics, this third dream, together with the fourth, seems to have a dark hint of some sort of Oedipus complex, Soseki's sense of guilt.[1] Even if we do not go that far, this piece is as Freudian as it is karmic.

How Soseki came to conceive of these ten night dreams is hard to conjecture. Some are apparently his own experiences in dreams or otherwise. Others might have suggested themselves while he was reading or thinking. Certain motifs recur: the anxiety of waiting, falling from the cliff, water, some secret guilt. They all suggest something deeper, darker, and vaster than personal remembrances—something almost primordial and universal as memories of the human psyche which abound in dreams. After *The Poppy* and especially his exploration through the maze of *The Miner,* Soseki probably felt the need to write these dream pieces. Many might wish Soseki had gone on to write other works like these dreams, or at least incorporate them into his own novels. But Soseki did neither.

CHAPTER 4

The First Trilogy (1908–1910)

I Sanshiro

1908 was one of the most hectic years in Soseki's career as a professional novelist. Early in that year he wrote *The Miner* and delivered a lecture, "The Novelist's Attitude," which, revised, appeared in *Hototogisu*. Then he wrote a beautiful personal sketch in *shaseibun* style, "The Rice Bird" (June 13–21), and "Ten Nights' Dreams." Throughout, he managed to make himself available for many magazine interviews. And if this were not enough, only weeks after "Ten Nights' Dreams," Soseki announced his forthcoming novel, *Sanshiro*. In his announcement of August 19, Soseki stated:

A graduate of a local higher school, Sanshiro now enters Tokyo University, and this exposes him to a fresh atmosphere. His varied responses result from his contact with college friends, elders, and young women. My only task is to let these people free in this particular atmosphere. The rest is up to them—as they swim around freely, there will be a drama. In the meantime the readers and the author getting used to the atmosphere will come to know its inhabitants. If it turns out that neither the atmosphere nor its inhabitants is worth all the trouble, we shall have to resign ourselves to our want of luck. It is simply commonplace. I cannot possibly work wonders.

His is the casual, relaxed pose of an amused observer alert to record the free movements of various inhabitants in a human aquarium. There is little of the tenseness he showed when he set out to erect a world of polished artifice in *The Poppy*, or to probe into the secret of human nature in *The Miner*. This probably is because Soseki, after his two previous ventures, now returns to the world familiar to himself, and this feeling of return makes the first of Soseki's first trilogy a work of perennial charm and freshness.

The novel, which is the story of Sanshiro's first year in Tokyo, begins appropriately with his departure from his tradition-bound home town, Kumamoto, where he left his aged mother alone. On a journey to sophistication this youth of twenty-three meets strangers who sufficiently jolt him out of his innocence and naïveté. One is a woman with whom he spends a night in a hotel room under peculiar circumstances, whose parting comment is, "You really are chicken-hearted, aren't you?" The other is a bearded man who boldly predicts doom to Japan emerging victoriously out of her war with Russia. Once in Tokyo, Sanshiro discovers two entirely different worlds: one, the world of Nonomiya, a scientist from his home town, who is alone experimenting on the pressure of light, and of Hirata, "a great darkness," who turns out to be the bearded man on the train, and who is puffing out his "philosophical smoke," equally alone beyond the mundane; the other, the world of Yoshiko, Nonomiya's gentle sister who practices the violin, and of Mineko, who pleasantly tantalizes him, and whose strange personality reminds Sanshiro of the woman on the train. If one is the world of misty knowledge, the other is the world of gay society. And it is Sanshiro's new friend, Yojiro, "a lovable prankster," who offers to guide him through these two worlds which seem as different from each other as they are attractive.

So now these two worlds, together with a third, that of Kumamoto, beckon to Sanshiro. As the world of Kumamoto means the past, the world of an ivory tower signifies the present, and the world of young women, the future. It is only natural that Sanshiro turns toward the future, the privilege of youth—timidly but eagerly. And Sanshiro's attraction to Mineko, who seems to him to hold the key to the future, becomes the main plot of the novel, while Yojiro's scheme to instate Hirota as a university professor serves as a subplot. Always at the mercy of Mineko's whims and caprices, Sanshiro can never be sure about her heart. When, however, he makes up his mind to declare his love, it is too late. Just as Yojiro's scheme fails, Sanshiro loses Mineko not to Nonomiya as he had thought he might, but to a man with gold-rimmed glasses, of healthy complexion, who once proposed to Yoshiko.

Whatever our impressions, *Sanshiro* is a dialectical synthesis of *The Poppy* and *The Miner*, not in that *Sanshiro*, like *The Poppy*, depicts the world of contemporary intellectuals, nor in that *Sanshiro*, like *The Miner*, treats the ordeal of initiation. *Sanshiro* relates back to both works in point of Soseki's narrative technique. That Soseki here is trying to work out a suitable narrative technique—especially in a novel which is also a newspaper serial—is clearly indicated in one of his interviews while he was writing the novel. In it Soseki compares Sudermann's works (*Der Katzensteg, Frau Sorge, Es War*) and Merejkowski's trilogy in terms of plot progression and panoramic extension. He suggests that a harmonious combination of both methods is essential for a good novel. Such a novel could satisfy the reader's interest in the plot development, as much as his desire for the fullness of unfolding scenes. The same, in his opinion, can be said about the contrast between the *shaseibun* and the traditional genre called "straight story." And surprisingly enough, both techniques had already been employed by Soseki in *The Poppy* and *The Miner*, with an alternating emphasis; so that the one became an example of plot formation, the other of extension. Now in *Sanshiro*, Soseki attempts to combine both methods without falling again into either the former's artifice or the latter's rambling, and thereby creates the unity of accelerated interest.

This peculiar combination of two different, apparently conflicting techniques suggests two possible approaches to the novel. First, *Sanshiro* as a young man novel or a novel of adolescence, for it deals with the hero's year in the world of metropolitan sophistication. The title of the novel suggests that; so does Soseki's own announcement; and "The Youth," one of the three alternative titles proposed by the author, also suggests it. Yet how different *Sanshiro* appears from its Western counterpart, the young man novel, one of the most intensely explored genres in modern Western literature, including such classics as Joyce's *Portrait of the Artist as a Young Man* and Lawrence's *Sons and Lovers*, both contemporary with Soseki's novel. Despite their individual variations, those Western heroes have one common pattern of experience: rebellion, emancipation, and search. They invariably rebel against the established authorities, such as family, school, state, and church. With this rebellion goes their emancipation, which begins symbolically with that of their sexual instinct, shaking the foundation of their existence, and ultimately ends in the search for their own identity. That many of these heroes are also aspiring artists indicates their creative search for life. They are mostly precocious adolescents; their break with the world at large is sharply dramatic; and their self-assertion is always violent. In comparison with them, Sanshiro is disappointing in every respect. Far from young and precocious, this student of literature is already twenty-three and is notoriously naïve. He seems to feel no intense urge to break with the world into which he was born. He thinks he can still go home. The furthest he is willing to go regarding the world of his past is plain when he says to himself while wondering which of the three worlds to choose: "There everything is peaceful and sleepy. No trouble in going back there. At any time he can return if only he wants to. The only thing is that he doesn't feel like going back unless. . . . It is a shelter to take refuge in, so to speak. In this shelter Sanshiro sealed off the past he had now shed. Realizing that he had buried even his own mother there, he began to feel sorry. . . ." And likewise, the slight touch of Minako's arm is sufficient thrill. His boldest confession of love to Minako is "I have just come to see you."

To us who are long used to the violent outburst of passions common to his Western brethren, Sanshiro is awkward, clumsy, naïve, and almost anemic. Yet for precisely the same reason he has his own kind of charm; he is so natural, so unassuming, and so commonplace that many may easily identify themselves with him. This aspect of Sanshiro indicates partly his own society, which tends to suppress violence, but also Soseki's conscious design. To be commonplace was Sanshiro's destiny, and Soseki decided to choose one of the most commonplace names for his own hero. In spite of his commonplaceness, Sanshiro has his own eccentricity, a quality which cannot be overlooked. Sanshiro, as Soseki describes him, is "a rambler rather than a studious worker," consequently a desultory reader of books. But when he comes across a worthy scene, he enjoys mentally reviewing it over and again, for it gives him a feeling that his life has depths. This side of Sanshiro as a rambling observer provides the novel with a panoramic extension, making it a novel of manners as well. Socially its scope extends over two concentric circles: the first and inner circle is the university world dotted with ivy-covered libraries and dark, cellar-like laboratories, also animated by athletic meets, theaters, ateliers, exhibits, student lodgings, and social gatherings. The second and outer circle is bordered by Sanshiro's three worlds, the intelligentsia, the country folks, and new women. Both circles represent the kaleidoscopic social panorama of the postwar Meiji Japan which contains the seeds of future conflict between the old and the new. The inhabitants are not yet embittered by the conflict, since there

is still time before it turns into a clash; rather they are brightened
by their indescribable sense of emancipation. It is a brave new
world Meiji Japan courted with such spirited enthusiasm; and
Sanshiro is rambling around the threshold of it. In short, Sanshiro
is a symbol of Meiji Japan, at least the early Meiji Japan which is
experiencing a sense of wonderment and exhilaration. It is the
moment of awakening, the experience of the brightness and freshness rather than the darkness and bitterness of a new world. This
is what Soseki evokes in the novel.

Sanshiro's three worlds set the stage for his pilgrimage to sophistication; three sets of people, each representing a world of its
own, dramatize it as their *genii loci*. There is his old mother, supported by Mitsu, a girl who loves him, reigning over the world of
Kumamoto, his past; there is Hirota, supported by Nonomiya,
reigning over the world of the intellectuals, his present; and there
is Mineko, also supported by Yoshiko, over the world of new
women. The first of these is out of the question as far as Sanshiro
is concerned because it is the world he has just left for a new and
larger one. To him there are only two worlds, the one he is experiencing and the other he is dreaming of. Hirota and Nonomiya,
whose relationship is somewhat similar to that of Kushami and
Kangetsu, though Hirota is more serious and apparently more
profound than Kushami, represent his intellectual challenge. This
bearded man, who is often considered Soseki's mouthpiece, con-
tinually puffs out his "philosophical smoke," viewing the world
around him with complete detachment. An original critic of civilization and society, as well as a confirmed bachelor, he at once
shocks and attracts Sanshiro with his provocative opinions about
love and marriage, Japan and the West, man and the world; there
seems to be some dark past behind his philosophical mask, as his
nickname, "a great darkness," suggests. And his is the kind of detachment which is too remote yet to Sanshiro, fresh from his cra-
dle. His heart is drawn more toward the world of new women.
Mineko and Yoshiko, who symbolize the world of the future, a
symbol of life itself. Viewing this world from afar, Sanshiro often
wonders: Could this world be complete without him? Doesn't he
have a right to play a leading role somewhere in it?

Mineko and Yoshiko remind us of Fujio and Sayoko in *The
Poppy*, not that they are rivals like their early counterparts, but in
point of personality contrast. Yoshiko is a combination of Sayoko

and Itoko, with a touch of modernity; she is gentle, fresh, and familiar; she makes Sanshiro feel at home, the kind of girl who could certainly make him happy as her husband. There is no shadow of mystery about her person, however. For this reason Sanshiro's heart goes out to Mineko. She is Yoshiko's opposite; she is Fujio without her overpowering egotism; more subtle and refined, she may bend at her own will yet cannot be bent by force. Now she beckons to Sanshiro but retreats as he advances. If Yoshiko is fresh and attractive, Miniko is sophisticated and fascinating. To him every move she makes seems to have some meaning which he cannot fathom. She is at once fascinating and tantalizing —as if she were a riddle of life. Much has been said about her personality. She has been labeled as a sort of "unconscious hypocrite," the term Soseki used in referring to Sudermann's heroines. Some critics have taken it to mean that Mineko instinctively loves Sanshiro, but deceives herself by believing she despises a country bumpkin like him. Others have taken her for an exhibitionist, the brand Hirota used in criticizing the self-assertiveness peculiar to emancipated modern youth.[1] Or if one doesn't mind adding further confusion to the issue, Mineko is gypsy-like, somewhat reminiscent of Turgenev's Zina, the enigmatic heroine of "The First Love."

The novel closes as Sanshiro's first year in Tokyo nears its end, with his return home for the summer. But he is willing to return, not because the past is strong enough to pull him back, but because he is an obedient son as he has always been. But his return will be only temporary; he is no longer the same old Sanshiro that left Kumamoto a year ago; he is now a young man feeling that life has more than one possibility. It is this awareness, or rather this feeling, that really matters—the bitter sweet feeling every youth, poetic or prosaic, experiences before the mystery of life—constantly beckoning and eluding. It is a sense of yearning and longing for the life that is still unknown. If *Sanshiro* is to be considered a young man novel, it must be said that Soseki focuses not on the moment of passionate pursuit which grips its Western counterparts, but rather the mental state prior to that moment, the state of awakening and longing which we tend to take for granted. If we look for those moments of high passion in *Sanshiro*, we are actually expecting a different kind of hero. He is a participant, of course, but he is also a rambling observer. Suppose Yojiro were the hero of this novel—Sanshiro's alter ego who always runs, never rambles, always acts, never observes—we would nevertheless prefer Sanshiro. *Sanshiro*, as its hero suggests, involves no active engagement with life; it only raises problems; for the novel is Sanshiro's preview of life, Sanshiro standing before its three-mirrored walls of past, present, and future.

II Spring Miscellanies

According to the contract with the *Asahi*, Soseki was to write two novels per year, each running in the neighborhood of a hundred installments, or three novels of lesser length. But the *Asahi* apparently kept pressing Soseki in their eagerness to print more of his writings. Soseki was willing to meet their constant requests without complaint; he rather welcomed this opportunity to write in a relaxed mood between his novels. Under such circumstances were written "An Evening Arrival in Kyoto" before *The Poppy*, "The Rice Bird" after, "Ten Nights' Dreams" after *The Miner*, and now *Spring Miscellanies* after *Sanshiro*. All of these occasional pieces served no doubt as an outlet for what could not find its way into his novels. In them we feel closer to Soseki the man, without his professional mask.

The twenty-five pieces in *Spring Miscellanies* written evidently without any particular order in mind, show the range of Soseki's interests and accents—from sketches to reminiscences, from short stories to fantasies. Pieces like "A Snake," "A Fire," and "Mind" retain the weird, if not dark, atmosphere of his earlier grotesque and arabesque "Ten Nights' Dreams." Pieces like "*Mona Lisa*," "Persimmon," "A Kakemono," and "A Voice" lean in the direction of the short story, whereas "New Year's Day," "A Thief," "A Cat's Grave," "I Am a Man," "A Copper Pheasant," "A Procession," and others are distinctly sketches dealing with trivial but amusing incidents in the author's life. But more than one-third of the collection is filled with his reminiscences: only two, "Empire Day" and "Vicissitudes," record the author's experience as a child and as a youth, respectively; the rest, "A Boarding House," and its sequel, "An Odor of the Past," "A Warm Dream," "A Fog," "By-Gone Days," and "Mr. Craig" relate Soseki's experiences in England: the painful family drama he witnessed as a boarder; a suspended dream world at a theater; a London fog in which he lost his way; a brief idyllic moment he enjoyed in Pitlockley, Scotland; and a humorous character sketch of the Shakespearean scholar Soseki had as his tutor. Artistically set forth, they all radiate subdued sweetness without bitterness; they are personal reminiscences to be enjoyed for their own sake.

In our literary history these pieces would properly fall under the genre of miscellaneous writings, the genre at which modern critics tend to cast a suspicious glance, and which not many writers consider worth practicing, for concentration on major genres has been regarded as the primary task for both writers and critics. But Soseki took a different view of the matter. While writing these pieces, Soseki responded to an interviewer's query about the types of writing he wished to do: "I want to try my hand at anything, whatever. I want to try as many varieties as I am capable of. I want to try as many directions as suit my nature and my temperament." These short pieces are therefore the result of Soseki's efforts to express his total personality. There is little doubt that Soseki took them seriously. He had an observing eye, an intelligent mind, and a sensitive heart for people, things, and places. Above all, he was a consummate stylist. These are some of the qualities which make these ephemeral pieces graceful as art, and place them side by side with Soseki's novels.

III   *The Taiyo Popularity Poll*

Soon after "Vicissitudes," the last piece of the series, left his pen, Soseki, keeping his promise, began to think about his next novel. He was busy turning over this yet unwritten novel in his mind for more than two months. An incident happened about this time which was a tribute at once to Soseki's fame as a novelist and to his uncompromising nature as a man. Soseki found himself the top vote-getter in the contemporary artist popularity poll sponsored by the influential monthly *Taiyo*, as part of its twenty-second anniversary project. When the magazine, accordingly, presented him with a gold cup as first prize, Soseki rejected it, much to the surprise of others, and felt it proper to explain his own stand. To any artist, Soseki first admitted, this honor would surely be appealing and gratifying, in view of the reputation and integrity of the sponsoring magazine. But the temptation, however great, Soseki would not allow to overrule his personal principles regarding popularity polls. A poll is "the tyranny of the majority," which has no regard for the free will of the persons involved. "Especially in the civilized community of today, where everyone is allowed the freedom of evaluating his own worth, it is most proper to see that he continues to do so. A poll may degenerate into a means which, in the name of the majority, some may use indirectly in order to infringe on this very freedom." Further, polls such as this may come in handy to those ignorant outsiders eager to simplify the situation for their convenience and curiosity; yet the realm of literature is varied and complex; it defies such a readymade categorization; it needs no such intrusion nor interference from without. For these reasons the practice of popular polls, Soseki concluded, is harmful and dangerous.

IV And Then

And Then has been described in various ways, but critics agree on at least two points: that it is Soseki's first attempt at the so-called love story, and that it is, furthermore, a first-rate work. Some critics have indeed contended that *And Then* signals Soseki's first true expression as a professional novelist. Whatever the validity of their contention, one fact stands out: Soseki's unusual care. On planning alone he spent two months; and he revised some portions of the novel which was rare with Soseki, who seldom retouched his works except for some minor connectives which might obscure the context. His existing notes indicate with what care he considered various aspects of this novel; and his outline, which he followed with fidelity, confirms the thoroughness of his preparation. That even at an early stage of writing Soseki could see the whole novel through is evident in his announcement of June 21, 1909, a week before its serial appearance: "The novel is entitled *And Then* for various reasons: first, *Sanshiro* was about a university student and now this is about what 'then' followed; secondly, the hero of *Sanshiro* was very simple-minded but this one is beyond that stage; and thirdly, in this novel some strange fate befalls him, but nothing is said about what will 'then' follow."

Daisuke, the protagonist of the novel, is a bachelor of about thirty, blessed by wealth and intelligence. Unlike his less fortunate former university friends, such as Terao and Hiraoka, he has chosen intellectual pursuits as the only meaningful occupation because that alone would save him from any compromise with reality and from loss of individuality. He is resolved to maintain this complete independence, and he can afford this since, second son of a wealthy capitalist, he is relieved from those obligations tradition imposes on the eldest son, and moreover he is allowed to maintain a separate household, though, of course, at the expense of his father. Thus Daisuke represents the precarious status of the new intelligentsia in modern Japan—precarious in that his individual freedom is constantly threatened by the world which does not understand him and which he thoroughly despises. Inward criticism such as this is his only defense mechanism. This is exactly Daisuke's relationship with his family, more specifically his father, who regards him as one of the revolving satellites within his private solar system; a shrewd financier who conveniently ascribes his success to his feudal morality (his favorite motto is "Sincerity is the way to Heaven"), he is, all in all, an arch-symbol of that incongruous mixture of feudalism and modernism called Meiji Japan. Beside him stands Daisuke's brother, a man of the world not necessarily sharing his father's feudal mentality yet operating smoothly within the same framework, and his wife, an odd mixture of the old and the new fashion, who, though a good mediator between Daisuke and his father, adds an indirect pressure on him by way of her meddlesome kindness. Beyond this immediate family circle stands also Hiraoka, who has just returned to Tokyo, exacerbated by failure in his struggle for existence; Terao, Daisuke's foil, who must sacrifice his artistic ambition to the necessity of survival; and, finally, Kadono, Daisuke's house-boy, strong in muscle but not brains, whose dullness is the epitome of the philistines. To all of these, Daisuke is but a privileged loafer born in the lap of luxury, a man of taste (*"arbiter elegantiarum"* as Daisuke was nicknamed in his university days).

Isolated from these manifold circles of characters, Daisuke remains aloof, keeping to himself a feeling of inexplicable emptiness, a sort of ennui which he accepts as the fate peculiar to those who have reached the state of *nil admirari.* Then suddenly the situation changes, sweeping the hesitant Daisuke into a drama in which he has to choose between duty and instinct, and society and nature. And this happens with the reappearance of Michiyo, his old love, whom the young Daisuke sacrificed for the sake of his friend Hiraoka. Facing Michiyo, now crushed physically and morally, Daisuke realizes that his was really a false sacrifice, and that this was the cause of his ennui. For her sake and his own, Daisuke feels it is imperative to follow the dictates of his heart, and yet

cannot but be frightened by the obvious consequences that would
follow in relation to Hiraoka, his own family, and society in general—especially now that he is forced to accept or reject a marriage proposed by his family. The world is narrowing its circles,
closing in on Daisuke, demanding his final choice. Torn between
his love and his friend, between his love and his family, and between his conscience and society at large, Daisuke desperately
seeks an easy way out by trying to go on a trip, forgetting himself
in the world of the gay quarters, bringing Hiraoka back to
Michiyo, and even considering consenting to the proposed marriage. But when he realizes none of these attempts can really solve
the problem, so long as Michiyo exists and his heart cries for her,
he at last decides to cease to be a man of will, but become a man
of nature.

Getting ready for his showdown with his father, he burns his
bridges behind him. Daisuke confesses his love to Michiyo with
characteristic brevity and force: "My life needs you; yes, I do indeed need you." Michiyo calls this belated confession a cruel one
and responds: "If you hadn't told me, there would have been no
hope worth living for." The world reacts harshly to Daisuke, a
knowing transgressor of its own sacred law. Hiraoka, while accepting the turn of the event as it came, forbids him to see Michiyo now ailing in bed; his father disowns him, and his brother
takes the same measure. The novel ends as Daisuke tells the bewildered Kadono, "I'm going out to look for a job," and rushes
into the dusty street under the scorching sun of a summer noon.
"And finally the whole world became flame-red, and blazing
tongues started flickering around Daisuke's head. Daisuke made
up his mind to ride the streetcar to the furthest limits until he was
consumed."

Compare this ending with the opening of the novel: "As someone rushed by the gate with hurried steps, there seemed a pair of
large wooden clogs hanging inside Daisuke's head. But they
slipped out and disappeared as the footsteps moved farther away.
Then he woke up." It is equally symbolic. If this beginning is well
in keeping with the life-rhythm of Daisuke, a man of leisure, the
whirling ending also corresponds to the determination of the hero
now transformed into a new man, a man of action. This dramatic
metamorphosis of the hero makes *And Then* a powerful novel.
This is something not present in *Sanshiro*. In *Sanshiro* an unful-

filled anticipation constantly frustrates us because so little happens, whereas in *And Then* suspense dramatizes Daisuke's choice. This difference alone would sufficiently show how fast and well Soseki matured as a novelist.

Yet *And Then* calls for comparison with *Sanshiro*. Indeed, much has been said of their continuity. For instance, it is fairly clear that Daisuke inherited Mineko's unconscious hypocrisy; which he now consciously seeks to eliminate; also Michiyo is not another Mineko, but really Yoshiko over whom Sanshiro chose Mineko, and so on. But this identification of theme and character seems all too inadequate to elucidate more basic points where both novels meet and part. Our real question is: Why was this novel as immediate successor of *Sanshiro* entitled *And Then?*

As we recall, *Sanshiro* is primarily concerned with Sanshiro's search for identity through those three worlds—the worlds of Kumamoto, of Hirota and Nonomiya, and of Mineko and Yoshiko—or the past, the present, and the future. At the end of the novel Sanshiro is not committed to any of these possible worlds, though he stands closer to the second than to the first, and for a while to the third than to the second. (This is one of the reasons why we are left unsatisfied with *Sanshiro*.) And this uncommitted pose of Sanshiro seemed due to Soseki's primary interest in the process of identification rather than its result. In *And Then,* on the other hand, Daisuke is shown as a man already committed fully to Sanshiro's second world, or Sanshiro committed to the world of Hirota. Therefore, he now faces only two worlds, the world of the past (his family) and that of the future (a large question mark).

Also in *Sanshiro*, Soseki seeks to combine two kinds of narrative technique, what he terms panoramic extension and progressive plot. Hirota as a critic of society and civilization becomes Soseki's main agent for the first, while Sanshiro's series of personal experiences (including his unsuccessful experience with Mineko) accelerates the plot progression. It is the constant distance between these two agents that serves Soseki's purpose, but at the same time frustrates the reader. In *And Then* this second source of our dissatisfaction is eliminated since Daisuke now represents at once Sanshiro and Hirota. In him are combined Sanshiro the actor and Hirota the critic. Daisuke as we find him at the beginning of the novel is Sanshiro with Hirota's critical eye, or Hirota with Sanshiro's empty heart. So with Daisuke society and individuality be-

come an inseparable entity, the process by which *And Then*
blends Soseki's two often conflicting narrative techniques. Placed
in more specific perspective, Daisuke is the Meiji intellectual in-
carnate, and his personal ennui reflects that of a class which has
lost or not yet found its *raison d'être;* and his decision to possess
Michiyo indicates one possible way of solving the general predicament.

Again in *Sanshiro* the hero is not yet forced to choose; his three
worlds simply beckon to him from various distances. As an observing rambler his participation is always halfway, as in his dealings
with Mineko. After a survey of his three worlds, Sanshiro thinks
thus: "Remaining in bed, [he] arranged these three worlds side
by side and compared them with one another. Then, mixing all
the three, he obtained one result: The best thing for him is to
bring mother up from the country, marry a beautiful girl, and
commit himself to intellectual pursuits." It is a wishful compromise
possible only to one who need not choose. Such a daydream is not
allowed Daisuke, or at least is no longer available to him. He is
forced to choose between these two worlds, or they are now closing in on him so that there is no other way out but to choose
between the past and the future, between his family and his personal happiness, between the way of the world and the way of the
individual. And what he chooses is the thematic core of *And
Then.*

At the beginning of the novel, when urged by his sister-in-law
to marry the girl of his family's choice, Daisuke unthinkingly remarks: "Well, it seems better still to marry as I wish, rather than
to please tradition." The remark, though made casually, anticipates the drama of Daisuke's choice. And with full consciousness,
Soseki weaves two symbolic patterns around the couple, as
though resting the weight of the entire novel on these patterns.
The girl is by no means the first candidate his family has chosen
for Daisuke, but the reason for their special insistence on her, as
his sister-in-law relates, is that she is a great granddaughter of a
certain Takagi to whom Daisuke's father owed his life. In an incident which happened some years before the Restoration, Daisuke's father and uncle, both young samurai, killed another young
samurai, of ill repute, in a brawl. Whatever their justification, they
had to commit hara-kiri, according to the samuarai code at the
time. But it was Takagi, a remote relative of their mother, who

interceded to save the two brothers from the worst and by using his own influence settled the matter peacefully. This marriage, they all point out, is something more than a mere arranged marriage; it would bring to fated fruition a relationship started between the two families years before. Daisuke's sister-in-law, a lover of Western music and a patroness of fortune-telling, is naturally enthusiastic; so is his brother, who cannot see anything but good in it. But most enthusiastic of all is his father, who points out that the marriage will serve as a token of his gratitude to the other family. At first Daisuke sees in his father an anachronistic but understandable remnant of the old feudal morality, but as his father in desperation begins to insist on the necessity of their alliance with a landed family, Daisuke can not but suspect that there is an ulterior motive behind this marriage of fate. In fact, it will be but a marriage of convenience to bring about an alliance between capitalism and landlordism. That he is to play the role of pawn in this shrewd business transaction is, to Daisuke, a shocking and disgusting revelation. At the same time it seems eloquent evidence to him of the hideous corruption deep-rooted in the moral structure of Meiji Japan.

Against this pattern of fate we can best grasp the ritualistic significance of two counter symbols, a ring and lilies, which recur throughout the novel, binding Daisuke and Michiyo inextricably in fate, and their conscience. These two symbols, now separately and now jointly, create their own world of ritualistic fullness, wherever and whenever Daisuke and Michiyo are together. On her first visit Daisuke finds Michiyo still wearing, besides her wedding ring, the one in a gold frame with a large pearl on it, which he had given her as a wedding gift three years before. The more painfully he remembers his old feeling toward Michiyo, which he sacrificed for friendship, the more their hearts draw to each other through their memory of those innocent days. And finally he realizes that they had virtually been married even before she married Hiraoka, as the symbolic ring suggests. Just as the ring serves as a symbolic pledge of their love, so the white lilies help restore their wounded hearts to their original purity. One day while half-overcome by the fragrance of the lilies-of-the valley, Daisuke dozes and yet subconsciously senses the presence of someone. It is Michiyo. A little later she returns with a bunch of white lilies, and in thirst drinks from the large vase of the lilies-of-the-valley, without waiting for him to bring a glass of water. Then, she draws near the lilies she has brought, and smelling them, says, "A good smell, isn't it?" Daisuke involuntarily bends back, telling her not to put her face so close. Then she reminds him of the lilies he brought to her house many years ago when she was a girl, adding that at that time he himself had smelled them just as she was doing. And when he makes up his mind to confess his love, the first thing he does is to put bunches of white lilies into vases, and then sends for Michiyo. While awaiting her arrival he gazes at the flowers, acknowledging its pervading fragrance. "A little later he said inwardly: 'Today for the first time I am going back to the naturalness of my old days.' The moment he could bring himself to declare this, a sense of peace such as he had rarely experienced for some time ran through his whole frame. Why could I not go back sooner? Why did I resist nature from the start? In the rain, in the lilies, and in bygone days now restored, he discovered life which was pure, immaculate and tranquil. Nowhere in that life was there any desire for gain, any selfish interest, any morality that would press down on him. There were, instead, the freshness of clouds and the naturalness of water. Everything was blissful; and everything was beautiful." And after she leaves, Daisuke brings the flowers out into the garden, strews them around, and crouches unthinkingly among the white petals under the clear moonlight. It is a sublime moment.

And Then is a love story in its most serious sense; it deals with the regenerative power of love, the love which forces a man out of his existential ennui, drives him into society and transforms him from a dilettante into a rebel; it also depicts a man's faith in a woman and her response to her "inner truth." No one could doubt Soseki's seriousness any more than that of his lovers. In grappling with this theme Soseki must have remembered one of his earlier reflections. In a fragment of 1906 Soseki analyzes his dissatisfaction with love literature in general. In such literature, Soseki points out, love tends to isolate itself from the world, creating its own private orb, as well exemplified in the extreme romantic "love is best" type of literature in which love often degenerates into flirtation. Yet love is a serious business, the artist takes it as a serious factor of life, and the reader also expects the same. Therefore, only those works which reduce this element of flirtation while relating love to the actuality of life can make a very serious issue of love, and consequently give their readers full satisfaction. This is the case with *And Then.* Here Soseki takes special care not merely to let his lovers follow the logic of the heart to its extreme but brings various forces into full play, for love is, after all, double-faced; it is a private affair and at the same time a social problem. Moreover, Soseki, not simply content with setting the lovers against their social background, brings their love and conscience into direct clash with the moral structure of the social organism. Theirs is no doubt a case of adultery, though both lovers are as decent as man and woman can possibly be, and their decency, completely in keeping with their strength of character, is not the fiction of Soseki's prudery. True, Soseki's powerful art enables us to suspend our sense of moral judgment while we read the novel, but equally true, Soseki is not the kind of artist who would elicit the reader's sympathy solely by his artistic hypnotism. To him art must be grounded in life itself, making it serious in the reader's view.[2]

In drawing Daisuke and Michiyo together Soseki knew he was actually impinging on a highly sensitive moral problem. (When one of his friends tried to identify Daisuke with his creator, Soseki said in a joking vein: "Well, the same Daisuke is going to commit adultery, I am afraid.") This is why Soseki weaves those symbolic patterns around the central situation with such care and binds his lovers with the ring, a pledge of love, and the white lilies, the ritual restoring their love to its original innocence. That is why Soseki remains the analyst of the lover's heart, telling the story entirely from Daisuke's point of view. Daisuke is as conscious of his delicate situation as Soseki. Soseki describes Daisuke facing the moment of decision: "He was fully aware of what dangerous social consequences would follow once he was to allow his relationship with Michiyo to ferment by the will of heaven; he was aware that such love, though sanctioned by the will of heaven, trangresses the laws of man and usually comes to be accepted by society only through sacrificing the lovers involved. He could not but shudder at the tragedy that might befall them both." Daisuke's justification cannot be dismissed as the commonplace excuse which many lovers in literature invoke. Daisuke is too serious a man and Soseki is too serious an artist to give way to this. In his notes on Sudermann's *Der Katzensteg,* apparently made about this time, Soseki jotted down: "(1) It is hinted in the conclusion that morality can hardly resist nature: here is the theme of the work. (2) The contrast between Regina and Helene is the contrast between the natural and the shackled love. I myself am now thinking of depicting similar constrasting loves, and I feel as if I have been forestalled. Shall I give it up? Or shall I go ahead?" This may help clarify the issue here. Soseki's primary concern is neither to sanction one love at the expense of the other, nor to determine the superiority of one to the other; of course, he is unequivocal about their priority not in terms of social morality but in the light of individual conscience, and equally aware of their struggle for supremacy. With artistic impartiality he dramatizes the conflict that will exist so long as man is earthbound.

But *And Then* is more than a love story; it is, more properly, a novel of self-discovery; it deals with the process of Daisuke's discovery of the natural self which asserts itself against the all-powerful social norm. That is why Daisuke believes he is right, absolutely right, in restoring his existence to its original purity, and identifying this naturalness of being with the will of heaven. Love merely serves as a symbolic catalyst to give the needed meaning to his empty existence. This is the real meaning of his confession to Michiyo: "My life needs you; yes, I do indeed need you." Just as in *Sanshiro* Mineko serves Sanshiro as an enigmatic symbol of life, so does Michiyo in this novel serve Daisuke as a symbol no longer enigmatic but as a restorative symbol of life. Soseki wrote in his notes for *And Then:* "Human emotion, in an instant, enriches the content of life, and one who experiences such an instant triumphs over his physical death." Through his faith in Michiyo, and her response in terms of her inner truth—their love —Daisuke experiences this noble instant. His ability to choose between the voice of his heart and the dictate of moral norms casts a sublime aura over his choice between "to be" and "not to be," the theme of *And Then.* This Soseki knew when he wrote in the same notes: "The proper reason to believe my work to be good—can be found under the large category: choice of individuality and its realization. In this sense my work is necessarily better than other writers' works."

V *A Passage through Manchuria and Korea*

Within a week after completing *And Then* in mid-August, Soseki had an attack of stomach trouble. As a result his planned trip to Manchuria had to be postponed for a while. On recovering, however, he left Tokyo on September 2, proceeded to Osaka, and arrived by steamer in Dairen, where he joined his host, Nakamura Zeko, an old college friend, then director of the South Manchuria Railway Company. Until his return home on October 17, Soseki saw various places, such as Port Arthur, Yingkou, Mukden, Fushun, Changchun (all in Manchuria), and Sinuiju, Pyongyang, and Seoul (all in Korea). It was a journey of a month and a half, a long one even for such a lover of travel as Soseki, especially when he so often had to overcome the recurring stomach trouble.

His travelogue in the present form began to appear in the *Asahi* from October 21, four days after his return, and came to a sudden end with the fifty-first installment for some unexplained reason. As the serial title suggests, Soseki evidently intended to cover the entire journey, but as it is, it ends where he is on the point of touring the famous open-air coal mine at Fushun (what he saw there would be interesting in view of his experimental novel, *The Miner*), thus leaving nothing about his travel through Korea. Judging from his own diary on which the present serial was based, the whole project could have been twice as long as that. But this incompleteness seems to have little to do with the fact that the serial has been the least popular of all of Soseki's writings. Not a few critics, even sympathetic ones, have criticized it on two scores: first, there is too much Soseki in it that often obscures his account of the lands and their people he came into contact with; second, there is nothing that indicates Soseki's awareness of political implications; he is apparently ignorant of the machinery called Japanese colonialism at work; if he really is he chooses to be indifferent to this disturbing problem.[3] (Not only that, Soseki, some may even charge, seems delighted in discovering the enterprising spirit among the Japanese "colonists.") Indeed, the period following the Russo-Japanese War (1904–5) was one of prime significance in the history of Japanese colonialism, and Manchuria and Korea were the first victims of this military, political, economic, and cultural expansionism. And last of all, the South Manchuria Railway Company, which his host was directing, was its half-official agency, and recent history has proved it to have been perhaps one of Japanese colonialism's most effective instruments. Soseki's strange silence may variously be accounted for, however; it was probably due to the nature of his trip, undertaken primarily

for his personal pleasure, or he may have unconsciously eliminated anything unpleasant about his experience. But a more plau-
sible explanation is Soseki's own non-political nature. In this travelogue, as in other writings, Soseki is always nonpolitical. If it is
true that here Soseki voices no criticism at all in this matter, it is
also true that he does not offer any eulogy either. In short, he
makes no overtures to either the pro-colonist or the anticolonist.

The work is not polemical; it is the record of Soseki's travel
many years before that part of the world became acutely conscious of the harshness of Japanese political aspirations. Even
those resident "colonists" among whom Soseki found old acquaintances and new admirers were not yet aware of their own
role in the drama. The Soseki we find here is the Soseki who reminisces about earlier days with old friends, as often as the Soseki
who records in his clear, light, and unassuming style sundry impressions and observations about lands and their sojourners. Thus
his travelogue teems with the peacefulness of the natives carrying
bird cages, forgetful of their own hunger; the patience and energy
of the native coolies laboring in sweat; the haunting beauty of
native girls of pleasure; the moving silhouettes of a blind musician
and a little dancer; the gentle outline of the earth singularly reminiscent of Sung landscape paintings. In describing these unfortunate natives Soseki shows no signs of the colonist's superiority. It
is a world of humble people to whom their daily existence means
so much, a timeless world beyond all political vicissitudes and one
for which Soseki has a matching eye, mind, and pen. The real
value of Soseki's travelogue lies in the very fact that it is the kind
of travel account Soseki alone could give us, and that it does have
so much of Soseki, and this more than compensates for the absence of a political consciousness.

VI *The* Asahi *Literary Columns*

In November 1909, the *Asahi* decided to create literary columns, and Soseki was asked to take charge of the project, much to
his delight. For some time Soseki had entertained a similar idea
and on various occasions had urged the institution of such columns. His reason was partly personal and partly practical. For
example, in November 1906, when the *Yomiuri Shimbun* approached him for the same purpose, Soseki was admittedly attracted, for that would enable him to give financial help to some

of the destitute artists around him. Probably with this in mind, Soseki had recommended these artists' articles to the *Asahi* for publication, while he himself contributed to other magazines and newspapers. Whether or not this latter factor served as an immediate impetus, the *Asahi* finally saw fit to provide some space for the venture, and Soseki, while responsible for the section, put Morita Sohei (who had virtually been buried since his scandalous novel, *Soot and Smoke*, 1909) in charge of it, assisted by Komiya Toyotaka. That Soseki's intentions were more than just to help those young writers around him is evident in the wide range of subjects (including sculpture, painting, and music) and contributors who eagerly responded to his requests. Through this channel, Soseki himself voiced his views on naturalism and other subjects, together with those of the younger writers in his circle, joined lately by such writers as Abe Jiro, Abe Nozei, and Mushyakoji Saneatsu. And in the next two years the *Asahi* literary columns, as Soseki had envisioned, served their contributors and readers as most respectable channels for the exchange of opinion and information on literature and other arts.

VII   The Gate

And Then ends exactly where Daisuke rushes into the whirling flames of a new world of vision. And this is in keeping with Soseki's initial announcement: "and thirdly, in this novel some strange fate befalls him, but nothing is said about what will 'then' follow." What will "then" follow? What will happen to Daisuke, to Michiyo, and also to their love? And in more general terms, what will happen to those who have defied the laws of man in the name of heaven? As long as they live bound to this earth, they must sooner or later pay for their transgression—a truth which permits no exceptions, as life and literature show. But what price must Daisuke and Michiyo pay? This question is Soseki's as much as the reader's. Soseki's answer is *The Gate*, a sequel to *And Then*, which completes Soseki's first trilogy.

But *The Gate* is a sequel to *And Then* only in a thematic sense. Otherwise, they are more different than they are similar. Although in *The Gate*, Sosuke and Oyone carry the burden of Daisuke and Michiyo, they, especially Sosuke and Daisuke, are altogether different persons, as different from each other as Daisuke and Sanshiro are. If in *The Gate* Soseki appears to negate what he

affirmed in *And Then,* it is because of the difference in the protag-
onists' character. Daisuke is capable of believing that he had symbolically married Michiyo even before she married Hiraoka, and
with this conviction he invokes the will of heaven in defiance of
the laws of man. His is a deliberate choice, and at this sublime
moment of choice he turns into a determined fighter. Sosuke, on
the other hand, does not seem capable of such a choice. Even
assuming that the following six-year struggle for survival had
changed him, Daisuke could not possibly be Sosuke: Daisuke
chooses to fight against society; Sosuke lets himself be forced out
of it. Furthermore, Sosuke did not have a heaven-given right to
Oyone, prior to that of his friend Yasui. The fact is that Sosuke
did steal Oyone, or at least her heart, from his trusting friend,
though he could justify it to himself by pointing out that Yasui
originally introduced her as his sister. In his dealing with the
whole affair, there is little of Daisuke's fundamental decency. Soseki's own metaphorical account indicates the difference of character and circumstance between these two sets of lovers: "Every
time he recalled those days, Sosuke wishfully thought it would
have been less painful had nature halted its course, had Oyone
and he been petrified as they were. The whole affair began at the
time when spring was raising its head from beneath winter, and
ended at the time when green leaves replaced cherry blossoms.
All was a life-and-death struggle, as excoriating as though squeez-
ing oil out of a green bamboo over a slow fire. A gale took both by
surprise and brought them down. When they rose, sand was all
over everything. But they could not tell when they had been
blown down."

Soseki does not release his well-wrought suspense by telling us
this until more than halfway through the novel, but he has been
carefully preparing us, while pretending to detail in a naturalistic
manner the daily tedium of a humble government clerk and his
gentle wife. Their rented house, the haven they have finally found
in Tokyo after six years of marital life in various cities, is situated
at the end of an alley, always muddy as in the time of thaw, under
the overhanging cliff that allows little sun and that may collapse
any moment. This physical surrounding itself bespeaks the social
position of its temporary tenants, who are isolated from the main
street, which is always blessed by the sun. Yet for this very reason

they are a fond couple "living in a city as though alone in the mountains." Not allowed to grow outward, their life has lost in extension but gained in depth.

All these six years they have not sought any distracting intercourse with the world; instead, they have devoted the whole time to digging into each other's heart. Thus, their lives have sunk down to the very dregs. In the eyes of the world they are still two separate human beings, but to themselves they have become one organic whole morally incapable of separation. Their nervous systems now synchronize to the slightest pulse. They are like two drops of oil spilled over the vast basin—which become one by repelling the water, or more properly, which the repelling water brings together and makes inseparable. And their mutual embrace, therefore, contains a sense of affinity and satiety seldom found in an ordinary couple, and at the same time it also contains a sense of ennui which goes with it.

Like their house under the cliff, their life is exposed to menace from within and without. The menace from within is the dark shadow of their past which often beclouds the tranquil surface of their life, the past which is also the source of their union. When, for example, Oyone reminds him that there will be sunny days, Sosuke says curtly: "We don't have the right to expect that sort of thing, do we?" Or when Oyone in desperation consults a fortune-teller about the sad fate of their babies, the man also deals her a crushing blow: "You have done something wrong to another person. For that sin you are accursed. That is why you can't raise children." The menace from without is Koroku, Sosuke's younger brother, whose intrusion into their little world aggravates their financial insecurity. To Sosuke, Koroku's impatience is a painful reminder of his own reckless youth. Sosuke suspects that his brother and even his own wife are really the human agents through which heaven intends to torture him. If Goroku re-creates an image of Sosuke's ruinous youth, Sakai, his good-natured landlord, suggests the Sosuke that might have been. Like his house over the cliff, Sakai's gay, large family is the world itself which Sosuke and Oyone can never hope to re-enter. For a while Sakai seems a welcome intrusion bringing an illusion of the world, especially when he offers shelter for Koroku. But he, too, turns out to be another cruel agent of heaven, perhaps the cruellest of all, since he revives the ghost of Sosuke's past. It is Sakai who casually informs him of the imminent arrival of his adventurous brother and his companion from Mongolia, a certain Yasui.

When the menace from without has reached its climax through a series of "accidents," or rather through what the Buddhist calls a chain of karma, the shadow of the past has also become a reality, shaking the foundation of Sosuke's existence. To his despair he discovers that time has not healed his old wound and that the past is not dead at all. There seems no one to whom he can now turn to recover his lost peace, not even his wife. As the last recourse he flees to a Zen temple in Kamakura. But the only thing he finds after a ten-day meditation or struggle is that the desired state of spiritual certitude is beyond him, and that he is not meant for that kind of bliss. On returning home he learns of Yasui's departure, a narrow escape indeed. But instinct tells him that "such insecurity is bound to repeat itself many a time and in varying degrees," and that if to have it repeated is the business of heaven, it is also his to be constantly on the run. Then comes a lull. Koroku accepts Sakai's offer; Sosuke also survives the readjustment of office staff and even gets a raise. There is a small celebration for the occasion. People are talking about the season's first nightingales. To Oyone's comment, "I'm really glad! So at last spring is here," Sosuke replies from the veranda busy clipping his nails, "Um—but winter will soon be back." The novel ends there.

Critics have been frankly severe about certain aspects of *The Gate*. Soseki's handling, for instance, of the series of "accidents" which leads to Sosuke's plight, they point out, is too obvious; and Soseki's own words, "too many accidents," suggest that he himself realizes the awkwardness in depending too heavily on coincidence.[4] The critics seem to miss the point here, though; Soseki's focus is on Sosuke, to whom the series of accidents, as they should to anyone in his state, naturally assume the outlook of a more meaningful chain of events much like a Buddhist cycle of karma. But Soseki's handling of the denouement, especially Sosuke's desperate flight to a Zen temple, poses a more serious problem. It has been pointed out that Sosuke's ten-day experience in Kamakura is virtually the same as the author's own of fifteen years before. On this basis some may assert that at this crucial point in the novel Soseki failed to resist his habitual temptation to use materials readily available to him, and that the temptation got the better of his artistic judgment. What Sosuke is facing at the moment is not the weight of society which he can stand just by sheer strength of character if only he remains firm, but the ghost of the past that some transhuman measure alone can exorcise. That is, faith or religion alone can solve Sosuke's predicament; in this Sosuke is as right as his creator.[5]

Then, why his failure to attain the desired state of spiritual certitude? First, Sosuke is mistaken when he believes he can gain relief simply by "strengthening his mind substance," instead of facing the ultimate import of his past, his double sin of betrayal and adultery. Trying to meet the immediate need, Sosuke takes a measure which is too abstract and indirect to be effective. It can result only in evading the issue itself. It is the mistake of putting the cart before the horse. He is also mistaken when he fails to realize that the nature of his problem is such that it can be solved by him alone, yet, ironically enough, runs to Zen, which insists on the primacy of self-reliance. But the final reason for his failure lies in his character, which is not cut out to tackle problems of this nature. Soseki describes Sosuke standing hopelessly outside the gate:

> "Don't knock; it's no use. Open it yourself and come on in" was the only sound he heard. He wondered how he would be able to unbolt the gate, and mentally contrived the necessary ways and means. But he could not muster the strength that alone could actually open the gate. Consequently his present position is nowise different from the previous one when there was no such problem. He was left alone before the gate, helpless and powerless as ever. So far he has lived solely by his own common sense. And to his chagrin, he was cursed by that very common sense. Now he envied the single-mindedness of those fools which, from the start, rejects discrimination and judgment. Or he marvelled at the intense self-application of those pious devotees which made them oblivious to wisdom and contemplation. As for himself, it seemed he was born fated to stand for a long time outside the gate. There was nothing he could do about it. But it was so ironic that he had come all the way to the gate which he could not possibly enter. He glanced back, but he had no courage to take his way back. He glanced ahead; there the solid door stood in front, ever obstructing his view. He was not meant to go through the gate; nor was he meant to content himself without going through the gate. In short, he was an unfortunate who, transfixed under the gate, was awaiting only sunset.

The Gate is thus a tragedy of character. There is a world of difference between Sosuke and Daisuke: with Sosuke, Daisuke's "will of heaven" degenerates into fate. Daisuke dares to face his destiny, whereas Sosuke takes flight. Incapable of attaining the state of transhuman values, he always follows the same course, on the same level. As long as he remains in flight, he cannot free himself from the cycle of punishment. He is a fatalist. On so many occasions he applies the word fate to those characters and events which seem to him agents of heaven to pursue him. But Sosuke is not a born fatalist. He has made a fatalist of himself, or allowed his youthful experience to do that. When younger, Sosuke was a firm believer in the present and future; he was either free from the past, or had no sense of it. When he heard of a certain village surrounded on all sides by mountains, he laughed at the complacency of its inhabitants: "Well, I wonder how anyone can live in that sort of place." Then he became a firm believer in the past, although he was not aware of it. Their small circle of life under the cliff, invisible and visible, had been limited by their past, as the horizon of those villagers by the mountains. If this acceptance of fate makes Sosuke and Oyone such a peaceful couple, it is also what endears them to many readers whose small world knows nothing of God or the Buddha. Sosuke is a kind of fatalist who already foresees the shadow of winter in the approaching spring, as shown in the conclusion of the novel. (The novel, symbolically enough, begins in autumn and ends with the departure of winter.) Even in the seasonal cycle of nature, only two, autumn and winter, are his, while he shies away from spring and summer. When on his return from the temple Sosuke calls on Sakai for the obvious reason, his host amusingly relates a story about frogs: every spring there are thousands of frogs born in the stream of a certain park, many of which in the midst of hustle-bustle become lovers. And these creatures of love, some heartless passers-by stone to death. Sakai's comment is all the more ironic to his guest: "That is why we talk about piles of dead bodies, all of them fond couples, I regret to say. That is, in a couple of hundred yards' space you come across many a tragedy. Compared with them, well, we must say we're very fortunate indeed. No one is going to crush your head with rocks just because he doesn't like to see you are a fond couple. . . ." Sosuke and Oyone, certainly, are their human counterparts, dreading the same deathblow.

There is an interesting episode suggesting how the novel accidentally found its title, though no reader would question its appropriateness. When the novel was to be announced, Morita Sohei and Komiya Toyotaka, at their mentor's request, had to concoct something suitable without any knowledge of the still unwritten novel. It happened as if by chance that they opened Nietzsche's *Zarathustra*, hit upon the word "gate," and chose it as the title for Soseki's forthcoming novel. Some time after he started writing, Soseki complained that his novel was becoming less and less what its title suggested. But this complaint turned out to be unfounded. As it is, *The Gate* is an eloquent example of Soseki's ability to incorporate into a work in progress anything he happened to find potentially usable; that brilliantly symbolic scene describing Sosuke vainly hoping for admittance through the gate is a tribute to this ability. The gate, as this particular scene and the entire novel suggest, functions on at least two levels: it is the gate of society, the human world within which every man, because of his mortal nature, must obey the laws of man; it is the gate through which Sosuke is forced to seek his further flight from the world; and it is also the gate to the realm of God or the Buddha in which alone Sosuke felt his sin could be absolved and where the will of heaven reigns, remaining always beyond his reach. The very pose of Sosuke standing in despair before the gate suggests the nature of his dilemma, the dilemma he faces as a transgressor of the laws of man—without being blessed by the will of heaven. It is the pose of a fatalist, a man who has allowed fate to shape his own life.

It has been customary among critics to designate the significance of *The Gate* as Soseki's first genuine confrontation with the world of the common man, whose life is constantly subject to the pressure of society.[6] But this view requires revision. It is not society but the ghost of the past that is ultimately responsible for Sosuke's perennial flight. *The Gate* dramatizes the vengeance of the past on a coward who refuses to believe in its reality. If the novel signals Soseki's first recognition of the reality of the past whose ghost is pursuing him, the significance of the novel also lies in the fact that in it Soseki for the first time recognized the meaning of the past and its possible use as artistic material. *The Gate* attests not only to Sosuke's, but also to Soseki's, discovery of the past; to Soseki, as to Sosuke, it is only a discovery, for the work that follows *The Gate* is in a way the result of his frustrated attempt to face the force of the past without which there is neither present nor future. It also suggests Soseki's acceptance of the past as sin. In this Buddhistic cycle of karma, sin is not separable from love any more than the past is from the present. In *Within the Sash-Door* Soseki relates his childhood dream in which he had been tortured so unbearably by his failure to make up for someone else's money he had stolen, that he cried for his mother. Even as early as in 1905, he recounts another dream in which he was appalled when reminded of the terrible murder he had committed long before. One critic has labeled Soseki's sense of insecurity as a derivative of original sin.[7] Whatever the case may be, it is certainly true that even in the works prior to *The Gate* we can find some hints of this sense of guilt, especially in Ono, Mineko, Daisuke, and other characters; but only in *The Gate* does it begin to assert itself as the central theme. In this sense the novel, while winding up Soseki's first trilogy, relates its theme to his second trilogy.

CHAPTER 5

The Second Trilogy (1910–1914)

I Random Recollections

WHILE working on *The Gate*, Soseki on several occasions complained of his stomach condition which forced him to slow down his writing pace to about one installment a day. In June 1910, immediately after completing the novel, Soseki was hospitalized for some forty days for treatment of ulcers. In August he went to Shuzenji for convalescence. There his condition took a sharp turn for the worse; after a series of haemoptysis, he lapsed into a coma on August 24. Somehow he managed to survive this crisis but had to stay there until October. On returning to Tokyo he was hospitalized for further treatment until the following February. After this prolonged illness Soseki was no longer the same. The trouble recurred regularly almost every year from then on, and each time he was forced to be idle a month, until in 1916 it finally took his life.

This is Soseki's so-called Shuzenji crisis, one of the most hotly debated Soseki problems, which has divided critics into two camps. One camp asserts that Soseki was no longer the same either physically or spiritually; that the crisis also turned out to be the most decisive point in Soseki's life as a man and as an artist; and that it signaled the emergence of his philosophy, *sokuten kyoshi* (conform to heaven and foresake self), whereby he was to seek to combine his life and his art. This group takes the crisis as a crucial point in Soseki's metamorphosis. The opposing camp flatly rejected this view as sheer myth, sheer fantasy, sheer fiction contrived by Soseki idolators.[1] For a consideration of either case, it is wise for us to turn to Soseki's own records, *Random Recollections*, which appeared in the *Asahi* from October 29, 1910 to February 20, 1911.

Random Recollections, based largely on the author's diary, consists of thirty-three chapters. As its title suggests, these chapters were written without any particular order, but they do revolve around certain central preoccupations. First, they are Soseki's thank-you notes to his friends, his admirers, and his readers for their profound concern over his well-being. As he calls his survival a sort of providence, they are pervaded with his unconditional gratitude for life itself, experienced only by one who has nearly missed his footing on the tightrope of life.

. . . As I was lying in bed and staring at the ceiling I realized that the world was more generous than I myself; with this realization there rose a sudden stir of warm breeze in this world which I had believed to be unlivable. It was beyond my dream that this hustle-bustle world could spare so much time and show so much kindness to a man well over the age of forty, who was virtually marked out by the law of natural selection, and who had no deserving past. As my body survived my illness, so did my spirit. I thanked the illness; I also thanked those who had spared so much trouble, time, and kindness. I wishfully hoped to become a good soul; and made the pledge to myself that whoever destroys this happy thought of mine shall be my eternal foe.

With this sense of gratitude Soseki wished to relate some of his experiences and thoughts during the confinement.

Secondly, these chapters convey an exquisite sense of discovery, or rather Soseki's rediscovery of his own self. Thanks to those around, Soseki was able to live what Eucken terms a free spiritual life. Critical as he was of the philosopher's academic abstraction, Soseki's physical confinement served him as a laboratory in which he could experiment with this free spiritual life in its unalloyed mode. What he discovered is in his opinion worth reporting. It is something he rediscovered rather than discovered, though currently out of season and rarely found; it is a world totally unfamiliar to Gorky, Andreyev, Ibsen, Shaw, and their like—makers of what Soseki calls a literature of pain; it is the world familiar, perhaps too familiar to be novel—to the Oriental mind; it is the world of poetry which has been discarded by advocates of modernism. Soseki is convinced that this spirit of poetry should come to our rescue by adding a fresh dimension to life. As he states, he will attempt to remember as soon as he can, record as soon as he can, "this ancient fragrance to share with those modernists and those sufferers who are so many in today's world." Those innumerable *haiku* and Chinese poems scattered over the chapters are the mementoes of Soseki's journey to this realm of poetry. It is his return to the ancient tradition of the East; it is also his return to childhood; it is even his return to the homeland of his soul which is the homeland of the Oriental soul. While relating his early interest in Sung landscape painting, Soseki gives us a glimpse into this Xanadu:

On the silk canvas there was a house with a garden where plum trees are blooming in the bright sun; with a sedge gate in front of which a stream is flowing gently along the hedge; and facing a roundish blue hill far away. When I mentioned my wish to live in such a place once in my life, a friend, glancing at my serious look, seemed very sorry to remind me of the inconvenience I might experience. This friend was a native of Iwate. While ashamed of my own stupidity I nevertheless loathed the practicality of my friend who ruined my sense of poetry.

And thirdly, *Random Recollections* is a unique record of Soseki's brief experience of death, with his personal reflections on the untranslatable intimacy between death and life. Returning from death, as Soseki called his thirty-minute coma state, he was shocked to discover the violent contrast of life and death, and their apparent discontinuity, and even more alarmed to realize the fact that the same self had been subject to these two sharply divided separate phenomena simultaneously. Transiency, he discovered to his fright, is characteristic of death, as well as of life. But in the transiency itself Soseki experienced a sort of absolute state. With clinical precision Soseki described the gradual process of the merging of his self with the blue, clear autumnal sky:

It became my daily ritual to gaze at this sky. Eventless and altogether empty, this vast sky cast its silent shadow wholly on my mind. Equally eventless and equally void was my mind. These two transparent things came to embrace each other, becoming one. And what this oneness left to me was a certain feeling I might call ineffable. As soon as the quiet corners of my mind shaded off, the color of my focusing consciousness also faded off. A misty veil lightly overspread all; and consciousness of the entire existence grew thinner. It was not as substantial as an ordinary dream; nor was it as disorderly as normal consciousness; nor was it the heavy shadow wavering in between. To say the soul leaves the body would seem a gross mistake. It was rather the kind of state removed far from sensory awareness as the soul, pervading even the ends of minutest nerves, lightened and purified the muddy inside of my body. I seemed aware of what was going on around me; at the same time I also seemed aware that awareness was something very special, peaceful and unearthly. My mind rose, of itself, from the bed —along with my body which carried it, like a floor mat rising of itself, as if due to swelling water underneath the floor. Or more properly, while the weight of the mattress against my waist, shoulders, and head, disappeared, my mind and my body were lingering at ease in their original position.

This brief but recurring experience, which was supposedly caused by his anemic condition, Soseki compared to the sense of bliss, the complete harmony of self and the world, which Dostoevsky experienced during his epileptic fits, his "sacred ailment," the sensation one experiences as he slips over the edge of the heavens down into the boundlessness of space. Another reason Soseki felt an affinity with Dostoevsky was that they both had a narrow escape from death: "This joy of a narrow escape was something special, in ratio to our fear of death. Such a juxtaposition of the fear of death and the joy of life always reminded me of Dostoevsky." All in all, to Soseki this was a rare experience, rare but real since it was his personal experience. Through it he also experienced a state of absolute harmony which obliterated the painful barrier between man and nature. Just as Dostoevsky was all his life grateful for his experience, so was Soseki, apparently, grateful for this crisis in Shuzenji. In his diary entry of September 26, 1910 Soseki wrote: "As I sit up in bed for the first time, the world which I have seen only horizontally, now appears vertically —a refreshing experience." In his desperate wrestling with death Soseki, it seems, learned priceless lessons about himself, others, and life, all of which were to revitalize his inborn zest for life. *Random Recollections* is Soseki's attempt to eternalize in words all these personal experiences.

II *Five Summer Lectures*

From the fact that in 1911 no novel came from Soseki's pen, we may hastily conclude that for him it was a restful year. In this we are deceived. True, Soseki needed rest, but the world would not give it. That is perhaps the price he had to pay for his fame and talent. In fact, 1911 was as eventful as any other of the strenuous golden decade which ended only with his death. He was ever busy discharging his tangible and intangible obligations to the world, worrying about his own precarious health, and coping with his personal problems, which were by no means pleasant.

The first of these unpleasant experiences took him by surprise—quite literally, in February while he was still in a Tokyo hospital recovering from the Shuzenji crisis. The Ministry of Education delivered a note requesting Soseki's presence for a Doctor of Letters degree which its committee had decided to confer on him. To others it might have been a pleasant surprise, but not to Soseki. Immediately he informed the authorities of his refusal. But the Ministry refused to withdraw the degree on the grounds that it had already been made official. As neither party was willing to yield, the matter dragged on into April without satisfactory settlement. It was one of the most publicized events at the time. Some accused Soseki of being too obstinate, or of courting publicity, while others admired his personal eccentricity. In the midst of this James Murdoch, his old college teacher, wrote congratulating him on his "moral backbone." He was one of the few who could grasp the issues involved.

It was a matter of principle as Soseki pointed out on more than one occasion. First, it is a violation of the individual's right; government authorities have no right to force even an honorary degree on him without regard for his personal feelings. Therefore, as an individual he wished to reserve the right to refuse it. Soseki was convinced that such a degree system, no matter how effective in promoting scholarship and arts, could do more harm than good to the future of the country, since it was bound to create a false impression about scholarship, and moreover, to leave it in the hands of a few learned monopolists. And above all, it was his sincere desire to remain a plain citizen in the present and future, as he had been in the past. In this matter Soseki was the same Soseki of two years ago when he reacted to the *Taiyo*'s popularity poll. This time, as then, Soseki proved to be an individual who "regards freedom as part of his nature." Both incidents again reveal Soseki's determination to preserve this right against encroaching force from without, whether it be official or popular.

Most of the summer Soseki was on lecturing tours. In June he journeyed to Nagano and delivered the first of the series, "Education and Literature," at the invitation of the local educational association. In August he journeyed to the Osaka area under the

Asahi's sponsorship and delivered four more lectures, "Vocation and Avocation," "The Enlightenment of Modern Japan," "Substance and Form," and "Literature and Morality." These five lectures, which some may equate with a novel, mark the midpoint of Soseki's career as a lecturer. They are a valuable extension of his early lectures, both academic and popular. The only difference is that while in the early lectures Soseki was primarily concerned with the theoretical aspect of literature, he is now intent on dealing with its practical aspect. As a practicing artist, out of the ivory tower, Soseki considered many problems about literature, such as the nature of the artist, art and society, art and morality, and the dilemma of modern Japan.

"Education and Literature" anticipates many of the issues he would discuss in the rest of the series. In this first lecture Soseki takes education broadly, relating it to the sphere of literature. Traditional education prior to the Meiji period was, by and large, idealistic and emotional, always upholding certain abstract virtues for the common people to emulate. Because of this essentially deductive spirit it is impregnated with many difficulties which defy any easy solution. New education shows an opposite orientation: because it starts with facts it is inductive, reflecting a modern critical and scientific spirit. Hence its marked tolerance toward individual variations and differences. The same difference of orientation is also apparent in the rivalry between romanticism and naturalism, two major literary schools which dominate the Japanese literary scene. Champions of both schools often contend that literature has nothing to do with morality, but in this they are mistaken. Although, Soseki points out, art and morality do part company in certain areas, they must come to terms on the ultimate and fundamental level. Truth is always obscured by reaction, which characterizes the present schism. If naturalism can justify its existence by its dedication to veracity, romanticism can also claim its existence as long as man retains his basic need for spiritual aspirations. The future, Soseki concludes, must seek their harmony, not their divorce, in the form of neo-romanticism, but it cannot be a mere repetition of romanticism, since history never exactly repeats itself. There are many echoes of the old Soseki, the artist of independent mind, but there is also an emergence of Soseki the moralist.

In "Literature and Morality" Soseki restates his case and develops his thesis along the same lines, but takes another forward step in urging a synthesis of the romantic and naturalistic views of man. Although promotion of morality is not the primary function of literature, literature does deal with the stuff of life, which allows moral judgment. Ironically, Soseki continues, it so often happens that romantic literature, despite its pretended concern with morality, contains some elements of immorality, whereas naturalist literature, despite its professed indifference to morality, reveals much moral concern. No society can do without some sort of ideals, but these ideals must, first of all, be hospitable to reality. Japanese society needs some such ideals, after having forsaken its rigid, demanding, and impossible feudal ideals. The Japanese should, in Soseki's opinion, accept realizable ideals which would insure future harmony with their neighbors and fellow human beings, inspire sympathetic tolerance for their past weaknesses, and enhance the intimacy of individual contacts.

In "Vocation and Avocation" Soseki touches on the more general problem of individual independence in modern society. The more modern civilization develops, the greater diversity and complexity it creates in vocation. Proportionately, modern man becomes deformed in the process of specialization, finally losing his independence as a whole man. The peculiarity of modern society has come to reverse the original relationship between vocation and avocation; modern man chooses his vocation for the sake of others, while reserving his avocation for himself. It becomes increasingly difficult to unite his vocation and avocation, but exceptions to this trend are perhaps the scientist, philosopher, and artist, whose vocation is also their avocation. Soseki's critique of modern society, unexpectedly, turns out to be an apology of the artist.

In "Substance and Form" Soseki first takes issue with Eucken, or rather with the Euckenian mode of thinking prevalent in contemporary Japan which urges a choice between man's desire for substance (i.e., individual freedom) and man's desire for form (i.e., order and organization). To Soseki this means rather the possibility of harmonizing man's polar desires so as to gratify both sides of life; it is no mere contradiction which demands our choice. Or it may be called a contradiction, but only in a logical sense. This is Soseki's existentialistic protest against the tyranny of formal logic which is responsible for philosophical abstractions.

Life rejects such abstraction. (In one of his notes Soseki writes: "Art includes philosophy. Philosophy abstracts substance from life, whereas art constructs life. Therefore, philosophy possesses no living power.") In this particular instance, as in others, common sense should be a wiser guide than intellectual abstraction. Form exists for substance; not vice versa. When substance changes, form must follow its suit. By applying this truth Japan may be able to grasp the conflict between the old and the new, and resolve it to some extent.

In these four lectures Soseki constantly returns to the present state of Japan, whether he speaks as an artist, as a social critic, or as a man of the twentieth century. But in "The Enlightenment of Modern Japan" he keeps close to this subject, which has been dear to him as an artist and as a man of Meiji Japan. The paradox of modern Japan, says Soseki, is that thanks to the current enlightenment, which is, in this case, synonymous with Westernization, Japan is enjoying higher standards of living than at any period of her past; but from this it does not necessarily follow that the suffering or pain of existence has been proportionately allayed. On the contrary, it has only increased due to the universal war of economic competition. Her Westernization, moreover, is superficial at best because the initial impetus came from without, not spontaneously from within. All this is probably historically inevitable, Soseki admits, but the point is that this peculiar situation is the cause of universal emptiness, malcontent, and uncertainty. Meiji Japan, as he continues his analysis, is trying to digest, in a matter of decades, Western civilization which took centuries to evolve to its present status. Japan, then, is attempting something impossible from the start, even though there is no alternative. Precisely herein lies the real cause of nervous collapse. What is worse, there is no ready solution; it is a tragedy without any hope of solution. But his is a voice of warning in the wilderness, which was largely wasted on his fellow Japanese who had by now gained confidence in their own achievement, especially since their victory over Russia.

Soseki was a born conversationalist and a born lecturer. These lectures show this. They display his gifts of scintillating wit and humor. They are also long and serious, certainly too long and too serious even for his charmed audience. But they all exemplify Soseki's logical and candid mind which refuses to compromise his deep convictions. As a body of significant views and opinions, these lectures are closely related to his creative works immediately preceding and following.

III   Until After the Spring Equinox

This strenuous summer lecture tour did not leave Soseki's health unaffected. With his ulcers recurring, he found himself hospitalized again, instead of returning to Tokyo. Back home in mid-September, he had to undergo surgery again, this time for hemorrhoids, and he was under treatment until the following spring. In October, Ikebe Sanzan, the editor of the Tokyo *Asahi*, who had been instrumental in bringing Soseki to the newspaper, resigned after a clash with his colleagues over Morita Sohei, then in charge of the literary columns. Soseki saw fit to discontinue the columns, deciding that his original conception had been thwarted as it had turned into a stage for polemics. Also out of his obligation to Ikebe, Soseki tendered his resignation to the *Asahi*, though he was eventually dissuaded. Later in November his fifth daughter, Hinako, died suddenly of an unidentified cause. These events, evidently, shattered Soseki. "My stomach has cracked. Even my spirit seems to have suffered the same. Every time I recall it [his daughter's death,] I feel an inconsolable sorrow and pain." Under such circumstances, Soseki set out to write *Until After the Spring Equinox*, at the pace of one installment per day, never certain of his own health.

In a foreword to the novel, which was to open his second trilogy, Soseki touched on various points in a reflective manner. First, apologizing for his failure to discharge his obligations toward the *Asahi* and his readers over a period of time, he expresses his desire to make the novel as interesting as possible, though he is in no way confident about the result. Second, declaring that he is neither a naturalist nor a symbolist, nor a romanticist, he intends to produce only his own kind of novel. Third, Soseki regards it as fortunate for him to have those readers who, more or less strangers to the backstage of the literary world, live the decent and peaceful life of plain human beings: it is his privilege to write for those educated and ordinary readers. Fourth, the title has no special meaning other than that the novel begins with New Year's Day and will continue until after the spring equinox. And last, in the present serial he hopes to try out his long-cherished view that

a novel consisting of several short stories might be highly readable
as a newspaper serial. But inasmuch as a work of art often follows
its own course rather than the author's intent, his own work will
be no exception to this. Even if he fails, there will still be a series
of short stories.

If this last point indicates Soseki's interest in the possibility of
structural experiment, it is also one important common denomina-
tor of all the three novels in his second trilogy. *Until After the
Spring Equinox,* as Soseki initially intended, consists of six short
stories of varying length, plus an epilogue designed to tie them all
together. It is what we might call a point-of-view novel. In order
to give a sense of continuum and unity to it, Soseki creates a character called Tagawa and conceals himself behind this agent. To
the extent that in these six pieces Soseki simply narrates what his
agent personally discovers in each of the six episodes, the novel
can be called Tagawa's story because it concerns his first encounter with the world.

As the novel begins, Tagawa is a bachelor of law recently graduated from the university, seeking a job—but halfheartedly. He is
equally a bachelor of life, so to speak, more avid for the romantic
side of the world, often daydreaming of fantastic exploits and adventures in a faraway region in which he is naturally the sole hero.
But for the time being he can find enough excitement right
around himself, and in present-day Tokyo, that stimulates his romantic curiosity. First, there is Morimoto, his fellow boarder,
whose weird experiences in various parts of the world he can
share in imagination, and who now suddenly vanishes, leaving his
rent unpaid, and also his cane with the carved snake head, as
Tagawa's legacy ("After the Bath"). Looking for a position he is
introduced by a university friend Sunaga to his uncle Taguchi. He
is pleasantly surprised as this successful businessman assigns him
to report back every move and conversation of a certain couple, a
middle-aged man and a young woman. This assignment he duly
performs, far more completely than Taguchi suggested ("The
Streetcar Stop"). But on making a detailed report Tagawa finds
out that the couple is really Taguchi's daughter, Chiyoko, and his
brother-in-law Matsumoto. His disappointment has its compensa-
tion: Taguchi turns out to be a good-natured prankster, and
through his generosity Tagawa secures a position ("The Report").

If these three stories chronicle Tagawa's factual experience as a

viewer of life, the next three transcribe his emotional experience
as a listener to the depths of life. If the former make an outer
circle along which Tagawa roams, the latter create an inner circle
whose intense human drama holds him spellbound. In the last
three stories Tagawa still remains Soseki's agent, but his function
is reduced to that of a listener to three stories told by Chiyoko,
Sunaga, and Matsumoto, respectively. Matsumoto, to whom Taguchi sends Tagawa, is a confirmed idler, the exact opposite of
Taguchi. The reason he does not receive a visitor on a rainy day,
Tagawa learns from Chiyoko, is that his daughter died on such a
day, the death for which Chiyoko holds herself responsible ("A
Rainy Day"). (This often anthologized piece is admittedly Soseki's tribute to Hinako, whose death he refused to accept as a
fact.) Then follows Sunaga's confession about his fated relationship with Chiyoko. Obviously a foil to Tagawa, Sunaga is sensitive, intellectual and brooding to excess; he loves and yet fears his
cousin Chiyoko, who passionately loves and at the same time despises him. He convinces himself that he does not care for her, but
it comes to nothing the moment a rival appears on the scene ("Sunaga's Story"). Now it is Matsumoto's turn to relieve our increasing sense of suspense concerning Sunaga's dark past. Sunaga is the
child of his now deceased father and a housemaid. For this very
reason his mother, or rather his foster mother, is determined to
bring him and her own niece Chiyoko together as husband and
wife, so that their mother-son relationship may be made more
permanent. In retribution for his own negative influence on Sunaga, Matsumoto reveals the whole secret to assuage his young
nephew's anguish. Finally Sunaga sets out on a journey in search
of inner peace ("Matsumoto's Story").

It is highly probable that the narrative structure of the novel
was inspired by R. L. Stevenson's *New Arabian Nights,* a collection of seven stories all centering around an adventurous Bohemian prince. (Soseki had previously admired Stevenson's ability to
dramatize his situation, and in the story itself he mentions Stevenson's work as the only English text Tagawa read in college with
any amount of enthusiasm.) Beyond this, they are as different as
any two works can be. Soseki's work can hardly be called pica-
resque and picturesque, two qualities which make Stevenson's
work what it is. Unlike Stevenson's Bohemian prince, Tagawa remains an observer hardly involved with the unfolding human

drama. Viewed from his angle, the novel is a series of six episodes loosely strung together; consequently, its center of interest blurs. Although we vainly wait for Tagawa's involvement, the author does not want it. The result is that while the novel develops from the physical into the psychological sphere, there is little appreciable change on the part of Tagawa. Soseki himself may have dreaded our expectation. In the epilogue he reminds us, and perhaps himself, that Tagawa is only an inquirer of the world, avid but distant because his means of contact is a sort of earphone. True enough, Tagawa learns something about life from these episodes, and each episode is different from and deeper than the one immediately preceding. From Morimoto he gets a glimpse of nomadic life; from Taguchi and Matsumoto, two polar characters, a sense of the breadth of society; from Chiyoko, an exquisite sense of sorrow blended with the beauty shrouding death, a feeling far removed from the terror normally associated with it; from Sunaga, an entangled story about the relationship of mother and son, man and woman, which gives him a sense of depth—without affecting his inner being; and from Matsumoto, the fact that an idler can be a man of keen awareness. "In short," concludes Soseki, "all his latest knowledge and sentiment about life has come through his ears. A series of stories which begins with Morimoto and ends with Matsumoto, at first engages him lightly, then gradually deeply, and finally comes to a sudden end. But he hasn't been able to step inside, to his relief as much as to his disappointment. Disappointed, he cursed the snake's head atop his cane; and now relieved, he blessed it, too. Gazing at the vast sky, he pondered the future course of the whole drama which ostensibly came to an abrupt halt."

But the reader shares only Tagawa's disappointment, not his relief. The implication here is obviously that the novel is an artistic failure, or at least that it fails to give us the sense of unity and fullness we experience with a good novel. For this we may venture various theories: we may ascribe it to the circumstances under which the novel was conceived and written, notably Soseki's shock of pain over the death of his favorite child and also his own deteriorating health; we may relate it to his misplaced desire to write an interesting story; and again we may explain it as something inherent in the author's structural experiment itself. The most probable reason, however, is that in the process of creating "extension" which would provide the novel with the necessary breadth, Soseki by chance struck a supposedly central situation far richer than he could foresee; but it was a bit too late when Soseki found himself drawn irresistibly to his character Sunaga, and his complicated relationship with Chiyoko. Indeed, it is "Sunaga's Story" that dominates the entire novel, so much so that one may suggest that it is the only story Soseki really cared to write, the rest being simply to build up a sense of suspense around it. The result is that the novel falls apart, dividing our attention between two characters, Tagawa and Sunaga. This lack of unifying interest, if we use Soseki's own terms, accounts for its lack of fullness.

Whatever Soseki's original design, it is Sunaga who commands our attention; it is his predicament that saves the novel from being a complete failure. What is it in Sunaga and his situation that fascinates us, as well as Soseki? Later in the novel, Matsumoto recalls a certain scholar's speech in which, on analyzing the enlightenment of modern Japan, he declared that under such conditions one is bound to suffer a nervous breakdown unless he is superficial.[2] When the lecturer compared his conclusion to the old truth that ignorance is bliss, and knowledge often causes sorrow, Matsumoto remembered his own nephew: "It's bad enough that we Japanese were forced to swallow down such a bitter truth; but a youth like him, afraid to grasp his personal secret and yet trying to do just that, must be worse, indeed far more miserable and wretched." "To tell the truth, his star was clouded from the very day he was born"—so saying, Matsumoto reveals the secret surrounding Sunaga's birth. Only now can we understand the nature of Sunaga's agony. His inborn introspective tendency, his incapacity for dazzling action, his so-called modern malady—all these factors have helped to make him what he is. But there is one more basic factor that has gnawed at his heart, whose nature he could not identify, much as he tried, whose presence he could not but sense. The only thing he did feel certain of is that it hovered between his dying father's advice: "Ichizo, after I'm gone, you must depend on your mother's care. Remember that," and his mother's promise at his funeral: "Your father is gone, but I'll love you as before. Don't you worry." Even as a child, Sunaga sensed that these strange words had stuck in his heart. His is the agony and frustration of a patient who, because of his pain, senses the presence of some unknown disease and yet has no access to its cause because his doctor remains deaf to his desperate supplication. Then finally, Sunaga begins to discover that all his life he has been a man with a past, and that his is a struggle with the past. Here he is close to Daisuke and Sosuke, but their similarity is less than their difference. Although Daisuke and Sosuke suffer under the shadow of the past, their past is something within their reach, something they are able to identify because it is their own doing, whereas Sunaga's past is beyond his personal reach because it started even before his birth. Unlike Daisuke's and Sosuke's past, his is not the past he made himself, but something he must accept as part of his existence and learn to live with. In Sunaga, Soseki pressed Daisuke's and Sosuke's confrontation with the past as far as man's struggle with his true nature, or his search for identity.

If Sunaga's search for identity is the warp of his story, his relation with Chiyoko is its woof that reinforces and enriches the texture. It is Chiyoko who forced high praise from Masamune Hakucho, one of the most severe Soseki critics, that in her Soseki for the first time created a living woman, a character of flesh and blood—compared with Fujio, whose gorgeous costume conceals her empty frame; with Michiyo, whose shadow outshines her person; and with Oyone, who has only a shadow.[3] In this Masamune is right. Soseki takes pains to expose several aspects of Chiyoko, Chiyoko with Matsumoto whom Tagawa observed, Chiyoko at the death of her little niece, and Chiyoko confronting Sunaga. Especially in her clash with Sunaga over a certain Takagi, she not only drives Sunaga to face his own inconsistency, the inconsistency between heart and head, but also reveals in full her own passionate nature. Yet there is one quality she shares with her predecessors, Fujio, Michiyo, and even Oyone: it is the quality of fearlessness, and it is this that attracts and at the same time frightens Sunaga, who knows only fear.

This contrast between the fearful male and the fearless female is Sunaga's own; and he extends it to that between the poet and the philosopher. "Her sense of judgment," remarks Sunaga on Chiyoko, "is completely independent of education and experience. Simply intuitive, she goes direct to her object. That makes the other party feel as though he were struck by lightning. By the force of her drive I mean that a mass of purity, huge and voluminous, can shoot out of her heart, not that it is thorny, poisonous or corrosive. The proof is that so many times in the past, while facing her anger, however violent, I felt the inmost part of me cleansed by her purity; I even felt I had just encountered something sublime. Standing alone before the whole world, I am willing to defend her as the most womanly of all women." "I have always held that nothing is as beautiful as pure emotion; and nothing is as strong as beauty. The strong, naturally, do not fear. If I were to marry Chiyoko, I couldn't possibly stand the powerful ray issuing from her eyes. The ray does not have to be anger; it can be pity, love or adoration. I am sure I'll be petrified by the ray. That is because I am a man of emotion too feeble to return in gratitude as much as, let alone more than she gives." Here Sunaga virtually paraphrases Hirota's cryptic remarks: "A woman can be pure; the trouble with a man is he can never be as pure."

On hearing Sunaga's story about his relations with Chiyoko, Tagawa rightly wonders whether they were "meant to be husband and wife, or to live as friends, or to face each other as enemies." To this Matsumoto replies: "I don't think they can escape from this conflict, and the conflict is a sort of karma that binds their birth. Unfortunately, they are very much attracted to each other, and yet those around them have no power over the fate that governs their attraction. They are a sorry pair who meet only to part, and part only to meet. Whether or not you can understand my point, if they marry, they marry only to beget unhappiness; if they do not marry, they are as much dissatisfied, in the sense that they continue to be unhappy. Therefore, I think it would be wisest to let nature take its course." Through this relationship between Sunaga and Chiyoko, Soseki dissects the phenomenon of love itself, which with Daisuke and Michiyo, with Sosuke and Oyone, he had taken for granted. The result is that in *And Then* and *The Gate* he affirmed the reality of love, and now in *Until After the Spring Equinox* he subjects it to relentless scrutiny. The fact that Sunaga and Chiyoko were since childhood meant to be husband and wife by others merely indicates Soseki's intent to bring the image of love under closer analysis. There was no such problem with Daisuke and Michiyo, with Sosuke and Oyone; they were fated for each other. The question rises when we suppose, as with Sunaga and Chiyoko, they are not. Matsumoto advises us to let nature

take care of their fate, but that makes sense only in the novel.
Soseki is not content with the problem as it stands. He must carry
it into his next work, *Kojin.*

IV   Kojin

Soseki always felt both fascinated and repulsed by the profession of detective.[4] As often as he condemned it, he tried to justify
it (or his own fascination) as a pathological symptom of self-
consciousness, which he called a modern malady. Whether or not
this strange ambivalence was due to his alleged persecution complex, two points deserve mention: one is the possibility that there
is a relationship between Soseki's attitude and his favorite technique of suspense in many of his works; the other is the fact that
Until After the Spring Equinox is in a way a detective story and
Tagawa is a detective. Even prior to Taguchi's assignment, Tagawa thought about this possibility but ruled it out. When Sunaga
suggests that he be a detective, Tagawa's reaction is thus described: "Keitaro in earnest explained why he could not possibly
make it. By and large, the detective is as it were a diver plunging
underneath society; the profession would ensure better access to
human mysteries. Conveniently, there is no danger of getting involved since his sole task is to observe the dark side of others. All
he wants is to remain a student of man, or rather to observe with a
sense of wonder the way a strange mechanism called man gropes
through darkness." Sunaga's aloofness irks Tagawa, but he cannot
keep away from his friend for more than a few days. Tagawa's
return to Sunaga is the key to the entire novel, for with his circle
of private search gradually narrowing down to its focal point, he
finds none other than Sunaga. Like Tagawa, Soseki returns to Sunaga, now convinced that there is something in the character he
created. At the same time he wants his agent to step within the
drama itself, instead of merely observing from without. Thus Tagawa becomes Jiro the narrator of *Kojin;* likewise Sunaga becomes Ichiro the hero of this domestic drama, being a married
man. And as Soseki tightens up their relationship, they become
involved in one central situation, a kind of Paolo and Francesca
situation. This is the basic pattern around which Soseki develops
Kojin.[5]

If *Until After the Spring Equinox* is Soseki's attempt to combine
two things, a point-of-view technique and a novel composed of

short stories, or more properly to unify short stories into a novel by way of this particular narrative method, *Kojin* indicates Soseki's intent to press this technical experiment further. Its four stories, "Friend," "Brother," "Return and After," and "Anguish" are all narrated from Jiro's point of view. As the novel opens, Jiro arrives in Osaka with two things in mind: to meet his friend Misawa in order to carry out their planned pleasure trip and to expedite, at his mother's request, the pending marriage between Osada and Sano, which was initiated by Okada and Okane, the couple who married in a similar manner. The latter problem, however, which comes to a successful solution, is only of secondary importance. The primary focus of this part is really Misawa, who has ruined his stomach at a wild party and now is in a hospital for treatment. Into this small hospital world comes another patient for the same purpose, a geisha whom Misawa forced to drink at the party. Misawa's uncommon interest in her, as Jiro finally finds out, is caused by her resemblance to a young divorcee, mentally deranged but now dead, whom he came to love in secret.

Misawa's departure for Tokyo coincides with the arrival of Jiro's family—his mother, brother, and sister-in-law; and when Jiro joins their trip to Wakanoura, the novel suddenly unfolds its central drama for which the second part, "Brother," sets the stage. Unlike his architect-brother, Ichiro is a scholar who has been suffering from failure to establish an intimate rapport with his wife, Onao, whom Jiro had known prior to their marriage. It is here that Ichiro expresses his suspicions that his wife may love Jiro, whose integrity he says he trusts, and confronts him with an unheard-of request that Jiro test her honor. Jiro rejects the request, but a peculiar turn of events forces him to do more or less that. When he accompanies his sister-in-law to Wakayama, they are caught by a hurricane and compelled to stay overnight at a hotel. Although Soseki subtly exploits their delicate situation, nothing really happens and they return. Jiro reports to Ichiro that his wife's honor is beyond doubt.

"Return and After" details their situation, which turns from bad to worse to worst amid a succession of trivial but complicated family affairs, all of which seem to run their normal course. Three events stand out, however: Osada's wedding, which fares precisely the way it should; their father's story about a blind woman intent on ascertaining her former lover's heart; and Ichiro's story about the Paolo-Francesca episode in terms of the law of society and the law of heaven or nature. In the meantime Jiro moves out of the house, while Ichiro becomes more and more isolated from his family. His parents realize something has to be done before the worst overtakes Ichiro, and this is a feeling which Jiro also shares. As a means of dragging him out of his shell of isolation, they beg of his friend H to take him traveling. H succeeds in the attempt. His long report on Ichiro during their travel occupies most of the last part, "Anguish," the drama of a modern intellectual facing three alternatives: suicide, madness, and faith.

To summarize a novel is always a thankless task, for oversimplification and distortion are bound to result. This is especially true with *Kojin*, which simply defies any sort of retelling. However, even this summary, though inadequate, presents a few points of interest: first, Jiro succeeds Tagawa, but is developed beyond the latter's role as observer; second, Ichiro inherits Sunaga's problem, and their difference is that Ichiro must wrestle with the problem raised by Sunaga. Ichiro and Onao, as husband and wife, in their domestic impasse clarify and intensify the impossible relationship between Sunaga and Chiyoko. And third, the relationship between Ichiro and Jiro, in relation to Onao, realizes the potential love triangle of Daisuke-Hiraoka-Michiyo. All these points indicate that in *Kojin* Soseki attempts to press his previous themes and character relationships to their logical limits. The entire novel suggests the urgency with which Soseki as a man and as an artist felt it necessary to tackle the problem. It is this feeling of urgency that pervades the novel, compelling every reader to identify himself with its central hero, Ichiro.

In past decades critics have heatedly debated whether or not *Kojin* is an artistic success, both technically and thematically; opinion is still sharply divided. Some dismiss it as a failure, despite its thematic significance; others designate it as one of Soseki's most mature works, with all its obvious flaws.[6] It cannot be denied that *Kojin* is by no means a perfect work, even to those enthusiasts who regard it as one of the author's best works. When judged by our standards it has some serious flaws. To us who are used to Western fiction, especially contemporary fiction, *Kojin* may appear but a series of sharply etched tableaux without the dynamic rhythm of action. We may go as far as to argue that in this novel there is only a situation but no action that should develop from the situation, that Soseki in effect creates a potentially explosive Paolo-Francesca situation only to bypass it, and that the novel builds up our sense of anticipation, but leads us nowhere. Aside from such over-all objections, there are still more specific points to be made. For example, there is an apparent cleavage between the first part and the rest of the novel, and then between the first three parts and the fourth and last. Some may wish that Soseki had been more specific about Ichiro's and Jiro's profession so as to make better use of them in the novel, and also about the previous relationship between Jiro and Onao, and further, that Soseki had not abandoned Jiro's own problems, including his relationship with Onao, and left them unsolved. And last of all, some may express dissatisfaction with the denouement itself, which is merely suggested in H's letter in the last part. Some of these criticisms may be sound; however, one must bear in mind that a perfect work is usually an artist's dream and a critic's hypothesis. It would be more profitable for us to probe into those qualities which make *Kojin* powerful literature.

In *Kojin,* as in its immediate predecessor, Soseki is intent on creating a novel which consists of short stories or episodes. And in tightening his work without damaging its organic wholeness, he is far more successful here than in *Until After the Spring Equinox.* His narrative method in *Kojin* is what we might call an oblique method. And it is employed in two ways: first, in order to unfold the over-all drama Soseki creates Jiro, who is sympathetic toward Ichiro because they are brothers, and at the same time prejudiced because he himself is involved in the situation. Until he receives H's missive, Jiro remains imperceptive. Then, to complete Jiro's broken vision, Soseki introduces H and places him in an inner circle—far closer to Ichiro than Jiro, and far closer than any other character can ever be. By way of H's detailed report concerning Ichiro, Soseki heightens this basically domestic tangle to the level of an intellectual, cultural, and metaphysical issue. By the same means he disposes of what he once regarded as an important but difficult subject in modern fiction, namely the treatment of religion or a religious state. In *Kojin* Soseki deals with this state quite successfully. And his success is due largely to the oblique method which enables him to offer just sufficient indications as to the direction in which Ichiro's spiritual release might lie.

Equally noteworthy is Soseki's sense of structure. As a devoted student of Western fiction he knows how to make those seemingly unrelated episodes and ancedotes function organically, circling around the central situation. As one whose ambition once was to become an architect, he also knows how to bring into play his sense of balance—contrast as well as parallel—to make intricate the pattern of symmetry and thereby enrich and elaborate rather than confuse or obscure the basic theme of the novel. First, the impossible marital tension between Ichiro and Onao is made sharper by introducing two pairs, Okada and Okane, and Sano and Osada, one already established and the other in process. These two couples, indeed, are made to serve as the norm dictated by long feudal tradition which they all matter-of-factly accept. Presumably Ichiro and Onao married by arrangement, just as Okada and Okane did, and just as Sano and Osada do, but their marriage resulted in deviation from the social norm, for Ichiro and Onao are a classic example of an incompatible couple forced by tradition to live together as husband and wife. Furthermore, they are, unlike their foils, the new man and the new woman dissociating their individual selves from society and seeking to value their hearts on their own individual terms. Yet the trouble is that they are not and cannot be completely free or modern. In the world where everything is in rapid transition their selves and hearts know only their conflict. Worse still, Ichiro, instead of quitting in compromise, tries to settle once and for all his personal problem on the absolute level, whereas Onao is not as forthrightly free a woman as, say, Ibsen's Nora.

Second, two other episodes, both pathetic and telling, that of Misawa's deranged divorcee and that of the blind woman, also stand in contrast to Ichiro and Onao. Misawa's happiness is due to his remaining ever poetic and romantic, and his never trying to translate experience into absolute terms. As Ichiro is a philosopher, so Misawa is a poet. (It is well to recall Sunaga's contrast between the philosopher and the poet; also his self-analysis: "My head is meant to suppress my heart.") Misawa is content with what he knows to be an illusion, because as a man of poetic temperament he instinctively refuses to dissect the beauty which is the essence of that illusory image of the insane young divorcee. This contrast of attitude between Ichiro and Misawa becomes pronounced when Ichiro reacts to the blind woman episode. When Ichiro denounces his father's practical expediency, it is be-

cause to him his father's dealing is despicably cheap in comparison with the intensity of the blind woman's single-minded desire
to grasp absolutely the heart of her lover who deserted her some
twenty years ago.

Onao's tragedy lies precisely in the fact that by virtue of her
own egotism she can never be insane like Misawa's young divorcee and thus release her passion; at the same time, she is just
sufficiently freed from tradition to keep her heart in silence as the
blind woman does. As Jiro describes her, she is extremely elusive
because she accepts the dictates of tradition, an acceptance which
in her case is a silent defiance, and almost by instinct she keeps
her heart to herself—as her only measure of self-protection.

Ichiro, on the other hand, suffers from an excessively cultivated
intellect and an introspective sensibility. He has his own share of
passion for his wife, but like her, he is also incapable of discarding
his own self. Neither Ichiro nor Onao, thus, knows an easy compromise; nor is divorce conceivable under these particular circumstances; nor does it lead to any solution. Theirs is the battle of the
sexes, as with Strindberg's characters. And what is worse is that in
their society the battle cannot be fought in the open; it is a constant duel of two minds that allows for no finality.

It is true that the domestic impasse of Ichiro and Onao is the
common tragedy of a new man and a new woman caught in the
violent transition of Japan from feudal to modern society. Yet in
Kojin this domestic tragedy is not the cause of Ichiro's plight;
rather it is the symptom of the general malady of an age Ichiro
happens to represent. This point is vital for a correct understanding of the novel. For this reason Soseki depicts the personal situation by way of Jiro, and then by way of H's letter places it in
suprapersonal perspective. Due to the latter device, *Kojin* becomes something more poignant, incomparably more profound
than a mere domestic tragedy. While working on the novel, Soseki, as was his wont, had to struggle with an ever recurring nervous strain, a third attack of chronic ulcers, and a deepening sense
of loneliness; so that the last part, "Anguish," was completed only
after an interval of five months. In the past, critics have sought to
hold this interruption responsible for weakening the continuity
between the last part and the rest of the novel.[7] Quite contrary to
their contention, however, it is really a plus rather than a minus
factor because it elevates the theme of *Kojin* to another plane.

And that significance is, first of all, sociocultural in the sense that in Ichiro Soseki creates a modern Japanese intellect, a product of Meiji Japan, the period which is comparable not only to Russia in the second half of the nineteenth century, but also to Renaissance Europe still under the shadow of the medieval world. Only in these terms can we view the sociocultural dilemma of Meiji Japan as an impossible hybrid of Eastern and Western culture. Here Hamlet is more germane to Ichiro than Raskolnikov, for instance. Ichiro is a modern Japanese Hamlet to whom the world is veritably out of joint.

It would also be a gross mistake to explain Ichiro's nervous tension and his sense of loneliness as no more than Soseki's personal problem. Soseki himself said as early as 1906 that the nervous breakdown is a malady peculiar to modern man, and he also said that the more faithful one tries to be to himself the more acute the malady becomes. From this it becomes clear that in terms of his own experience, Soseki was actually diagnosing the disease of his own Japan, his public testimony being his lecture in 1911, "The Enlightenment of Modern Japan." In *Until After the Spring Equinox,* Matsumoto casually refers to this in relation to Sunaga—casually because this sociocultural background still only serves there to accentuate Sunaga's wretched condition. But in *Kojin* it becomes the very stuff that makes the novel and its central character, Ichiro.

"Why, then, 'tis none to you; for there is nothing either good or bad, but thinking makes it so; to me it is a prison"—what Hamlet here says of himself may also apply to Ichiro. (Incidentally, Jiro says to his suspicion-ridden brother: "Brother, isn't it your own thinking that makes it so?" And Ichiro, in an ascending elevator, comments: "This is just like a prison; so is life.") Ichiro's plight is the plight of the intellectual. He excels in the abstract, but fails in the concrete; when he re-creates a night scene in Osaka he is altogether incapable of grasping people, places, and events in their proper context. His memories of these, graphic as they may be, remain fragmentary. Take for example those foreign names scattered all through the novel, such as Dante, Shakespeare, Meredith, Nietzsche, an aspect which certainly reminds us of those Russian novels by Turgenev, Dostoevsky, and Tolstoy. Certainly we cannot justify their frequent appearance merely as the result of Soseki's known practice of creative reading or artificial inspiration, for that would prove to be only pedantry. In order to do him justice in this matter, at least two points must be noted. First, the allusions are completely functional in the context. Ichiro's request that Jiro test Onao's honor echoes situationally and thematically that meaning-packed episode of the impertinent husband in Cervantes' *Don Quixote*. Both Ichiro and Anselmo are attempting something impossible. In a way *Kojin* contains the metaphysical theme of "El Curioso Impertinente" superimposed on the romantic situation of Paolo and Francesca. Second, and more significant is that in *Kojin* all these foreign names, with a few exceptions, are supposedly an integral part of Ichiro's own thinking process. All his references, while highly functional in their respective contexts, take on an air of outlandishness. These names appear as alien in the novel itself as, according to Soseki's speech of 1911, Western civilization is in the cultural landscape of Japan. They have failed to sink deep roots in the soil of Japan. They are not completely blended. It is this failure of cultural interfusion that indicates the source of Ichiro's tragedy, a tragedy of a modern Japanese intellectual isolated from his own world. These foreign names are as much in keeping with Ichiro's intellectual background as with his tragic situation which is symbolic of that of modern Japan.

Yet Ichiro's plight has a further significance, a universal one. His is also the plight of modern intellect and of modern man in general. His plight bespeaks the predicament of modern man in hopeless isolation from his own family, society, culture, and ultimately his own cosmos. This deeper implication becomes clearer when Ichiro puts his personal case in the light of modern science, which acknowledges no rest and only drives man on and on. In his talk with H, his Horatio, so to speak, Ichiro states: "Man's insecurity stems from the advance of science. Never once has science, which never ceases to move forward, allowed us to pause. From walking to ricksha, from ricksha to carriage, from carriage to train, from train to automobile, from there on to the dirigible, further on to the airplane, and further on and on—no matter how far we go, it won't let us take a breath. How far it will sweep us along, nobody knows. It is really frightening." The theme here, we know too well, has been one of the major themes of Western literature since the turn of the century. The significance of Soseki's art is, then, that while describing a most concrete domestic situation, he expands its implications across many levels of human existence in the modern world, without losing its immediacy. This is what he accomplishes in *Kojin*.

In his speech on modern Japan, Soseki designated her dilemma as a tragedy with no hope of solution. Soseki might have believed this to be still the case—at least on the collective level. On the personal level, however, it is likely that Soseki had by now come to see some possibility of it. This is suggested in Ichiro's travel, the possibility which was still not evident in Sunaga's. It is Ichiro himself who said in unequivocal terms: "To die, to go mad, or to enter religion—these are the only three courses left open for me." To Ichiro the absolutist, any practical expediency is out of the question. Yet no ordinary solution is possible in his tragedy of self. It calls for some sort of transhuman measure which alone can deal with self to any satisfactory degree—on the fundamental level. And Soseki prophetically suggests that the only humanly possible solution is the last of the three alternatives, namely religion in its purest sense as the only human way in which man can surpass himself—by surrendering his own self to something larger than himself.

This would appear to contradict Ichiro, who demanded in desperation that his friend H name any god as trustworthy as even a ricksha man. Just as in modern literature so many heroes in a like dilemma return to their traditional faith, so does Ichiro seem to turn toward his. The solution suggested in *Kojin*, unsatisfactory and incomplete as it may seem to some readers, is authentically Oriental. Soseki's hint as to this matter is given when H suggests that Ichiro be possessed by surrendering rather than asserting his small ego. (In fact, Matsumoto said something similar to this as one possible way of Sunaga's salvation.) The crab scene, where Ichiro experiences a momentary release, is a case in point.[8] Soseki seems to agree with H in suggesting self-absorption as the only possible human solution—at least for Ichiro who knows no god to whom he may turn. This solution, however, has nothing to do with Rossseau's return to nature; it simply points to the possibility of absolving the cursed self by way of the so-called esthetic or mystic union, for in this union there is no longer any schism between "thou" and "I." This sort of solution might appear to the Western reader no better than an escape from the issue itself, or worse still, the obliteration of the very self. But the Orient has traditionally viewed the problem in a different light, always asserting this mode of self-absorption as a divine state because it simply means to expand, not obliterate, self, which becomes as large as nature, the divine source of individual life. It is comparable to what Christian mystics term one's total surrender to God. In this sense many of Soseki's nature descriptions, especially of mountains and water in the last part of the novel, may be thematically as significant as his foreign names. Nature is as much Ichiro's birthright as those foreign names are alien to him. Thus considered, Soseki's solution in terms of union with nature (ultimately in a metaphysical sense) would be as valid as Dostoevsky's solution in terms of return to Christ.[9]

It must be remembered that in *Kojin* Soseki is content with only offering this hint of solution. The solution here, vague as it may seem, is unmistakably in that direction. Soseki has come a long way from the conclusion of his early novel *The Gate*. There Sosuke the hero, seeking a way out of his personal impasse, hopelessly knocks at the gate of a Zen temple. The solution suggested in *Kojin* is therefore doubly meaningful. He is now able to take a positive step forward; and his forward step is not in the direction of formalism, which is often not free from its own theoretical or dogmatic basis, even though it be Zen. Further, Soseki's solution here definitely points to his much-discussed and often-distorted philosophy, *sokuten kyoshi* (conform to heaven and forsake self.) Whether or not Soseki personally attained this state, it will suffice to say that in it Soseki seems to have finally seen the possibility, no matter how remote, of salvation for his hero, Ichiro.

V Kokoro

Art begins and ends in self-expression. Because art is an act of self-expression, the artist draws strength from existence itself, and whatever art is not faithful to its creator is hollow indeed insofar as he is concerned. So Soseki declared in 1912 shortly before setting out to write *Kojin*. It is this conviction that made *Kojin* such a compelling piece of literature. Ichiro, protagonist of the novel, who cries out, "Einsamkeit, du meine Heimat Einsamkeit!" apparently speaks for Soseki himself, the Soseki confiding to some of his friends: "Much as I wish to be content with loneliness, I am naturally happier if I can win even one friend to my side. That's probably because I lack a purely artistic temperament"; "Although I feel the urgent need of such an existential conviction, I am still astray in the realm of incertitude. Something ought to be done, I feel, and yet I am helpless"; and "Now I am trying to go on in search of truth." This sense of loneliness only deepened as he witnessed the passing of Meiji Japan with the death of Emperor Meiji in July 1912, and as he fought against his third attack of ulcers which interrupted *Kojin* for several months. Soseki felt like a man who had outlived his time and his life. It undoubtedly was the darkest period of Soseki's life as a man and of his career as an artist. And out of this darkness of heart he created *Kokoro*, the darkest and yet perhaps most moving of all his novels.[10] This he himself must have sensed when he decided to make it literally his own book by doing everything (design, etc.) by himself, printing it half at his own expense, and also writing his own recommendation: "To those who wish to grasp their own heart I recommend this book which has succeeded in grasping the human heart."

Kokoro consists of three parts: "The Sensei and I," "My Parents and I," and "The Sensei and His Testament." According to Soseki's initial plan, however, *Kokoro* was to serve as an over-all title for a series of short stories which would have only thematic continuity. While working on "The Sensei's Testament," the first story in the initial plan, Soseki realized that the piece needed its own development; consequently he changed his mind and decided to give it full treatment.

In this novel about the mystery of the human heart, Soseki does not specify the names of his main characters so as to enhance our intimacy with their inmost pulses. Although his acquaintance with the *sensei* started by chance in a summer bathing resort, the narrator, then a university student, feels some strange attraction toward this elderly person. The more he comes to know the man and his beautiful wife the more attached he grows, even though he fails to get the desired response. There is indeed something mysterious about the *sensei*, apparently withdrawn from the world but altogether devoted to his wife; the *sensei* shocks the trusting narrator with casual observations: ". . . but do you know that love is a sin?" or "Do you think that there is any breed of people born wicked? No, there is no such a thing as a born villain. Normally everyone is good. Or at least he is just like everyone else. But sheer chance can turn him into an evil creature, terrible as it may seem"; or "I was once deceived; I was deceived by no other than my own blood relations. I can never forget that. . . . I learned to hate not just them, but humanity in general which they respresent." All these remarks suggest to the young narrator some dark past that is evidently heavy on the *sensei's* mind. But what exactly it is, the narrator does not know any more than the *sensei's* wife, who modestly declares that no one could possibly make her husband as happy as she herself could. In his younger days the *sensei* was a different sort of person, not at all like what he now is, she says, and the only reason she can think of for such a complete change in his personality is the violent death of a certain friend of his. Once, when the narrator complains of his reticence the *sensei* says: "Because of what happened to me I distrust others. In fact, I distrust you, too. But I do not wish to distrust you. You seem so innocent. Before I die I should like to find even one single person I can trust. Can you be such a person? Would you be? Are you really sincere?" Then the *sensei* promises to tell his story, should the proper time ever come.

Upon graduation the narrator returns to his home where his father has been suffering from a kidney disease. Like other simple country folk, his parents, against the narrator's wish, plan a feast to celebrate his graduation, but must forgo it in deference to the passing of the Emperor. The tedium of country life becoming unbearable, the narrator resolves to return to Tokyo, but his father's illness takes a serious turn. So he stays on, despite a telegram from the *sensei* expressing a desire to see him. At the moment the patient reaches a crisis a long letter arrives from Tokyo in which the narrator's hurrying eye catches the following passage: "By the time this letter reaches you I shall no longer be in this world. I shall be dead." This is enough for the narrator to desert his dying father and hasten to Tokyo. On the train the narrator reads the *sensei's* letter.

It is in this letter that the *sensei*, keeping his word to the narrator, unfolds his past. The *sensei* was once a carefree youth who could have lived comfortably on the inheritance from his deceased father. When, however, he discovered that he had lost a good portion of it through his uncle's deceit, he could no longer trust others. But this first wound was gradually healed, when, back in Tokyo, he came to live with a respectable widow and her beautiful daughter (the *ojosan*). Into this now intimate circle the *sensei* quite unwittingly brought his old friend, K, a disowned and starving student of philosophy, who was as serious-minded as the *sensei* was easygoing. One day K confided to his friend and benefactor his love for the *ojosan* in whom the *sensei* himself took not a little interest, though he was then not quite conscious of it. By taking advantage of K's trustful nature, the *sensei* got ahead of him in asking for the *ojosan*'s hand. And he was readily accepted. All this, of course, was done without K's knowledge. Later, when informed of it, K committed suicide. On graduation the *sensei* married the unsuspecting *ojosan*, his present wife. Theirs, apparently, was a life of intimacy and contentment, but the truth is that the *sensei* was no longer the same person. In order to allay his gnawing sense of guilt he tried everything: he applied himself to his studies; and even took to drinking, but all to no avail. Finally he resolved to go on living as if he were dead. Then Emperor Meiji passed away, and following his death General Nogi committed suicide. The *sensei* felt that the time had at long last come to put an end to his already dead life.

From the vantage point of time we may agree that Soseki's decision to pursue only "The Sensei's Testament" after discarding his original plan was a wise one, for the moment he recognized this necessity he also perceived its thematic center more clearly than when working on any of his previous novels. All he had now to do was to explore his theme by a method which could embody it adequately.

Kokoro is built upon Soseki's sense of calculated suspense, and the intensity of this suspense increases in proportion as Soseki unfolds his story. From the outset the reader can identify himself with this naïve but serious-minded youth, thus sharing his attachment for the *sensei*. If the first part, "The Sensei and I," establishes this identity between the narrator and the reader, the second part, "My Parents and I," further exploits this intimate rapport by way of the contrasts and parallels between the *sensei* and the narrator's father. Throughout the second part we, like the narrator, are made to feel the presence of the *sensei* both by the narrator's family who unknowingly refer to him and, paradoxically, by his very absence. Then through the *sensei*'s own voice comes the final revelation which helps complete our image of him. Through such a three-stage development Soseki comes to grips with his theme. There is nothing that sidetracks our growing interest; there are neither digressions nor ramblings, which have often tended to impede the natural progression of plot in some of his earlier novels. Compared with these, *Kokoro* does gain greater concentration. Soseki's artistry here is such that in the end we accept the inevitability of the *sensei*'s death. It is indeed a work with classical restraint, clarity, and balance. In it Soseki shows himself to be a master of the economics of fiction.

Kokoro is in a way a story about the narrator not only because in the first two parts he speaks in person but also because his contact with the *sensei* forms a significant phase in his youthful exploration of life. While serving as the author's point of view, the narrator also lives his own life. Largely through the *sensei* he comes to face life itself, eager to wrest from life whatever lesson it can offer. On one occasion when he almost succeeds in cornering the evasive *sensei* the narrator declares: "No, I do not consider it another matter. I do value your opinions because they are born out of your own past. Otherwise, they would be worthless. I cannot be satisfied with a doll which has no soul." Quite unawares, the narrator is seeking what we might call the father image. For this reason Soseki provides the second part, "My Parents and I," so that the narrator may choose between his father and the *sensei*. As these two fathers react to life in their own characteristic ways, the narrator cannot but notice their resemblances and their differences as well. Both elders are suffering from diseases: his actual father is suffering physically, and his spiritual father, spiritually. Even in the first part their contrasts startle the narrator. On one of his visits home the narrator says:

I compared my father with the *sensei*. They are, alike, self-effacing, so much so that you can hardly tell whether they are alive or dead. Socially, both are non-entities. Yet my father, who loved to play the game of chess, couldn't satisfy me even as a companion; whereas the *sensei*, whom I had never sought for amusement's sake, exerted an influence on my mind, indeed a greater influence than if we had shared the common pleasure. Since the word "mind" sounds too cold, I should rather say "my heart." It would have seemed to me then no exaggeration to say that the *sensei*'s strength entered my flesh, or that his very life was flowing through my blood. All this in spite of the plain fact that one was my true father and the other, a stranger after all. By their contrast, I couldn't but be shocked as though I had for the first time discovered a great truth.

The narrator's decision to forsake his dying father in favor of his spiritual father signals his decisive maturation. It is a crucial moment of his life, because he chooses the spiritual truth over the physical fact. By this act, a shocking one indeed to those who adhere to the primacy of filial piety, the narrator becomes the one person in whom the *sensei* could confide his own dark past. Likewise, by this confidence the *sensei* proves to himself that he is still capable of trusting another human being, and thus humanity in general. In carrying out his old promise the *sensei* writes: "I shall regardlessly cast a dark shadow of life over you. But don't be frightened. Stare at this darkness and take whatever will be of help to you. By the darkness I, of course, mean moral darkness. I was born an ethical creature and reared as such. My ethics may be quite different from those of present-day youth. No matter how erroneous, they are nevertheless my own; they are not something I borrowed for temporary wear. That's why they may be of some use to you who wish to grow."

Shortly before *Kokoro* began appearing serially in the *Asahi,* Soseki defined a novel as "a faithful account of an individual's life or his fate." Such is *Kokoro,* no doubt. Moreover, it is a tragedy, a tragedy of character, as expressed in the person of the *sensei.* In a genealogy of Soseki's heroes, the *sensei* falls between Daisuke and Sosuke. His rivalry with K over the *ojosan* certainly reminds us of Daisuke's with Hiraoko over Michiyo, and also of Sosuke's with Yasui over Oyone. Had Soseki created in the *sensei* merely another Daisuke or another Sosuke, *Kokoro* would have been a work altogether different from what it is. The *sensei* is stronger than Sosuke, but weaker than Daisuke, supposing even that Yasui and Hiraoka follow K's course of violence. The *sensei* is not so defiant as to share Daisuke's so-called will of heaven; and yet in coming to face his own past squarely, he is far more steadfast than Sosuke, and therefore free of the latter's fatalistic resignation.

Soseki dramatizes with great care those two events which made the *sensei* what he is. First, when the *sensei* discovered his uncle's treachery he learned to loathe man. By his own admission he doubted humanity only in terms of money. At that stage he was but a disillusioned cynic who still maintained confidence at least in his own integrity. There was as yet room for this sort of moral luxury when he left his native town and those despicable folks for good. Then, through his dealings with K over the *ojosan* he learned to doubt humanity even in terms of love, and this time he could not find any room for refuge, because he himself was the object of his moral nausea. Deprived of the last vestige of a cynic's self-righteousness, the *sensei* now had to accept the reality of evil in his own heart. "Through cunning, I have won. But as a man, I have lost," writes the *sensei*. He succeeded in forestalling K's love by treachery, but failed in upholding his sense of self-righteousness. In K's suicide he witnessed the fate of a man who had just begun to live, supported by friendship and love, and whom he morally murdered by denying him this life support. As the *sensei* confesses, "My self-confidence was shattered by realizing that I was no better than my uncle. I had been disgusted with others, and now became disgusted with myself. I just could not move any further."

K's suicide dealt him a mortal wound; with the realization that he was K's real murderer, it also became a moral wound. With such a fatal wound deep in his heart the *sensei* rose or struggled to rise from the moral ruins of which he was the sole maker. But worst of all, by murdering K, the *sensei* really murdered himself. He knew full well that there were only two ways by which he could get out of this prison of conscience: either by laying bare his sin before his wife or by putting an end to his life. At the same time he knew equally well that he was incapable of choosing either of these two possible courses, or probably that he had no right to take either course. He sought something of a compromise, in keeping with his acute moral sensibility. In other words, he resolved to go on living as if already dead. This accounts for his refusal to confess his sin to his wife. When he says he could not bear the heartlessness of whipping a beautiful, innocent flower, and again when he says he found it too painful to stain his wife's memory even if slightly—though he was by now certain that she would be glad to forgive him, the *sensei* is not only justifying his own weakness. There is more to it than this. When, closing his letter, he explicitly forbids the narrator to reveal his secret to his wife, despite her lifelong suffering, the *sensei* proves himself to be a person of moral fastidiousness rather than a moral coward. He could of course have assuaged this spiritual agony simply by confessing his sin. Because of his puritanical moral outlook the *sensei* refuses to unburden even a small fraction of his sin onto his wife, the very trophy of his love and the very reminder of his sin. To him it is probably too easy a way out. It is his sin, not hers. With such a conviction he refuses to draw her into his sin, in spite of her undoubted willingness. In short, his is a life of moral masochism.

As a Japanese puritan the *sensei* reminds us of some of Hawthorne's Puritan heroes; and *Kokoro* bears a singular thematic resemblance to "Roger Malvin's Burial" (1832), one of Hawthorne's tales. (Although Soseki knew Hawthorne's works, there is no evidence that he had read this particular story.) Both works are psychological investigations of the moral impact of sin on the human heart. Yet in Hawthorne's allegory Reuben has a son who serves him as Isaac does Abraham; whereas Soseki denies to the *sensei* even this chance. (The *sensei* remarks to the puzzled narrator, "We'll never have one [a child] of our own," and laughing calls it "divine punishment.") More striking is the way both stories end. Hawthorne's tale is entirely allegorical. Especially so is its last scene, where the fall of an oak branch completes Reuben's expiation, lifting the curse from his suffering conscience, while Soseki cannot follow this solution for the reason that his world is not ruled by Hawthorne's God. Soseki's hero, instead, commits suicide as the only course of action available to him.

Yet it would be a mistake to explain away the *sensei's* suicide as the logical outcome of his dread despair that has accumulated over the years, and thereupon reject it on religious grounds. As the *sensei* came to realize, his friend K's suicide was prompted neither by loss of his love as such, nor by the clash between the ideal and the actual, but really by his unbearable loneliness, a loneliness beyond hope. The *sensei* himself, time and again, was frightened by the idea that he might be following the same path as K, but his was a loneliness beyond despair, as is evident in his resolution to go on living as if already dead. That is why he was able to bring himself to offer the best possible care to his mother-in-law, who was dying of an incurable disease. As he says, he did that of course for the sake of the patient, and also for the sake of his beloved wife, but largely for the sake of humanity. "Even before this," writes the *sensei*, "I had longed to do something, but I hadn't been able to do anything—just standing with folded arms. Since I was cut off from the world, it was the first time I had experienced the feeling that of my own volition I had done some good. I was, as it were, driven by a sort of feeling akin to the need for atonement." Also, that is why he could declare that he had dragged his life on and on for the sake of his wife, who was now alone after her mother's death, though all along he knew very well that his kind of love, no longer personal but merely impersonal, could never wholly satisfy her feminine heart. Yet as a man of acute moral sensibility the *sensei* was thoroughly convinced that there were no means by which he could sufficiently atone for his sin. While demanding nothing from others, he demanded everything from himself, as though he had assumed the role of God to punish himself. He became a caretaker of his own life. The only thing he could do under the circumstances was to await the proper time to release his charge. And when at last it came, he proved to be capable of self-execution. By this final act he became his own master. To him this signified a moral victory, since his trouble really lay in his initial failure to undo his error before K's suicide, the failure to act properly at the proper moment. There is Soseki's marginal comment in English on his copy of Nietzsche's *Thus Spake Zarathustra* which is in this regard highly revealing: "Our saying is 'it is dishonour not to die at the right time.' The question is to find out the right time. Moralists say that it is not one's life and therefore it is immoral to take away one's life by oneself. Very well, but our parents gave birth to us without our consent. Thus we find no reason why we should feel any obligation toward anybody as regards our lives. Our lives are our own and we are perfectly free to kill ourselves the moment we think it is the right time. Consider whether it is [the] right time or not and decide for yourselves." The *sensei* does precisely this with complete serenity. In writing his last letter to the narrator he discovers that he is still capable of trusting humanity; and in choosing death he also proves himself now capable of moral courage. If our final opinion of a man's worth depends largely on the way he dies, the *sensei*'s is no doubt a death of dignity, a death of triumph over moral ruin. In this sense *Kokoro* is a tragedy of character.

Yet, despite the aptness with which Soseki handles this theme, there is an artistically serious problem. It concerns Soseki's use in *Kokoro* of the death of Emperor Meiji and General Nogi's subsequent suicide as an immediate impetus to the *sensei*'s final decision. Did Soseki the artist momentarily lapse into Soseki the man? Did he intend it to be his artistic tribute to the Emperor whose death he took much to heart, and also to the General whose sincerity he never doubted? Or did he simply seek to capitalize on the topical interest? Soseki was too conscious and too conscientious an artist to dare such an artistic risk for mere effect. The fact that he deliberately chose this particular event as the proper moment for the *sensei's* suicide seems positive proof that he thought its use to be justified in the context of the novel.

The narrator's ailing father, who is in such sharp contrast with the *sensei*, cries out, on learning of the Emperor's death: "Oh, oh —our dear Emperor has passed away. I, too. . . ." And he gives up the feast planned in celebration of his son's graduation. Again later, on learning of General Nogi's suicide he exclaims, "What a terrible thing! What a terrible thing!" and in his hopeless delirium he declares, "Will General Nogi forgive me? How can I ever face him without shame? Yes, I shall come right after. . . ." If the narrator's father is the inarticulate voice of the common populace who lived under the Emperor's forty-five year reign, the *sensei* is then their eloquent spokesman. Of the Emperor's death the *sensei* writes: ". . . at that moment I felt as though the spirit of Meiji had begun and ended with the Emperor. I painfully felt that we survivors who had been most strongly influenced by the period, were now left behind the times." To his wife Shizu (her name incidentally is the same as that of the general's wife), who teasingly suggested *junshi* ("following one's lord to the grave") the *sensei* in fact stated that should he ever commit *junshi* it would be to the spirit of Meiji. At that moment he felt that he had poured a fresh meaning into this antiquated word. To the *sensei* the guns signaling the imperial funeral sounded like the knell of the passing away of the Meiji era. In General Nogi's *junshi* the *sensei* now found something very special. He writes:

In the paper I read General Nogi's testament. When I came across the passage that ever since losing the imperial banner to the enemy during the Seinan Rebellion he had constantly thought of suicide to atone for his blunder, I automatically counted on my fingers all those years Mr. Nogi had lived with the resolution of death. Since the Seinan Rebellion occurred in the 10th year of Meiji, there is a long stretch of thirty-five years between then and now. It would seem that all these thirty-five years he had anxiously awaited the proper time to die. I also wondered which could have been more painful to such a person, those thirty-five years he has survived or the moment he thrust the sword into his stomach.

A couple of days later I finally decided on suicide. You may not clearly understand my reason for suicide any more than I can fully understand General Nogi's. If so, it may be due to a difference of opinion because we belong to two different generations. That cannot be helped. Or more accurately, it is due to the unique character every individual is born with. In this letter I have done my utmost to make you understand this strange person who is myself.

This suggests that *Kokoro* is not only a personal but also a suprapersonal tragedy. In the *sensei's* personal tragedy Soseki also created another larger tragedy, a collective tragedy, a tragic conflict between two generations, the old and the new. Soseki is at pains to stress this point. For instance, the *sensei* writes at the outset of his letter: "I was born an ethical creature and reared as such. My ethics may be quite different from those of present-day youth." Speaking of K he also says that his friend held the past too precious to jettison, and that he moreover possessed stubbornness and perseverance, qualities seldom found among moderns. The conflict between the two generations here, needless to say, is the conflict between feudal and modern Japan, the conflict which characterizes the spirit of the Meiji period as a whole.

In his lectures of 1911, especially "Education and Literature" and "Literature and Morality," Soseki designated the contrast between feudal and modern Japan as one of two clashing ways of life. As he explained, the feudal way is deductive in that it starts from a set of moral precepts for the people to follow; it is idealistic and emotional; its romantic aspiration leaves little or no room at all for moral laxity, and is therefore exacting and intolerant. The modern way, on the other hand, is inductive in that it accepts a set of facts confirmed by new sciences; and its realistic and naturalistic approach, while responsible for lowering our ethical standards, shows considerable latitude toward human foibles and failures. If one is collective, the other is eminently individualistic; they are bound to conflict with each other. It is this conflict between the two diametrically opposite views of life that makes the Meiji period so vibrant, violent, and tragic, for both views inhere in the very fiber of the Meiji mind.

The *sensei* and his friend K are no exception to this. Both are too demanding, especially with regard to themselves. In this respect they are still part of the old generation. Yet as enlightened children of modern Japan they also belong to the new generation; they are in search of individual happiness. When they clash with each other over the object of their personal happiness, there can be no easy compromise. What is particularly significant about their love triangle is the conflict between friendship and love. If friendship is a feudal ideal for collective solidarity, love is then a modern ideal for individual happiness. Between these two ideals the moderns may find little or no conflict whatever, because to them friendship is but a faint memory of an erstwhile ideal, now completely overshadowed by love. As our perennial Browning-esque slogan, "love is best," implies, love justifies nearly everything. However, this is not the case with K and the *sensei*. To them, friendship and love have equal force; more often than not, friendship proves to be stronger than love because one represents the reality of the past while the other merely promises the potential future, no matter how alluring. The *sensei* is correct when he states that should he dare *junshi* it would be to the spirit of Meiji. Thus, combining a personal and a collective tragedy, *Kokoro* also becomes Soseki's artistic tribute to the spirit of Meiji.

In *Kokoro*, Soseki created a novel which is unquestionably "a faithful account of an individual's life or his fate." Soseki's stand in the novel is that of a moralist, not of a dogmatist. As a moralist he is content to subject to probing analysis the mystery of the human heart. He does nothing less and nothing more. Yet some critics have debated about Soseki's intentions concerning the character of the *sensei*, or more specifically, Soseki's attitude toward his tragic protagonist. Some have suggested that Soseki intended us to consider the sensei a noble character; others have flatly rejected such a view.[11] The truth is that the *sensei* is at once weak and noble, just as every man is. This is one of the reasons that through the narrator we can so readily identify ourselves with the *sensei*. In "Imitation and Independence," a lecture of 1913, Soseki said that if a criminal or a sinner can record the process of his mind and heart, and with the truthfulness of it, impress others, he is no longer a criminal or a sinner, for his very act of recording absolves his crime or his sin, thus entitling him to salvation.

CHAPTER 6

Another Vista: Last Years (1915–1916)

I Within the Sash-Door

TOWARD the end of July 1914, when *Kokoro* neared its completion, World War I broke out. In the months following Japan also joined the war and played her small part. But if the war was of such significance that it shattered the Western world, it still seemed far off as far as Japan was concerned. In mid-September Soseki had his fourth attack of ulcers and stayed in bed for about a month. Late in November he delivered a speech under the title "My Individualism" at the Peers' School. Shortly after this he contracted a cold and was confined to his house. Within the sash-door, that is, his private study, Soseki wrote a series of thirty-nine short pieces which appeared in the *Asahi* from January 13 to February 23, 1915.

In the first piece Soseki wrote somewhat apologetically: "To write I have to dare the scorn of those who have only a very limited amount of leisure at their disposal. . . . If I write, I am pushing aside politicians, soldiers, businessmen, and wrestling-fans. But I do not think I can pluck up that much courage. Only because I was asked to write something for the season, am I going to write about these trivial things concerning no one but me." This sets the general direction and mood for *Within the Sash-Door*, the last of Soseki's cycle of personal writings. There is little of either the rich variety of *Spring Miscellanies*, or Soseki's eagerness to convey his thoughts to his readers, so characteristic of *Random Recollections*. In effect there are no fantastics or grotesques, no prose poems or short stories. More often as a man than as an artist, Soseki records many events he has known, but neither his unpretentiousness nor what is almost a monotone can conceal the subtlety of his personal observations and recollections, filtered now through his contemplative mind.

They fall into three groups. The first group is composed mostly of the pieces describing scenes and recent events around the au-

thor—a magazine photographer who somehow managed to catch
Soseki's smile, a house dog called Hector whose drowned body
was buried near the grave of his cat, one of his college friends
who visited him after a long silence, a woman with literary aspirations, a man who insisted on having a sample of Soseki's handwrit-
ing, a fee for a recent speech (which he refused to accept, to the
other party's consternation), a woman who asked for his advice
on her mental confusion, a New Year's visitor who related with
admirable candor a sad affair with a geisha, a certain authoress
whose beauty and death he recalled, a man who expounded a
monistic view of the arts, a pet cat whose unpredictable health
reminded him of his own, a sunny Sunday which created a delightful state of self-irony, and so on.

To the second group belong Soseki's reminiscences of his own
childhood, none from his London sojourn. He remembers a band
of eight robbers that his neighbor directed to his house, a barber
who knew his family, an attempt to revisit his childhood home
of which he found no trace, his brother whose death as a bachelor
gladdened a geisha, and his own complicated childhood. All these
help conjure up his old family house which, in his memory, seems
so rustic, and somehow chilly and sad. One dominant image is
that of Soseki, the child who was fascinated by the *nagauta* lesson
of a girl next door. "When I walked over the stepping stones before our entrance into the street, I often heard Okita-san singing;
too young to tell whether she sang well or not, I remember those
spring afternoons, absentmindedly leaning against the white wall
of our godown—in the bright sun, soul enraptured, half listening
to her singing." Together with the house surrounded by blooming
plum trees in the spring sun, which Soseki envisioned in *Random
Recollections*, this evokes a Xanadu beyond the tyranny of time.
Another important image is that of the child rescued by his
mother from an evil dream in which he despairingly failed to restore funds he had misappropriated. "Even now I wonder
whether this incident happened entirely in dream or half in reality. But I clearly remember that I really did call to my mother for
help, and she actually came to offer me solace. Then, as usually in
my vision, she was wearing an unpatterned silk gown of dark blue
with a narrow black velvet sash." One is Soseki's dream-in-life; the
other is his life-in-dream. One is his soul's paradise; the other his

hell. And his guardian angel has the semblance of his own mother whom he lost at the age of fourteen.

The pieces in the last group are all of a reflective and meditative nature. There is the desperate voice of Soseki the man cursing his own opaque vision and supplicating the Almighty either for divine intuition to see through everyone or for power to transform others into beings of pure innocence. And there is Soseki facing a dilemma when a woman, having related her personal impasse, asks whether he would choose life or death for a fictional heroine in a like situation. Although death is dearer than life in his private thought, he urges her to follow the flow of time that carries away all human wounds. "Thus," writes Soseki, "while I believe death is always dearer than life, my wish and advice could not transcend this life which is full of unpleasantness. This would prove that in practice I am after all a half-hearted naturalist. Even now I stare at my own mind with half-suspicious eye." There is still another Soseki reiterating his most familiar subject, his own ill health, his life under the shadow of death. In one place he muses on the funerals of his friends, all of whom had seemed in better than average health. "But once in a while my own survival seems unnatural; it makes me wonder if fate is making fun of me." Soseki is delighted to find a better way of describing his own health than "Oh, getting along somehow"—"Still at work," to which people react in their own ways. "Isn't it possible that somewhere within ourselves all sorts of things are going on, things neither I nor they themselves are aware of? If these things suddenly explode with shattering roars, what would their reaction be? Memories no longer speaking, their past consciousness would have vanished forever. In such a state, how would they take themselves—who are incapable of perceiving the continuum between the present and the past, between the past and . . . ? After all, holding a bomb manufactured in our dreams, we each walk toward a remote destination called death—talking and laughing, don't we? Our only blessing, then, is that neither they nor others are aware of what they hold inside."

Soseki was correct here in saying that his ailment was "still at work," for in late March while visiting Kyoto, he succumbed to another attack of ulcers, which was to take his life in less than two years. While still in bed, he learned of the death of his half-sister,.

Fusa. In fact, throughout *Within the Sash-Door* one can hear the approaching steps of death. Many a time Soseki returns to this point as he touches on his friends' funerals, and even the burial of his housepet Hector. His every gesture in this series seems to show a man who is glancing backward, from the end of his life. There is little of the exquisite delight in life which pervaded *Random Recollections*. Instead, there are signs of his intimacy with death itself, an affirmation that death is the only reality. Even in a New Year's card he jokingly said: "This year I may really die." It is a kind of joke that contains a grain of truth. When one of his friends argued about what he had said about death in the current series, Soseki replied: "I do not mean that I won't die; what I meant is all of us will die. About this I have nothing in common with Spiritualists and Maeterlinck who all insist on the continuance of individuality after death. All I want to say is that only in death can one enter the state of the absolute, and that state, in my opinion, is very dear indeed, compared with the world of the relative." [1]

Whether or not Soseki was aware of it, *Within the Sash-Door* is highly symbolic because his private circle within the sash-door serves as a mirror of life itself. It is a monologue of Soseki the man, and it suggests that he is nearing another vista. With death approaching, Soseki becomes more conciliatory toward life—the world of the relative. In such a mood Soseki wrote in June 1914, shortly after he set out to write *Loitering:* "Many things displease, annoy and infuriate us. And to clean them all up is beyond any human being. Wouldn't it be more admirable to accept than fight them? If so, I hope we all will work in that direction. My spirit is young for my age, but I have lately turned my steps that way." Soseki has come a long way from the period of his desperate struggle for a fuller creative life, when he declared war against his compromising self and the world at large. Soseki has now reached the time of inventory; and this also applies to Soseki the artist, for to him life and art have been inseparable, and his existence has been shaped by their dialectical development. In January 1914 he wrote to one of his admirers: "I have written all sorts of things in these ten years since I started as a writer. As I glance back, there are many things that I wish to rewrite altogether, and some I even wish to destroy from the artistic point of view. But since mine is shame in an artistic, not moral, sense, I can tolerate them." But the truth is that to Soseki his shame is both artistic and moral. *Loitering* proves that such was the case.

II Loitering

Loitering, composed of 102 chapters, appeared in the *Asahi* from June 3 through September 14, 1915. It details the difficult life of Kenzo, besieged by his wife Osumi at home, and outside by his foster parents, his half-sister and her husband, and his own brother. Fresh from his years' stay abroad, Kenzo has much difficulty settling down. In this state, one rainy day he runs into a bareheaded man. Kenzo immediately turns away and looks ahead, continuing his walk. But the other party stands still by the roadside, showing no sign of resuming his walk, and stares after Kenzo. Kenzo does not want to speak to this ordinary-looking old man whom he once regarded as his foster father. Later, running into the man a second time he says to himself: "This is not going to be the end of it." This opening of *Loitering* foreshadows what is to come.

Sure enough, Shimada sends a man to sound him out, and then appears in person. By various means he makes it clear that he has a claim on his erstwhile foster son. Now he appeals to Kenzo's sense of obligation by referring to the old days; now he threatens Kenzo, hinting at a certain document still in his possession. Then even his foster mother appears, long divorced from Shimada. Kenzo does his best to keep them off; somehow he manages for the time being by giving them a sum of money out of his by no means full pocket. The more desperately he seeks a solution to this situation, the further he is dragged back toward the past he believed to be safely dead. He is surrounded by the familiar faces, his impoverished brother, his asthma-ridden half-sister and her wayward husband, and now his father-in-law—all expecting something from him. To his dismay, these ghosts turn the dead past into the living present, ever darkening the future.

These intruders from the past put a strain on his already tight budget, and worse still, further alienate him from his wife Osumi. They secretly despise each other, and they know it; they blame each other, each believing himself right in their undeclared war. In an effort to meet his increasing family expenses, Kenzo takes on another job, a part-time teaching position, with the result that he retreats further into his own world. As for Osumi, her hysteria increases as her pregnancy advances; she grows jealous of the daughter of Shimada's second wife once expected to become Kenzo's bride (who is discovered to be dead); and finally she attempts suicide.

When the baby is born, things seem to brighten up a little. Kenzo and Shimada reach a compromise; Kenzo offers Shimada a hundred *yen* in exchange for Shimada's document; they agree to sever their relations. The concluding scene between Kenzo and Osumi is as symbolic as the opening. To Osumi, who seems relieved at the settlement, Kenzo declares bitterly: "In this world you just can't settle anything—hardly anything. Things, once started, go on forever, changing only their shapes and becoming unrecognizable. That's all." She makes no response. She only holds the baby up. "O what a good baby! I cannot understand a word your papa is saying." With this his wife repeatedly kisses the baby's red cheeks.

Loitering is generally considered a faithful account of Soseki's own life, or more accurately, the life Soseki lived during the period from 1903 to 1905, from the time of his return from England to his debut as author of *I Am a Cat* and "The Tower of London." Komiya has said that Kenzo is a candid portrait of Soseki, and that in what Kenzo experiences in the novel there is indeed nothing that Soseki himself did not experience.[2] To this, all Soseki students agree, unfailingly referring to *Loitering* whenever they attempt to reconstruct the Soseki prior to his debut as a professional novelist. What is suggested here is that *Loitering* is an autobiographical novel, if not an autobiography; this is one of the reasons why some critics have often rated it probably the best and most perfect of all Soseki's novels. In fact, *Loitering* is one of the few novels in the Soseki canon which many naturalists admired frankly.[3] To them it meant Soseki's final capitulation to their own cause; they decided that in it Soseki wrote a sort of *shishosetsu* ("I" novel) which was their stock-in-trade.

Yet *Loitering* is nothing like a *shishosetsu;* it is no *pièce de scandale;* Soseki, and for that matter his protagonist Kenzo, seems unqualified to be the author or hero of an exhibitionistic piece. Nor does *Loitering* resemble what we might call an artist's self-portrait. It is altogether devoid of self-assertion, self-defense, self-torture, self-pity—all those qualities we often associate with this particular genre; and most important of all, it reveals virtually nothing of an artist's frustrated but exalted struggle in his chosen vocation; in brief, nothing of art and the artist. Still less is it an artist's memoir, which usually relates a literary history of his times exclusively from his personal point of view. Instead, *Loitering* contains all that would make it a failure as an artist's self-portrait.

Like Goethe, we can say that all works are to a degree fragments of their authors' great confession. Soseki appears to be no exception to this. In spite of this, *Loitering* occupies a peculiar place in the Soseki canon—as his *only* autobiographical fiction. Soseki's other works then should be called autopsychological. This difference between *Loitering* as an autobiographical novel and the rest of his works as autopsychological novels is important. That is, what made this most impersonal writer attempt a novel like *Loitering*? In the past Soseki has very freely used materials that came his way, and openly admitted this practice. Yet *Loitering* is the first and last, the sole attempt of Soseki in this manner. Some critics have tried to explain it as Soseki's lack of artistic materials, and asserted that the work marks Soseki's decline as an artist, although his next work, *Light and Darkness*, refutes this theory.[4] What, then, is Soseki seeking to accomplish in this novel?

The key to this question could be found in *Within the Sash-Door*, which preceded *Loitering*. Winding up this series of personal writings, Soseki states thus:

So far I have written about others as well as about myself. When I wrote about others, I had some fear it might cause them inconvenience; but when I wrote about myself, I could afford to feel comparatively free. Nonetheless, I was not yet at that state where I could be entirely free of conscious pose. While not succumbing to the vanity of falsifying to deceive the world, I still could not bring myself to confess some of my shameful faults. Someone has said of such confessions as St. Augustine's and Rousseau's, and De Quincey's *Opium Eater*, that no human being can humanly describe true facts. What I have written, of course, is by no means confessions. My sins, if we can so call them, may have been recorded from a very agreeable angle. And this point may cause some a sort of unpleasantness. But as of now I am overriding that unpleasantness and with a smile glancing over humanity at large. With the same eye I am smiling at myself who have so far written nonsense—as if it were another person.

In *Loitering* Soseki for the first time is resolved to write about himself without any illusion and prejudice, and objectify himself with ruthless detachment. Only in this sense can we call it Soseki's confession or, more accurately, Soseki's experimental confession.

This point, that *Loitering* is Soseki's experimental confession, cannot be overstressed, for an experimental confession means a confession as art. Herein lies a significant difference between Soseki's confession and other artists', the difference being that most writers write their artistic confessions primarily as human beings, whereas in *Loitering* Soseki writes his human confession as an artist. For this reason the ultimate value of nearly all literary confessions is biographical. The case with Soseki's *Loitering* is basically different, for it must be approached as a work of art. Its primary value, to us, is an artistic one. Their difference, then, is that of history and poetry. The problem Soseki copes with in this novel is how to experiment on the relationship between history and art, or how to reconcile the dichotomy between fact and fiction.

To examine in this light, even roughly, the relationship between fact and fiction in *Loitering* would seem not only interesting but essential for a correct understanding of the novel. In order to register whatever truth there was in his life, Soseki the artist does exercise his freedom over the material at hand, even if that be his own life. The names of all the characters in the novel—including the protagonist Kenzo (by the way his family name is not given) are without exception fictitious. This, Soseki seems to be doing in an effort to distance himself from his material rather than in deference to those involved. The same consciousness is apparent in his use of the third-person narrative, though the first-person method should be more appealing to those readers who prefer history to art. The entire novel is encased in a symbolic frame. The very opening is overshadowed by a ghost out of the past which in the course of the novel turns out to be a menacing intruder—the past that seems to stretch back into the dark wherein lies Kenzo's origin. The closing scene, on the other hand, foreshadows the uncertainty of the future with which the present is but a temporary truce. The entire novel, as its title suggests, is hovering between the past and the future. Within this over-all symbolic pattern Soseki creates a pattern of character relationship —in two ways: outwardly, Kenzo and Osumi as husband and wife face Shimada and his former wife, Otsune, intruders from the past; behind Kenzo stands his brother, his half-sister, and her husband; and behind Osumi stands her father. Inwardly, however, Kenzo stands alone, facing two formidable forces, Shimada and Osumi. Shimada represents the force of the past, while Osumi, that of the present; one force is temporal; the other is spatial. Kenzo stands at the point of intersection of time and space.

But Soseki's artistic license is most pronounced in his technique of condensation. It is not really accurate to say that *Loitering* covers the 1903–5 period of Soseki's life, for the period only serves as Soseki's point of contact between past and future. It was actually in 1909, when Soseki was getting ready for *And Then* that Shiobara (his foster father) sent a man to request a sum of money and, after nine months' complications, agreed to the final terms. In *Loitering* Soseki moves the event back to the period 1903–5 with a view to providing the novel with a necessary plot, and then effects a greater artistic result by condensing the period from 1903 to 1909 into one year, still with the central focus on Kenzo, facing the two forces, Shimada and Osumi. This technique of condensation is further supplemented by another, the flashback, which helps re-create Kenzo's past in order to retrace his origin. "Is Shimada still living where he used to?"—to this natural question his sister is unable to give any more satisfactory answer than he himself. But this casual question creates a shift in his time perspective. "Along one side of the street ran a wide, deep canal for a hundred and twenty yards. The stagnant water was very unpleasant with smelly mud. And patches of bluish color fermented, now offending his nose." The ditch described here is the symbol of Kenzo's past. To his surprise the past constantly invades the present. Soseki's use of this flashback technique is far from mechanical; it is in accord with the law of association, which makes the present a point of confluence. Here again Soseki proves to be a master of the economics of fiction; and also a master of human psychology who knows the truth that so often in life, chronological time must give way to psychological time.

From these factors it would be more correct to conclude that *Loitering* covers the whole of Kenzo's thirty-six-year past, and Soseki's past up to this particular point. If Kenzo, like Dante, finds the meridian to be the darkest moment of life, the symbolism here also has the weight of fact. When Soseki returned from England, he felt the need for rebirth without knowing how to realize it. It was the most critical point of his life. Soseki describes Kenzo reliving his life: "All the while walking through an obscure street with little human traffic, he thought of nothing but himself. 'For what purpose in the world were you born?' asked a voice from somewhere in his brain. He did not dare answer it; he tried to avoid it. Soon the voice started hounding him, repeating the same question. He said at last, 'I do not know.' The voice immediately gave a derisive laugh. 'Not that you do not know. Even if you do know, you simply cannot go back. You are trapped on the way, are you not?' 'It's nothing I did, nothing I did.' Kenzo hurried on and on as though he were fleeing." Here Kenzo is indeed a straggler frightened into constant flight, unable to face the darkness which is really the shadow of his past. What he is is the result of what he has been. The past must be reckoned with before he can go on as a new man. Shimada is the symbol of the past that pulls Kenzo back; likewise Osumi is a symbol of the present that collaborates with the past, putting shackles around the fleeing Kenzo. There is only one way he can deal with the situation. Turning back, he must now face the past. Earlier in the novel, Kenzo states in a talk with one of his visitors: "We men normally live on the future only, but at a certain critical moment that future is blocked. So, realizing we're finished, we turn our eyes back to the past. Then and there the whole past returns to our mind. That is the theory." In the story Kenzo refers to Bergson's as an interesting theory, not relating it to his own life. But Soseki, as Kenzo's creator-analyst, sees that the entire novel hinges on this, since Kenzo is the person to whom the future is blocked, who is forced to glance back at his own past, and whose past is invading his future. And there we notice the merging of Soseki's technique and theme.

Kenzo is Soseki facing the most critical moment of his life, and from the vantage point of time Soseki views this Kenzo without illusion. If the past, to Kenzo, consists of "one-third nostalgia and two-thirds pain," it is only the first third that Kenzo wishes to remember, while burying the rest. But Soseki denies Kenzo even that and forces him to face the remaining two-thirds of his past which is only pain. At first, Kenzo receives Shimada as a man of the past lit by an already outmoded lamp; he feels more or less the same way about his own brother. He half-pities and half-despises his ignorant wife and sister. He believes in his intelligent and logical mind; he has his share of pride and vanity as an educated man; he thinks he has done with his "prison life," the prison of the past as well as the present. Yet he is still driven as a slave of time. Soseki relentlessly pursues Kenzo to the dead-end of the present, and strips him of his personal trappings, one after another, until he, in his nakedness, admits that he is no better than any of those whom he secretly despises. Now he is forced to accept all that is left for him, his own past. This apparent acceptance is suggested in Kenzo's words: "In this world you just can't settle anything—hardly anything. Things, once started, go on forever, changing only their shapes and becoming unrecognizable. That's all." [5]

Kenzo is not merely the other half of the Soseki who wrote *I Am a Cat*, although he has often been identified as Soseki without his feline mask. He is the matrix out of which all of Soseki's works grew, since Kenzo's acceptance of his past symbolizes Soseki's rebirth, or birth, as an artist. All his works from *I Am a Cat* to *Kokoro* are really what has evolved out of Kenzo's world. Kenzo's relationship with Shimada was carried forward by Hirota, Daisuke, Sosuke, Sunaga, and the *sensei*, all of those Soseki characters who dramatize Soseki's increasing concern with the weight of the past. Kenzo's relationship with Osumi, on the other hand, continued evolving from the basic pattern in Kushami and his wife, through Shirai and his wife, Sunaga and Chiyoko, and Ichiro and Onao. *Loitering* thus covers Soseki's long cycle of novels. And Soseki writes about Kenzo with the eye of the *sensei* revealing his dark past in *Kokoro*. In that novel the *sensei* writes to the narrator: "Not for you only, but also for myself, I have thus far tried to disentangle an enigma called me." In *Loitering*, Soseki characterizes Kenzo's problem (actually his own): "But how have I become what I am?"

The moment Kenzo asks, facing a sphinx called self, "How have I become what I am?" Soseki the man is reborn as Soseki the artist—destined to pursue this most human question. All his works from *I Am a Cat* to *Kokoro* are but the result of his attempt to solve the mystery of self in his chosen medium of art. Almost all the Soseki heroes are indeed a race descended from Kenzo; they are invariably cursed with their progenitor's obsession with self. When Soseki pursued this cursed race as far as his art would permit, it became clear that they could free themselves from their hereditary curse in three ways: through suicide, madness, and faith, as Ichiro, its most articulate member, declares. The *sensei* of *Kokoro* chooses suicide; Ichiro nears madness as he gropes for faith. To go beyond is in fact to go beyond art. After his decade's pursuit as an artist, Soseki had to face the very limitations of his own art. At this crisis as an artist Soseki found it imperative to return to his point of departure, to re-examine the foundation of his art, and to diagnose the human originator called Kenzo, whom Soseki the artist had once taken for granted. *Loitering* was born out of this act, the only act by which Soseki the artist could free himself from the cursed obsession bequeathed by Soseki the man a decade before. This rite of self-purification makes *Loitering* a confession which promises another new vista. And *Light and Darkness*, which followed, proves that Soseki came through his self-imposed ordeal successfully.

III   Light and Darkness

In "Here Again the New Year," which appeared in the *Asahi* for January 1, 1916, Soseki wrote: "Since life is not something you can control, it is of course unpredictable. Sickly as I am, I am still ten years younger than Chao Chou when he set out in search of truth; even if I may not be able to reach the age of 120 as he did, I feel I can accomplish something if I strive as long as my strength permits. So I am resolved to strive à la Chao Chou as long as my allotted time allows. To emulate the man nicknamed an old Buddha [Chao Chou] and live as long as he did, may not be my lot, but while accepting my sickly nature as it is, I shall be grateful in every way for time that unfolds itself before me, and strive to work with whatever I was born with. This much, I declare in this first piece of my 'New Year's Thoughts.'" Although at the same time he wrote elsewhere jokingly, "Well, I may die . . . ," Soseki probably would not have believed that he had less than a year to live, and that even this would be a year of physical suffering. His "New Year's Thoughts" had to be halted on account of his rheumatism. But in April it was found out that the pain was really caused by diabetes, and his treatment continued for the following three months. In the meantime he had to think about his next novel. "It seems I was born to be sick," he wrote in early May. Soon he had to stay in bed because of his stomach trouble. In the midst of all this Soseki started writing his novel, *Light and Darkness*.

As was his wont, Soseki spent morning hours on the novel, at the average pace of one installment per day. The rest of the time he took up his old interests, calligraphy and painting, and tried his hand at Chinese poetry, as he said, in order to get rid of the taste of worldliness that came from his creative work. In August he thought the novel would be completed sometime in October, but as he went on, it became clear that he was wrong, for there was no end in sight. On November 16, there was a gathering at his home, which was to be the last of the Thursday circle. Within a week he had an attack of ulcers, and gradually took a turn for the worse. November 28, he had a serious hemorrhage, and on December 2 another, taking a turn now for the worst. Absolute rest was ordered and no visitors allowed. On the eighth it became known that his condition was hopeless, and on the following day he died. At the time of his death there was on his desk a blank sheet of paper marked No. 189 of *Light and Darkness.*

Light and Darkness is thus Soseki's last and unfinished novel. It is also a work which turned out to be longer than Soseki had expected; even in its unfinished state it is the longest of all of Soseki's novels. How much longer it might have been, Soseki himself possibly could not have told. Nor can we tell how it would eventually have developed. Yet two things are evident. First, Soseki was unusually ambitious about this novel, indeed so much so that he begged of impatient readers to reserve their judgment until its completion; second, the novel was nearing its climactic moment at the time of his death. In spite of this, or probably because of this, more has been written about this unfinished work than about any of his previous works. Opinions are as many and as different as there are critics, as is usual with such an unfinished work. For example, Viglielmo said in his study of the later Soseki that the novel indicates too clearly that the author has nothing new to say.[6] But his is a minority opinion. The majority opinion is that the novel, despite its incompleteness, is definitely one of Soseki's best works; and some even go further, stating that, if completed, it would have marked the highest peak of accomplishment, not only among Soseki's works, but also in the whole range of modern Japanese literature.[7]

The plot of *Light and Darkness,* stripped of its impressive extension and psychological depths, is deceptively simple; it evolves around ten days in the life of a young couple, Tsuda and Onobu,

who have been married only six months. The novel opens with a
casual but highly unsettling talk between Tsuda (thirty years old)
and his physician about his hemorrhoids. "It's no use," declares
the physician after an examination, "just cleaning up the hole as
we've been doing. No chance for fresh flesh to come out, you
know. This time we've got to change the treatment, and do a radical operation. There seems no other way." To Tsuda's relief, the
doctor assures him of a good chance of recovery since his hemorrhoids, luckily, are not tubercular. This scene sets the tone for the
entire novel in that Tsuda must go through a radical operation,
both physical and spiritual. His recovery must be in both areas.

Tsuda and Onobu, outwardly, are an exceptionally well-suited
and loving couple, but in the course of their brief marriage they
have already experienced an increasing tension because of their
incorrigible vanity and unyielding ego. Onobu is passionately determined to love her husband and make him love her in return,
but Tsuda fails to respond. Impatiently she asks herself: "Is every
husband a sponge which exists only to soak up his wife's love?"
She wants to possess him, to monopolize his love as though she
were the only woman in the world. She vainly tries everything to
this end, using every means she is capable of, whether it be ac-
cusation or supplication. While consciously and unconsciously
parading as a happy couple, neither is willing to admit this existing tension to outsiders, let alone to themselves. But unlike Tsuda,
Onobu goes out of her way and takes every opportunity to convince them what an ideal couple they are.

Theirs is a strange balance which exists between inner tension
and outward harmony. But this balance is upset with Tsuda's hos-
pitalization, which coincides with an ultimatum from his father in
Kyoto, notifying them of the suspension of their monthly allowance. Their shock is material as well as moral. Soon they find themselves exposed separately and together to the assault of three
outsiders: Tsuda's sister Ohide, his friend Kobayashi, and his patroness Mrs. Yoshikawa. Ohide has always been critical of Onobu's
vanity and holds her responsible for his alienation from the
family. Evidently unconscious that her attachment to Tsuda
and jealousy of Onobu were partly caused by her own frustration
with her philandering husband, she deems it her sisterly duty to
rescue Tsuda from Onobu's snare, as if she herself were the para-
gon of family virtue. When her financial offer is forestalled by

Onobu, she accuses her brother and sister-in-law of being selfish, to the extent that they have lost the capacity for accepting others' kindnesses with grace. Kobayashi's attack is formidable because he is completely ruthless in exposing their self-complacency. Crushed by the weight of life, he becomes an embittered prophet whose words can be at once biting and insulting. To Tsuda he declares: "All right, wait and see which is going to win. Instead of helping you see it, I'd better let reality itself punish you. That would be more immediate and effective, I tell you." To Onobu he proves to be unbearable: "Well, madam. If that is your feeling, watch out you don't become the town laughing stock." His is a voice rising from lower depths which neither Tsuda nor Onobu care to face. And Mrs. Yoshikawa is a meddlesome and often dictatorial guardian. Although critical of Onobu's artfulness and cleverness, she certainly does not like the lukewarmness of her young protégé Tsuda. As one who once tried to bring Tsuda and his former lover together, she claims her right to his life, and in effect commands that he go see Kiyoko to set the whole score straight, while she promises to re-educate Onobu as a good wife.

All this happens while Tsuda is resting in bed following what his physician called a radical operation. Just as the physician is making his diagnosis, so these three characters are attacking the case, diagnosing the patient's moral hemorrhoids from their own angles: Ohide from the front on the level ground; Kobayashi from the lower depths; and Mrs. Yoshikawa from above. They are, like their patient, human beings full of their own ego. Their diagnoses are half-correct and half-wrong—like many human judgments. But they agree on one thing: that the patient is suffering from a moral disease called egotism; on the basis of this diagnosis Tsuda is sent to another physician, the spiritual physician who alone can treat his moral condition.

So under the excuse of convalescence Tsuda journeys alone to a hot spring where he is sure to meet Kiyoko, who is recovering from a miscarriage. And from Kiyoko, who once depended entirely on him and yet suddenly turned her back on him, Tsuda must find the answer to a question that has kept recurring to him over the years: "Why did she, such a slow moving person, take to sudden flight? Why in the world did she make such an about face?" At their first chance meeting both step back in surprise. But at their second meeting Kiyoko regains her usual composure and her innocent smile, which easily disarms Tsuda. With her first name slipping out, Tsuda asks: "How long are you going to stay here?" "No plan at all. If a telegram comes from home, I must go back even today, you see." "Do you expect such a thing?" he asks, surprised. "That, I can't possibly tell" is Kiyoko's simple reply. Trying to make out the meaning of her smile, Tsuda returns to his room. With this, *Light and Darkness* comes to a sudden end.

Of this novel, one critic writes that "it is a work born out of Soseki's contact with Dostoevsky and one of the greatest novels in Japanese literature that have a Dostoevskian outlook." [8] True, since his Shuzenji crisis Soseki had shown increasing interest in and felt an affinity with the Russian writer. (In a fragment of 1916 Soseki noted: "I am surprised to come across the same ideas as mine in Russian novels [probably Dostoevsky's].") Also true, in *Light and Darkness* itself, Kobayashi refers to the same point: "Whoever has read Russian novels, especially those by Dostoevsky, should certainly know that profoundly intense and genuinely pure feelings often gush like a fountain from the most depraved and uneducated person. Do you think it is a lie?" Indeed, there seems to be a sense of kinship between the two minds. In *Light and Darkness* Soseki for the first time creates a cosmos of his own, just as Dostoevsky does, notably in his last work, *The Brothers Karamazov*. Or more properly stated, *Light and Darkness* has its own world, its own community. This is something new, compared with the works prior to *Loitering*. In them it is ultimately a certain thematic obsession that gives an enormous impetus to their movement, and also moves their characters forward in logical deployment. Instead, *Light and Darkness* evolves around a world of characters, even though each of its inhabitants is a victim of his own obsession. (More or less the same thing could be said of *The Brothers Karamazov* and the works that preceded it.)

The center of Soseki's fictional cosmos is the domestic world of Tsuda and Onobu, and around this center rotate the three different worlds of Ohide, Kobayashi, and Mrs. Yoshikawa following their own orbits. Beyond their outer limits there is still another world shared by two families, that of Fujii, Tsuda's uncle and that of Okamoto, Onobu's, whose contrast may remind us of Matsumoto and Taguchi in *Until After*. These two families remain immobile, unlike the three active characters, setting this society's polar norms. And these multicircles provide the novel with an extensive façade suitable for a social organism, propping Soseki's cosmos. Over his own cosmos Soseki casts a creator's vision, all-seeing, all-knowing but completely detached like an impersonal god over a human cosmos. But how different Soseki, how different his cosmos, from Dostoevsky and from his cosmos! Soseki is as passionless as Dostoevsky is passionate; and Soseki's cosmos seems as comic as Dostoevsky's is tragic.

Much as he admired Dostoevsky, Soseki was critical of his great Western *confrère* on one vital point when he said: "It would be proper to seek those truths which touch life—not at outwardly critical moments but in the midst of common humdrum everyday life." This remark sufficiently sharpens one important difference between the two artists, or rather Soseki's artistic vision in contrast with that of Dostoevsky. Soseki's cosmos in *Light and Darkness* is altogether devoid of any of the physical violence so peculiar to Dostoevsky's. Whatever violence there is in *Light and Darkness* has no physical quality; it is singularly transparent and ostentatiously passionless. None of his characters (perhaps Kobayashi included) is capable of extremes of violence; they are all as timid and tamed as the readers are in their daily world. These characters are much closer to the average reader than even Soseki's previous heroes, let alone Dostoevsky's. For this reason we are tempted to label *Light and Darkness* a novel of manners. Viewed in this light, it would appear an Austean or Thackerayean panorama of upper-middle-class life in Japan.

But *Light and Darkness* is more than a novel of manners, though like its predecessors, it can serve as an excellent miniature of modern Japan; it is rather Meredithean or Jamesian than Austenan or Thackerayean; it is first of all a psychological novel which reveals an exceptional insight into the shades of commonplace daily life. In this novel Soseki is doing to his characters exactly what he did to Kenzo, his former self, in *Loitering*. Every character in *Light and Darkness* pushes everyone else around, unaware that what he believes to be a noble act is really his own ego-assertion. Everyone carries his own ego, which is an atom of his being, and suffers from the chain reaction it creates. *Light and Darkness* is in a sense Soseki's *Egoist*. Unlike Meredith, whom he much admired, however, Soseki does not believe that the so-called comic spirit can be the most efficacious and perhaps only antidote to the universal malady called the modern cult of ego. Soseki is concerned with a more permanent way of salvation than that. Through *Loitering* Soseki learned that self-diagnosis is the best way to start. Now in *Light and Darkness* he seeks to diagnose the Soseki characters, that race descended from Kenzo cursed with its inherited malady of egotism. If he does this brilliantly, it is only because he did just that to himself. All these characters in *Light and Darkness* are more or less sick at heart, as modern man is. Hence the paramount importance of mental therapy. And this provides a sense of direction for the novel.

In *Light and Darkness*, according to some critics, Soseki returns to *The Poppy* just as in *Loitering* he did to *I Am a Cat*. On this basis they suggest that the last period, 1915–16, really marked a decline in Soseki's creative power. That their verdict is an unwarranted impression was evident from our discussion of *Loitering*. Even the assertion that *Light and Darkness* is a continuation of *The Poppy* without its melodramatic moral scheme, fails to express the whole truth. Tsuda is like Ono in a certain way; Onobu like Fujio; and Mrs. Yoshikawa resembles Fujio's scheming mother, whom Kono holds responsible for the final disaster. Especially the marital tension between Tsuda and Onobu is what might have happened to Ono and Fujio in marriage. For that matter, it is what might have happened to Sanshiro and Mineko in a similar situation. Their relationship is more strongly suggested in that of Sunaga and Chiyoko, of Ichiro and Onao, and again that of Kenzo and Osumi. Soseki's own analogy of their relationship with that of two rival wrestlers meeting every day in a ring epitomizes the relationship of all Soseki heroes and heroines. This theory is clearly stated by Fujii, an "absent-minded critic of life" and at the same time "its very sharp observer." As Okamoto in turn paraphrases it to Onobu, Fuiji's theory is that the disharmony of *yin* and *yang* is as inevitable as their harmony; in other words, a man and a woman attract each other only because each has something different, and since this something different is not self, they can't get along; inevitably they stand apart from each other. Much the same view was expressed in *Until After* as Matsumoto commented on the impossible relationship between Sunaga and Chiyoko, and also in *Loitering* regarding that of Kenzo and Osumi. Then, it would seem more proper to say that in *Light and Darkness* Soseki returns to all his previous works, not just to *The Poppy*, and that his last novel is the furthest exploration of the basic marital pattern that has occurred in almost all of his works prior to it.

In his first trilogy Soseki dealt with the discovery of love; in the second he dealt with the anatomy of love itself; and in his last works, *Loitering* and *Light and Darkness* he undertook the anatomy of matrimony. In all of these works Soseki was concerned with the relationship of love and marriage on the basis of his anatomy of love, and throughout his examination pressed his anatomy of love and marriage to their limits, taking nothing for granted. The result seems darkly negative indeed, since it is tantamount to proving the impossibility of love together with matrimony, or the incompatibility of love and marriage. Love, which was once affirmed by Daisuke and Sosuke, crumbles in Sunaga's anatomy of love; marriage, which was also once affirmed by Sosuke, dwindles in Ichiro's anatomy of marriage. Love, which once triumphed over marriage, must pay its price. Sosuke and Oyone, and the *sensei* and his wife seem the only exceptions to this, but they realize the compatibility of love and marriage only outside of society. And most of Soseki's heroes are in one way or another capable of choosing the will of heaven over the laws of man, which implies their failure to reconcile them. As a moralist Soseki refuses to accept the impossibility of reconciling love and marriage, the very conclusion at which he has arrived through his quest. In *Loitering* Soseki again pursues the relationship of Kenzo and Osumi in the light of this question. What he achieves here, however, is not reconciliation but compromise. To Osumi, who momentarily describes their trouble as the result of their own unyielding ego, Kenzo replies philosophically: "If separated, man and woman may be friendly, but that will be an end. If together, they are rivals, but somehow they can manage. Well, that may be human life." Thus Kenzo accepts their situation as fact. But Soseki, as well as we, knows this is no solution to the problem; the problem keeps raising itself. In *Light and Darkness* Soseki renews his efforts to find some sort of solution to this problem, as it were, "not at outwardly critical moments but in the midst of common humdrum everyday life."

This suggests a new vista Soseki has reached since *Loitering*—a vista wide enough to encompass society which insists on the primacy of the laws of man, the way of the world. Love is surely private, but marriage is not; marriage is at once private and public. The moment love develops into marriage, the lovers are no longer private individuals; they become part of their community. Soseki heroes are essentially uncompromising rebels whom society refuses to accept, leaving them to the will of heaven they proclaim. In *Kojin,* Ichiro, in his talk with Jiro about his wife Onao, refers to Dante's episode of Paolo and Francesca, contrasting love with marriage, and nature (or heaven) with society. Ichiro's is an attempt to seek the foundation of his marriage in love; and in this attempt to reconcile love and marriage, nature (or heaven) and society, he fails hopelessly. Ichiro here represents Soseki's attitude toward this problem—at that particular stage. As his solution he then suggests three alternatives: suicide, insanity, and faith. But Kenzo, as he appears in *Loitering,* is incapable of leaping to the height of other Soseki heroes. He stands on a level much lower than many of his predecessors (or his fictitious descendants), an anticlimax in the genealogy of the Soseki heroes. And Tsuda is worse than Kenzo, standing at the lowest point in the whole scale. His stature is cut to the normal size of an average person, an average reader. This, in fact, brings them much closer to us. He is committed neither to marriage nor to love. Or he is incapable of committing himself to either of them, unlike Onobu, who still demands absolute love, and unlike Ohide, who is resigned to loveless marriage. As he leaves for a spa, Tsuda considers three ways he can choose from: "From the start he had three alternatives, only three. First was to remain indecisive, so that he may not lose his past freedom; second, to go ahead, even if that's to make him a fool; and third, to find a satisfactory solution without becoming a fool." And he takes the third as his. Compared with Ichiro's alternatives, Tsuda's do appear petty; especially this choice, which is actually a wishful compromise between the first two alternatives. But significantly enough, Soseki chooses to follow Tsuda's way, instead of dismissing it as petty, for it is also the way of the world. To seek a solution within the framework of the community, to lead an average man on to his way of salvation without resorting to the violence of rebellion, is what Soseki is trying to accomplish in his last novel. As long as a man remains earthbound, he must be part of his world, and on that basis try to transcend his own ego. All indications are that Soseki believes in this possibility, the only possibility left for common humanity.

In *Light and Darkness* Soseki stamps finality on all his past works.

If each of these works is a sonata or a concerto to develop his chosen theme singly but intensely to its finale, these themes, situations, and characters are brought together to form a larger musical composition. *Light and Darkness* is a symphony, although unfinished, whose structure is far more complex than that of a sonata or a concerto. The composer-conductor Soseki does not tolerate any single member, no matter how important, to play solo. In this novel Soseki, as he once wished, rewrites all of his works. As regards his attitude as creator, Soseki is said to have stated at one of his last Thursday meetings: "Lately I have entered a certain state which I would call *sokuten kyoshi*, although others might label it differently. It is something like this: to forsake the small self which I usually regard as myself, and to leave it to the dictates of a larger and universal self, so to speak. But I cannot describe it fully in words. And in this state all assertions, all ideals, and all isms, however grandiose, begin to look trivial, whereas those things which ordinarily seem insignificant, find place for their own existence. From this angle one can view with impartiality, discriminating nothing. *Light and Darkness* I am writing in this attitude. I'd like to lecture on another fresh, genuine theory of literature—in this very same attitude—at the University." [9]

This is not the same Soseki who openly confessed his desire to kill Fujio, the heroine of *The Poppy*, who might be poetic but lacked moral sentiment. Compared with this, Soseki's view of Onubu, who is said to best resemble Fujio of all Soseki heroines, throws some light on the problem of Soseki's "impartiality." In reply to a reader who criticized his shift of emphasis from Tsuda in the hospital to Onobu at home, Soseki wrote a long letter in which he patiently detailed his reason, together with his view of Onobu, and his over-all intentions:

Of course, I knew I could concoct a novel by providing the heroine [Onobu] with some fantastic character or appalling defects, in the way you anticipated. But I avoided it purposely, for I'm not interested in writing that sort of novel. . . . Since we are not yet at the end of the novel, I cannot say much. In *Light and Darkness* (so far as you have read) I think I have proved that with all her appearances she is quite free of such dubious, such fantastic fabricated defects. . . . While you anticipate that behind such [an artful] woman there must be some enormous scheme, I should point out that this is not necessarily true; and that various, more delicate shades can also create the same result. I would not say that what you say is untrue, but that sort of truth has already been exhausted by many novelists. Let them write about it, however worn-out. But if the readers hastily decide that there must be a single truth, then these novels would certainly be misleading. I do not find your anticipation by any means unreasonable, since you have accepted novelists' usual methods as a single-line truth in life. What pains me is that you speak of my failure to make it possible for you to realize for the first time that there is also truth in other than one place, and that thanks to Soseki, you have experienced another, brand new truth.

Soseki's expressed intent here to let his characters live as they are, follow the way of their own nature, without intruding into their human world and simplifying the subtle complexity of their behavior, is that of an artist who can also view his own creations impartially. This difference of attitude toward Fujio and Onobu indicates the basic difference between *The Poppy* and *Light and Darkness*. It also suggests the maturity of Soseki the man and Soseki the artist; for all great works are always impersonal, although impersonality itself does not necessarily create a great work. This observation, made shortly before his death, also affirms his determination to remain always an artist capable of viewing his creation with an impartial eye.

As a creator of this microcosm Soseki tries to see that every member plays his part as best he can. In this he succeeds to a great extent. While probing into the mind of Tsuda, petty, indecisive, materialistic, clever, and the most unheroic egoist of all Soseki heroes, Soseki applies an equally searching analysis to that of Onobu, who resorts to every conceivable device to monopolize Tsuda's love. Of all Soseki heroines (except for Chiyoko in *Until After*), Onobu is the only female character who is allowed a status equal to that of a Soseki hero. Although this may be naturally expected of her as Tsuda's full-fledged rival and partner, the point is noteworthy since in previous works Soseki describes his heroines invariably over their male counterparts' shoulders or through their eyes. Apparently more confident about the workings of the female mind, Soseki discards this habitual oblique method, approaching directly from all sides. As a result, Onobu emerges as a round character, a character drawn in fullness, not in profile. The same may be said of other female characters, such as Ohide, Mrs. Yoshikawa. This is what made Masamune Hakucho, one of Soseki's critics, state that in *Light and Darkness* Soseki at last comes to understand women.[10]

Light and Darkness is a world of egoists in constant clash; it is a large battleground of egos. Wherever there are egos, there is tension that makes itself felt most effectively through dialogue. All the characters maintain their precarious balance in this tension which allows neither peace nor truce. The marital battle between Onobu and Tsuda is not the only one. There is another between Onobu and Ohide, and between Onobu and Mrs. Yoshikawa, of course, on different relational bases. One is the tension between a wife and her sister-in-law; the other, the tension between a young woman and a middle-aged matron. Battle is mostly in the form of verbal fencing in which all seem to be partial victors and partial losers with the tide in constant shift. Because even in battle they must follow accepted social decorum, their tension, thus deprived of its necessary outlet, creeps under the surface. While the women face each other at a modest distance, the battle between Tsuda and Kobayashi knows no such courtesy; but with Tsuda ever recoiling within himself, which is his instinctive means of self-protection, theirs often tends to be a one-man battle; Kobayashi wins in insult, but loses in tears. There are still more battles, one between Onobu and Kobayashi, and another between Tsuda and Kiyoko. One ends in an uncompromising clash because neither is willing to yield, whereas the other is over even before it is fought. Their difference is due to the difference in personalities. All these characters become alive through action, in this particular instance, through dialogue. Soseki chooses dialogue in order to insure psychological analysis, even though it may certainly bore those readers who prefer external action.

In this novel Soseki creates three characters, all interesting and memorable. First is Mrs. Yoshikawa, who channels her excessive energy toward her young protégé; she is a meddlesome, dictatorial, and yet well-meaning autocrat. Although she may remind us of Fujio's mother, a woman of pride and schemes, she is altogether different. She, too, is an egoist as all autocrats are, but unusually shrewd as an observer of human nature, and frankly indulgent as a self-styled protectress. She is more like a great mother-figure in mythology, and somewhat resembles Eliot's garrulous Julia in *The Cocktail Party*. Next is Kobayashi, who is really not as novel a Soseki character as many critics believe.[11] He is what Hiraoka in *And Then,* and again Yasui in *The Gate* could have developed into eventually. As it is, however, he is fuller than these predecessors, having become a genuine social underdog. His sardonic nihilism, his unpredictable plunge from pathos into bathos, from insolence into sentimentality, and above all his negative way of self-expression—bring him closer to those injured characters in Gogol's or Dostoevsky's novels who hate their self-invited loneliness and assert their existence mainly by making themselves nauseous to others. With all this, it would seem too farfetched to assert on the basis of Kobayashi that the novel, when completed, might have been an authentic social novel. And last is Kiyoko, whose slow demeanor, childlike simplicity, and unguarded naturalness take Tsuda by surprise and yet somehow make him feel at home with himself. She has been designated as Soseki's dream woman or his image of the Eternal Feminine, as suggested in his English poem of 1903: "I looked at her as she looked at me:/We looked and stood a moment,/Between Life and Dream." Whatever she is to Soseki, Kiyoko is in every way the opposite of Onobu. Why did she suddenly run away? It is a question for Tsuda, as well as for us. As it is, she seems the only exception in the entire novel in which everyone is suffering from his own egoism. Why does Soseki allow such an exception? Or would she have been another sufferer had the novel been completed? There is no way of forming any definite idea about her. One thing is certain, however, that she seems to hold the key to the problem Tsuda is confronted with. She is almost a symbol, the most symbolic of all the characters in the novel, and indeed of all Soseki characters.

Light and Darkness as a whole is a symbolic configuration of Soseki's themes, characters, and situations, old and new. If *Loitering* atomizes all of these in its symbolic frame, *Light and Darkness* synthesizes them into Soseki's symbolic cosmos. This symbolist art is what separates his last two novels from his two trilogies, from their predecessors, and again what separates *Light and Darkness* from *Loitering* itself. In *Light and Darkness* he creates a cosmos which itself is a symbol. The symbolic nature of its opening scene has already been touched upon. As Tsuda leaves his doctor's office, pondering his diagnosis, he suddenly realizes: "It is the same with the mental—yes, entirely the same thing with the mental world. No one can tell when and how a change may come over it. And that moment of turning I witnessed by myself."

Then, Tsuda goes through a radical operation. While his body is under medical treatment, his soul is also being diagnosed by three or four volunteer physicians, or more correctly fellow patients: Ohide, Kobayashi, and Mrs. Yoshikawa, and even Onobu. Being themselves patients, they differ as to the cause of Tsuda's malady. Ohide and Mrs. Yoshikawa hold Onobu responsible for his present condition; Onobu feels a certain person in his past (namely Kiyoko, whom she desperately tries to identify) is the ultimate cause; Kobayashi, on the other hand, generalizes his despicable friend's case in more social terms. With all these individual differences, they are agreed on one point, that Tsuda's case needs treatment. So he journeys to a spa for convalescence, physical and mental. It is, then, to no mere spa, but really to a sanatorium that Tsuda is sent off, much against his will. He must go alone, because spiritual therapy is an individual matter, beyond those diagnosticians.

The last section (chapters 167–188) is most symbolic of all the scenes in the novel. Tsuda's journey has manifold meaning; it is a journey from home, from Tokyo, and from the metropolis of the human world; it is indeed a journey from civilization into the heart of nature. As the night carriage moves into the depths of the mountains with roaring torrents, Tsuda feels he has regained part of his long lost memory. "Ah, there is such a thing in this world! I wonder why I have forgotten it all." The carriage itself piercing the darkness of the night, seemed to him to be his own pursuit of her lost image. The lean horse galloping under the driver's continuous whipping becomes more like his own mind, and himself. But who is whipping this wretched animal? Mrs. Yoshikawa? No, he could not be so certain about it. Then himself after all? As a distant light comes in sight he realizes: "A light of fate. There is no other way but to ride to it as my destination."

Tsuda's journey is a journey into the past he has lost contact with; it is also a journey into the wasteland within himself; and last of all, it is a journey into a land of dreams only half-remembered. On the very first night he loses his way in a mazelike corridor whose exit he remembers yet cannot retrace. Just then, completely unprepared, he is surprised by his ghostly image in the misty mirror, and by Kiyoko, who turns her back on him before he finds anything to say. To take a dip in the hot water, for which many patients come, Tsuda takes off his clothes, one after an-

other, because he must be naked.[12] Significantly he discards the
padded robe Onobu made expressly for his journey, her own talis-
man. The whole journey from beginning to end represents
Tsuda's process of baptism, necessary for the renewal of his being,
the rebirth of his soul. And the *genus loci* of Tsuda's destination is
Kiyoko, the ray from whose eyes seems to restore his lost memory.
The moment the whole ritual almost reaches its climax *Light and
Darkness* comes to an abrupt end.

Stepping off the train Tsuda wonders—between the scattered
night lights and the vast shadows of darkness looming beyond:

> I am not going to pursue this dream-like stuff. Even before my de-
> parture from Tokyo, or more strictly, before Mrs. Yoshikawa urged
> this journey, no, further back, even before I married Onobu—even
> that's not quite adequate—indeed since the moment Kiyoko suddenly
> turned her back on me, I have been haunted by this dream-like stuff.
> And now I am in the midst of chasing after that dream. This streak
> of dream carried on from the past as I glance back—will this dream
> vanish when I arrive at the destination? That was Mrs. Yoshikawa's
> opinion; and that must be mine since I agreed with her opinion and
> accepted it as my own. But is this going to happen in fact? Will my
> dream be erased, after all? With that conviction, am I now here in
> this dream-like dreary hamlet? All those things that come in my sight
> —low-eaved houses, a freshly pebbled narrow road, faint shadows of
> electric lights, sloping straw-thatched roofs, a single-horse carriage
> with a yellow hood,—a mass of these things, somewhat new, somewhat
> old—indefinable, all dreamily wrapped in this chill night cold and
> darkness. The impression that these misty facts create—is this sym-
> bolic of the fate I've carried over here? The past is a dream, the pres-
> ent a dream, and the future also, a dream—and that is what I carry
> back to Tokyo. That may be the outcome of the whole venture. That
> seems likely. If so, for what purpose have I come, leaving Tokyo be-
> hind in the rain?

This is a crucial moment not only for Tsuda and Soseki, but also
for the reader—now that we are dealing with an unfinished novel.
What is hidden in the unwritten part of *Light and Darkness*? This
is no idle query; it is the key to the meaning of Soseki's last work,
as well as to the vision of Soseki the artist and Soseki the man.
Many critics and readers of *Light and Darkness* for study or
for pleasure have attempted to complete it after their own fashion.

There are two sharply divided conclusions, both starting from the written portion of the novel, but ultimately based on their interpretations of it. Komiya, for instance, argues that the whole thing should turn out for the better, for Tsuda and also for Onobu. Onobu, as he says, is the kind of woman who prefers to die rather than live as the laughing stock of others and anticipates the day when she, for the sake of her husband, will certainly muster all her courage. Suppose she learns from Mrs. Yoshikawa about the past relationship between Tsuda and Kiyoko, and further, that they are staying at the same resort hotel; how would she react? That can be imagined, says Komiya though he refuses to say how. As for Tsuda, who, as Kobayashi warns, must be punished by reality, his spiritual malady can be cured since, as his physician discloses, it is not tubercular.[13] Objecting to this suggestion, Eto argues that in *Light and Darkness* Kiyoko is far from an angelic figure holding the key to Tsuda's salvation, and her appearance is probably Soseki's artistic device to complete his theme of disillusionment—similar to that of Austen's *Emma*. It is, Eto continues, not salvation but shock that awaits Tsuda. He is going to die because of the recurrence of his hemorrhoids; what he experiences is, then, not a reconciliation but a struggle, while victory goes to Kiyoko—in a certain sense to Onobu, too. This denouement alone, Eto concludes, saves the novel from the possibility of catastrophe. And he believes that this suggested solution should honor Soseki.[14]

All considered, Soseki does not intend to create another Daisuke out of Tsuda, who chooses the will of heaven over the laws of man. Tsuda's rebirth, whether it is going to be partial or whole, is certainly suggested in the opening scene; nor does Soseki seem to intend to turn Onobu into another Fujio, who collapses at the moment of revelation. Tsuda and Onobu, furthermore, must be treated not as separate individuals but primarily as husband and wife. As Mrs. Yoshikawa suggests, Soseki is here concerned with the education of husband and wife as a social unit—without pushing them together or separately to the ultimate of violence. After all, they are ordinary husband and wife who have lost their rapport. And this spiritual rapport, Soseki seeks to provide for them. They are citizens of the human community, a zone of moral twilight, between good and evil, and heaven and hell. It is in this world of man and wife, not lovers, that they must seek their way together, where tragedy meets comedy, comedy tragedy. Is this not what the title really suggests? Soseki once had the hero of "The Grass Pillow" say of his life: "After twenty years' living in this world, I found it worth living; and now after twenty-five years I have come to realize that light and darkness are like outside and inside; and that wherever light is, there is darkness." *Light and Darkness* seems to be Soseki's reaffirmation of this truth. Surely, nothing so drastic and so dramatic may come out of the unwritten part of the novel. The word salvation sounds too grandiose to be applied to those earthbound creatures clinging to their own small egos. After all, salvation is the end of life. What matters is man's progress toward salvation, because that is what we call life, and what man makes of his life, gaining bit by bit spiritual insight into the darkness of ego within himself. Life must be the process of continual rebirth. That is what Tsuda and Onobu seem on the point of discovering probably for the first time in their lives. (In his casual chat with Kiyoko and a hotel maid, Tsuda remarks: "On the contrary, many people are still alive and yet born again.") That is also what the world called human community expects of every member. Everyone can go on the road of salvation if he has a mind to, for its entrance is the very life he lives on earth, not beyond. In his 1915 fragment Soseki, choosing Dostoevsky over Nietzsche, wrote in English: "It seems to us beyond doubt that it [Nietzsche's superman theory] will and does operate to deepen all contempt, to lessen every kind of sympathy for those less fortunate and to lead to the most useless frittering even of individual gifts. For the most highly gifted person needs more, not less, of the community sense, if he is to be the service he might be; and that is the reason for the superiority of Dostoevsky." *Light and Darkness*, though incomplete, may serve as proof that Soseki the artist and Soseki the man have at last come to meet in good faith.

CHAPTER 7

Conclusion: An Assessment

I Soseki's Individualism

THE golden decade of 1906 to 1916, in which Soseki the artist was born, was also the period throughout which Soseki the man desperately fought off both his periodic tension and his chronic ulcers. Especially after his Shuzenji crisis in 1910, Soseki had to live constantly under the shadow of death, so much so that he was, as it were, on joking terms with it: "If I drive my brains hard, there will be too much acid that is bound to corrode my stomach." When he said this he knew that he was sacrificing his life for the cause of art. His was the kind of art created in a deliberate choice of death over life, or in his continual defiance of death. When that eventually came at last in 1916, Soseki the man disappeared, bequeathing only his art to posterity. Just before he lapsed into a coma, Soseki is said to have bared his chest, begging a nurse to spray water on it; and when she did he blurted out "Mustn't die." Was it Soseki the man or Soseki the artist speaking these words? This question has been asked repeatedly. That is because these words came out of Soseki. Some explained them away as the voice of a dying man's instinct for life, whereas others argued that it was the voice of Soseki the artist, accepting it as a symbolic gesture of a great artist. Soseki, they suggested, said these words because he wanted to complete *Light and Darkness,* whose chapter marked 189 waited to be written, or because he wanted to see the future of modern Japanese literature in whose creation he participated with such zeal, or even the future of modern Japan with whose emergence he lived his life. Whichever was the truth, it is clear that while Soseki the man died in 1916, Soseki the artist has survived.

Yet Soseki the artist cannot be separated from Soseki the man. This is especially true with an artist like Soseki who must constantly return to life which is the matrix of his art. When he said that "literature is life and life, literature," he was probably defining his kind of art, the art born in the dialectical tension between Soseki the man and Soseki the artist. Because, after many years' groping, he chose literature as his vocation in its original sense. Soseki hated it as his profession, and fought against anything that might cause his vocation to degenerate into a mere profession. In pursuing his chosen vocation as the only means whereby to develop whatever gifts he was born with, and round out his existence, Soseki demanded absolute freedom. As he stated in "Official Exhibit and Art," an artist dedicated to his art is in an absolute state, beyond human obligations to family, country, society, and even moral norms. He rejected outer authorities and exercised his inner authority over his own destiny; he called this an individual revolution. Only in this light can we understand Soseki's personal motto: *jiko-hon-i*, or "on my own terms." Proofs that he did his utmost to practice what he preached are many: his decision to forsake his scholarly career to accept an *Asahi* offer; his rejection of the gold cup as the highest vote-getter in the popularity poll; his rejection of the government-created Doctor of Letters degree. But the best proof that he did succeed in this is the permanence of his art.

Soseki's is thus individualism in the most basic meaning of the word, the conviction that he was born with free will; therefore he has the right as well as the duty to exercise his free will for completion of his being; it cannot be confused with a Victorian brand of liberal individualism, in particular its Japanese version which has in the course of history suffered a series of defeats in struggle against formidable opposition: nationalism, socialism, collectivism, totalitarianism, and other creeds. Soseki's liberalism has little in common with the one in current fashion, either. In the midst of ideological confusion Soseki did not hesitate to declare, "Love of freedom is in my nature." Standing by such individualism, Soseki often critically viewed trends in Japan and the world at large.

In the last decades perhaps the most serious criticism of Soseki the man and Soseki the artist has been that he lacked social consciousness. Although this criticism has no basis, many Japanese naturalists and proletarian writers, and also the postwar generation have exaggerated this point, since Soseki, after some attempts, refused to create their kind of art. But what is strange is that even some Soseki students have more or less accepted it as a proven fact. For this, the impersonal quality of Soseki's art is partly responsible. Although Soseki placed the primary function of art far above the level of social criticism, he made free use of all sorts of topical allusions as long as their use was justified in the context of his writing. Besides those scattered all through his works, Soseki also posed as a critic of contemporary Japanese society and civilization. How Soseki the artist incorporated Soseki the man into his art is evident: *I Am a Cat*, itself, as we recall, is Soseki's thinly disguised criticism of the contemporary social, economic, and cultural scene. In *Sanshiro,* Hirota takes up this role as a critic of Japan basking in victory after the Russo-Japanese War, thus providing the novel with a necessary background. In *And Then* the conflict between feudal and modern Japan finds its thematic climax in Daisuke's free choice. This theme of conflict is variously considered by Soseki in his summer lectures of 1911; especially in "The Enlightenment of Modern Japan," which carries it further to the problem of Japan and the West. (Later, this lecture and others were collected in a volume entitled *Society and I*.) In *Kojin,* Soseki creates Ichiro as a figure symbolic of Meiji Japan caught in her modernization and Westernization. In *Kokoro* he once again treats Daisuke's problem in a negative way, in terms of the *sensei's* denial of life. And these, only a few examples, indicate the cultural significance of Soseki's art, one of the most frequently neglected areas of Soseki scholarship and criticism.

Commitment, one of modern man's most precious commodities, is in itself neither a virtue nor a vice. All depends on what one commits himself to. To Soseki there was only one thing worthy of his commitment. That was himself. And this commitment he regarded as his right and as his duty to his own being. Soseki is indeed one of the few exceptional cases in the intellectual history of modern Japan, an unfortunate record of Japanese intellectuals who have willingly and unwillingly contributed their share to the rise and fall of Japanese militarism. As a child of Meiji Japan, Soseki openly bemoaned the passing away of his world with the death of Emperor Meiji, and in *Kokoro* he wrote his own tribute through the *sensei* and the narrator's father. Yet he was no believer in the cult of the Mikado. There are revealing entries in his diary of 1912. While attending a *Noh* performance, Soseki was shocked by the contrast between the general audience and the Imperial family which was also present. One was as thoroughly discourteous as the other was respectful. "As the audience left there were streams of automobiles, rickshas and carriages. So those who showed no sense of courtesy must be upper class society of Japan. What a pity!" But at the same time Soseki noted that while the Empress and the Crown Prince were smoking, no such freedom was allowed the ordinary audience. "In this matter the Imperial family ought to show deference to us common subjects. If they consider their own smoking to be proper, the same freedom ought to be given to their subjects." What disturbed Soseki most of all, however, was that even in filling and lighting pipes they were assisted by their attendants, as if they were "dead" or "disabled." "They had better be advised to abolish such practice. Are those in the Ministry of the Imperial Household not aware of this? Or if they are, do they not dare protest? Really shocking!" And then he stated: "The Imperial family is no collection of gods. They ought to be accessible and friendly. By appealing to our sympathy they ought to cultivate our respect. This is the surest and most enduring policy. By such excessive and ill-conceived measures, of the officials of the government in general and the Ministry of the Imperial Household in particular, the Imperial family may gain in weight, but will surely alienate themselves from their subjects." In another entry of July 20, Soseki is indignant about the impending decision by government authorities to order, in deference to the Emperor's critical condition, suspension of all public performances of drama and other popular entertainments. "His Majesty's condition does certainly deserve the sympathy of the whole populace, but they ought to be allowed to carry on their business as long as it does not aggravate His Majesty's condition. The authorities have no right to interfere with people, although they are of course free to interrupt business if their sympathy dictates it. If, on the other hand, they do this in fear of the authorities or the accusing mob, their sympathy and courtesy toward the Imperial family are only perfunctory; they will inwardly nurse their dissatisfaction and grievance. This is tantamount to fomenting causes for dreadful consequences. . . ." History shows that Soseki's fear was warranted and that it came true in the form of the national catastrophe which the cult of the Mikado brought on his country.

If these entries are private thoughts that Soseki probably never dreamed of making public, "My Individualism" is then his most forthright pronouncement on the problem. In this speech delivered at the Peers' School in November 1914, two years before his death, Soseki first elaborates his brand of individualism by way of his own experiences, and defines it as *jiko-hon-i*. Then turning specifically to his own audience, which represents both power and wealth, Soseki states: "To sum up what I have so far been saying: first, if one aims at developing his own personality, he must also respect others'; second, if one wishes to exercise power, he must recognize the obligations that go with it; and third, if one wishes to display wealth, he must also accept the responsibility that accompanies it." Soseki designates strength of character as the basis of individualism. As he states, moral individualism, being based on the principle of justice, rejects partisanship, and consequently often finds itself alone. That is the price individualism must pay. It is no easy, lucrative business to take up, but it can provide grounds of certitude for those who wish to develop their personality.

Soseki is not unaware of the force of nationalism that steadily rose with Japan's victorious emergence out of the wars with China and Russia. Probably for this reason he dwells on the relationship between individualism and nationalism, the major forces whose open clash was already in view. Distinguishing his kind of individualism from another kind, moral laissez faire, he points out that the latter, not the former, really does harm to a nation. "Indeed," he declares, "we are at once nationalist, cosmopolitan, and individualist." Yet individualism must be the starting point, for individual morality is higher than collective morality; it is the highest of all moralities.[1] In concluding the speech Soseki stresses that nationalism may make some sense at critical moments of national destruction or survival, but at a time of peace individualism must be the basis of our conduct.

Equally illuminating is Soseki's reaction to World War I, which, from the vantage point of history, we regard as one of the most significant events signaling the arrival of everything modern. Thousands of miles away from Europe, Soseki viewed the event with both an outsider's curiosity and a philosopher's detachment, jotting his thoughts down in his "New Year's Thoughts" of 1916: "Here Again New Year," "Militarism," and "Treitschke." While recognizing the war as an event on an unprecedentedly grand scale to be remembered in history, he nevertheless suspects it to be an event rootless and empty—as all wars have been in human history, especially when he wonders what sort of contribution this bloodshed will make to the future of humanity. But, lowering his view from such contemplation, Soseki cannot but ponder the future of militarism, now apparently triumphant over liberalism. Wars, without exception, are means, not ends; and therefore can never be the ends of humanity. Militarism as such occupies an inferior position on the scale of human values. It pains him to note the tragic impact Germany's expansionism has wrought on England and France which love freedom and peace. Then turning to Treitschke, a historian who provided an ideological basis for Prussian militarism, Soseki comes to a fundamental question: Did not Treitschke advocate militarism and nationalism, after all, for the purpose of unifying Germany? Was not that unification meant to prevent pressure from outside? Now that the unification was completed with the foundation of an empire, and Germany could exist without fear of invasion, should not his ideology have been discarded? If it is meant to be upheld for ever, there should, logically, be some value in the ideology itself, because that value alone can justify its existence. But what is that value? In other words, it may be that Treitschke determined to uphold his militarism and nationalism until Germany unified not merely Europe but the entire world. However, when humanity is conquered by Germany, what are we to expect from Germany in return? This question Germany and Treitschke must clarify.

II *Soseki and Modern Japanese Literature*

If Soseki the man is more a free individual than he is a Japanese, Soseki the artist, strangely enough, is more Japanese than Soseki the man. This statement, however paradoxical, does not contradict Soseki's own equally paradoxical statement: "Indeed, we are at once nationalist, cosmopolitan, and individualist." Man is a many-layered being. As an artist Soseki knew well that no art could be created in a vacuum; and that every artist is part of his tradition, whether he likes it or not. As a creative artist Soseki could not but give thought to the general state of arts and letters in Japan. As far as he could surmise, it was a wasteland where the traditionalists, blind in their shell of self-complacency, were repeating their old rituals now empty of spirit, while the modernists, paralyzed by the dazzling façade of Western civilization, were aping everything but their own selves, with no sense of identity.

Soseki was critical of both camps. In fiction he scoffed at some writers' attempted return to the tradition of Saikaku, Bakin, and even Lady Murasaki; at the same time he chided others' blind faith in the cause of literary naturalism, or more properly, in their version of it. In drama, especially in traditional drama, Soseki, though confessing his ignorance, pointed out the uncertainty of performing actors merely wandering between naturalness and artificiality, without deciding which to follow. It seemed to him indicative of the general state of native drama itself. On the other hand, on attending the performance of *Hamlet,* Soseki demanded that the translator decide whether he ought to be faithful to the original dramatist or to the audience. In painting he also believed that the old school excelled in skill but failed in intelligence, and particularly in expression of depth of character or dignity of spirit; whereas the new school, trained in Western tradition, was still unable to create its own art and merely produced the kind of painting that others did. In short, both the traditionalist and the modernist are guilty of one common error, namely, imitation, their only difference being that one imitates unconsciously; the other consciously.

Imitation is necessary at a certain stage; this Soseki accepts as part of human nature. In his lecture of 1913, "Imitation and Independence," he explains this problem by way of man's double nature: every man represents at once mankind and his own self. In the former capacity he loves imitation and is willing to follow the path of others. But in the latter, he insists on independence. Independence in this sense has nothing to do with eccentricities or idiosyncrasies. Genuine independence demands uncluttered freedom as well as solid background. From this it is clear that both imitation and independence are necessary for deliberate cultivation of one's tradition. Applied to contemporary Japan, this suggests that the spirit of independence is of special significance. Considering various indications, the outcome of the Russo-Japanese War included, Soseki wonders if the time is ripe for Japan to leap from the decades of imitation to a new period of challenge, the period of creative originality. That means the appearance of new talents and geniuses.

Born Japanese at this particular time in history, Soseki experienced all the bitterness of fate that invariably befalls one from a "backward" or "underdeveloped" country. All through his aca-

demic education he used English textbooks on all subjects, chose a
foreign literature as his special field, and on graduation, pursued
it as his means of livelihood. While abroad he felt the tragedy of
having been born in such a country at such a period. Even his
desperate groping for his own true identity in London had a significance both personal and general. In his own case, Soseki undoubtedly saw an individual example of what Japan as a whole
needed, what might be called national identity; it was all the
more acute because in Japan's efforts to catch up with the West
she went so far as to neglect, and worse still, possibly sacrifice, her
own cultural identity. The result was a tragic loss of confidence in
herself. Soseki's *jiko-hon-i* was an individual manifestation of
what his country was belatedly arriving at. Only in such historical
perspective can we fully understand the impact of the Russo-Japanese War: To Japan it was without doubt an issue of life and
death, political as well as cultural. Like all his fellow countrymen,
Soseki rejoiced at her victory over Russia, which was in their opinion part of the West. But Soseki was one of those few who could
see in this victory not the completion of Japanese efforts to
emerge as a modern state, but rather the beginning of another
more arduous period of genuine survival as a civilized nation,
genuine because without cultural identity her victory would
amount to little. This is what he stated in an interview with *Shin
Shosetsu* for August 1905, when Japan's victory over Russia
seemed to have become certain. In it Soseki declared that her victory was only military, because for this victory Japan had lost
another phase of the war; in other words, Japan had won the military war at the expense of her cultural identity. In order to rediscover, or to win, that other phase—peace—Japan had only one
way to take, to leap beyond the period of imitation toward that of
renaissance. In his opinion Japan must march forward, directed
by her regained sense of confidence, not turn back, as ultra-na-
tionalists suggest, toward her past, the tradition which had proved
its insufficiency at the moment when Japan was forced to open
her door. Japan, Soseki urged, should rather seek her foundation
in the present and continue to assimilate, not imitate, Western
civilization, and at the same time, if from this new angle she re-
examined herself, she would also rediscover her unique originality. Only by this approach, not by antiquarianism, would Japan be
able to enter another creative era, Soseki asserts at this point, as

England entered her glorious period of creativity following her victory over the Spanish Armada.

In charting the best possible way for his country at this critical moment Soseki virtually charted the way for himself. The subsequent decade, as we have witnessed from his career, was also Soseki's golden decade as the first professional novelist in modern Japanese literature. Equipped with Western literature, he launched into the unknown and, always guided by his own instincts, he produced a number of works, each time improving on what had preceded, learning his trade both fast and well. At the same time he guided young talents who began to gather around him, all eager to learn from their master. While taking charge of the *Asahi* literary columns, even though briefly during the period of 1909–11, Soseki introduced many obscure artists whose views he did not necessarily share, promoted new talents, and always sought to usher fresh air in the world of literature which so often tended to falter and stagnate. This he did not only in literature but also in other arts, including painting, sculpture, and music. In all these, by his own examples, he urged critics to encourage artists to discover their own strengths, instead of damaging them as they often did, so that their cooperation might eventually yield a new fruit hitherto unheard of in the whole range of Japanese literature.

A decade later, when his career neared its full circle, Soseki saw something close to what he had striven for. Around him he found an increasing number of artists, all of a new generation for whom he had done his share in the laying of the foundation. It was a heartwarming discovery for Soseki, who, in spite of all his admirers, had always been lonely. And in Akutagawa, Kume, and Kikuchi he saw the hope of the coming generation. Soseki's letters to the first two in particular bespeak his confidence in and high expectation of this rising generation. In a letter of August 12, 1916, addressed to Akutagawa and Kume, Soseki wrote: "Are you working hard? Are you writing something? You mean to be writers of a new generation. With this in mind, I am watching your future. I want you to be great. But don't get too impatient. I want you to go forward boldly like an ox; and that is what matters. I wish to breathe a more cheerful and refreshing air into our literary world, and help it get rid of the habit of prostrating itself before foreign literatures. I'm sure you both feel the same way about all this." In

another letter of August 24, again to the same writers, Soseki tried
to drive his point home: "I admire you for the great deal of reading you are doing, and all the more so because you are doing that
in order that you may get the better of those books. (This is not
meant to be a joke, but praise.) I think it is high time for writers,
too, to stop suffering from Russophobia since our soldiers won the
war against the Russians. This has been my pet theme for some
time, but this is the first time I've bothered you with it. So listen to
me at least once." Then Soseki returns to the same point: "We
have got to be oxen. So often we try to be horses, but it's very
hard indeed to be thoroughly oxen. Shrewd as I am, I am afraid I
am as of now no better than a sort of cross between ox and horse.
Please don't be impatient; don't wrack your brains. March forward untiringly. The world knows how to bow to perseverance,
but seldom takes notice of momentary flares. Push right on to the
death. That alone matters. Don't seek out rivals and try to beat
them. Then, there will be no end to your rivals; they will keep
coming one after another and annoying us. Oxen do push on and
on, always aloof. You say what to push on? Well, we push the
man within, certainly not the artist."

Then, how well did these three writers heed Soseki's advice,
which a critic called "one of the most beautiful prose pieces in modern Japanese literary history"? [2] Kume and Kikuchi did turn out to
be oxen, but never pushed hard enough. With an easy, halfway
compromise between life and art, both soon settled down as successful popular writers. Akutagawa, on the other hand, turned out
to be a horse rather than an ox; this impatient Pegasus did indeed
soar, charging the literary firmament with his *frisson nouveau*, but
after a momentary flight plunged into destruction. Throughout his
brief but intensely tragic career he upheld Soseki's intellectual tradition, though he regretted his failure to live up to his beloved mentor's expectation. There were also two groups of writers determined to carry on Soseki's legacy. One was the neo-idealist group,
comprised mostly of young thinkers and critics who frequented
Soseki's Thursday gatherings. Upholding Soseki's moral individualism, they have managed to survive the intellectually sterile dark
age of Showa Japan. The other was the Shirakaba (White Birch)
group, of Mushakoji, Shiga, and other practicing artists, which
incorporated Soseki's legacy into their own brand of humanism.
Otherwise, Soseki has remained a solitary figure in modern Japa-

nese literary history, just as he was during his lifetime. Perhaps this was the price he had to pay as a true individual, as he himself pointed out. But his is still an exemplary case, which may serve as the source of inspiration for many Japanese artists yet to come.

III *Beyond Japanese Literature*

In one of his early letters, indeed the earliest now extant, of 1889, addressed to Masaoka Shiki, the future leader of the new *haiku* movement. Soseki wrote: "To live is the sole end of man." Soseki was then twenty-two years old, still unaware of the real question, how to live. Yet it was this zest for life that sustained his precarious health through his arduous career. Then, he chose English over Chinese literature, the unknown over the known world, and the future over the past. His growing conviction of it as a right choice is also evidenced in the two articles on Laotzu and Whitman, written in 1892 in his senior year at college. In the former, standing by his evolutionist position, Soseki applies formal logic to expose the basic inadequacy of Laotzu's philosophy. He is especially critical of Laotzu's failure to discuss the absolute in terms of the relative and dismisses him as a philosopher with only one eye. Soseki's naïve scienticism naturally rejects Laotzu's mystic state. In the latter, however, Soseki calls Whitman one of the most welcome events in recent years, praising the poet's democratic egalitarianism which stems from his spirit of independence. Soseki is particularly enthusiastic about the way Whitman relates his all-inclusive concept of love back to the transcendental soul. If Soseki rejected Laotzu for his negativism, he also accepted Whitman for his positivism—in relation to life. In seeing no possibility of compromise Soseki at the end of his formal education was undoubtedly an intellectual rebel, in the sense that he willingly deserted his own tradition for a strange god.

The significance of these two essays lies in the fact that they mark the initial pattern of dialectics out of which Soseki's existential history evolved, the dialectical pattern of negation and affirmation, philosophy and literature, and East and West; finally toward their reconciliation on the ground of life itself. And Soseki's personal pattern, significantly enough, represents that of Japan itself, in its history from the Meiji to the Showa period. Soseki was a child of modern Japan who lived in his person the life of his country. Starting as an intellectual rebel, Soseki launched into the world; he went abroad, and when he returned he was still an intellectual rebel but more matured after his two years' stay in London. Accordingly, his dialectical pattern underwent a salient change. Now out of the dilemma between his academic and his creative career, which was itself a variation of this original pattern, or more properly, inwardly out of that dilemma, Soseki said characteristically, "My brain is half-Western and half-Japanese." So Soseki said in an interview of 1907 shortly before he decided to accept the *Asahi* offer, just before he chose a creative over an academic career, thus becoming a professional novelist. What his statement suggests is twofold: First, that while in life Soseki was still Japanese, in literature he was now Western; and that if life is the substance of his being, it is literature that can give form to its substance which must have form for its own fulfillment; second, more largely, that Soseki was now standing at the midpoint of the dialectical balance between East and West. Yet the statement as a whole indicates the precariousness of his position, for in order to round out his circle of being Soseki must be whole Japanese and whole man, not just half-Japanese and half-Western. Only in this sense could he say, as he did later, that life is literature, and literature, life, or rather that literature exists for the sake of life, not for its own sake.

If "To live is the sole end of man" bespeaks Soseki's youthful and unconditional acceptance of existence, he also has to face an inevitable question of how to live. Soseki's nearly two-decades-long search pointed to art as the most satisfactory means of solving this question. His art was born out of the process of his ceaseless efforts to offer his kind of solution. As he came to realize, there were no simple, neatly cut, readymade answers to it, because life itself is the process of unfolding its changing face in all directions. With what he was born, with what he acquired, Soseki attempted to solve the problem by dedicating his life to art, a strange paradox indeed of life and art which devour each other only to create another, higher form. This inseparability of life and art in the process of their endless unfolding is what Soseki meant when he stated at the midpoint of his career: "Art begins and ends with self-expression." By creating his kind of art in order to participate in the mystery of life, Soseki virtually replied to Futabatei Shimei's pathetic question: "Is art worth devoting the whole of a man's life to?"

Then, how is life crystallized in Soseki's art? Stated differently, what is the over-all outlook of Soseki's art? In concluding our study of Soseki, it would seem well to take a backward glance at this problem. As a child of Meiji Japan, Soseki accepted this most exciting period of Japanese history as the basic material for his art. For interested readers all of his novels can provide a telling panorama of the era, an era of dramatic transition from the old to the new Japan. It was a historic period when Japan, once aroused from her two-century-long feudal isolation, had to confront the rapidly changing complexity of the modern world in the second half of the nineteenth century. At this period of drastic re-orientation in all directions and on all levels, the most urgent problems for Japan to solve were modernization and Westernization, although in her case they were one and the same problem. With regard to Westernization, Meiji Japan had to face much the same situation as nineteenth-century Russia; with respect to modernization, Japan had to experience something similar to what the West had already come through four centuries before with the disintegration of medieval feudalism. It was this twofold reorientation that made Meiji Japan so violent, so complex, and so dramatic a scene of human history.

It was a period of revolution, rather than evolution, singularly enough, without bloodshed. For this very reason the period was charged with suppressed violence, the violence that contains greater disaster than any open violence. Against this vibrant political, social, and cultural background, Soseki sets his world, never ceasing to explore the moral dilemma of individuals caught in the historic vortex: those individual men and women emancipated for the first time from the iron grip of their feudal tradition and society. All of Soseki's heroes are delighted by their discovery of self. But their exhilaration is short-lived, for at almost the same time they have to seek their soul's salvation, too. Astray somewhere between these two points, point of departure and point of destination, they find no easy solution in dealing with their newly discovered selves. They are driven to experience life's birth and death at once, with few intervals for fulfillment.

The so-called Soseki hero, an archetype of all his heroes, is "half-Western and half-Japanese," the term Soseki used in describing his own hybrid mentality. To dismiss them merely as the idle rich would be as superficial as to find in James's cultural pilgrims nothing but leisurely esthetes, for theirs is a search for identity. Soseki's characters belong to a class of intellectual elite. By virtue of their intelligence and sensitivity they are painfully aware of the cultural reality of Japan, which Soseki designated as a tragedy with no hope of solution. In the midst of the masses won over by Western-ization and modernization, these characters only find themselves in isolation. The price they have to pay for their being cultural élite is their own suffering. Totally incapacitated by the insensi-tive world, they are unable to accept any ready compromise, seek-ing something more final and permanent for their life's goal. Equally relentless is Soseki's determination to press their suffering as far as they are capable—now to suicide, now to virtual insanity, and now to faith. What Soseki seeks in this is a new ethos which allows no compromise, and therefore is acceptable to them, how-ever violently it may vary from the norm of society.

But their new ethos, if it should come about at all, must be carved out of their immediate concrete situation. For this Soseki chooses their domestic world where they cannot be left alone in relation to their wives, brothers, sisters, and parents, thus helping to focus this conflict between a new and an old ethos, sharper than in the outside world. The domestic scene is thus charged with a sense of impasse, especially when Soseki brings new men and new women together face to face. In re-examining their rela-tionship, Soseki takes nothing for granted; because these new men and women must live as husband and wife, not as mere lovers, their world more often turns into a battleground than into a haven of harmony. Their selves, now newly awakened, only know their demands, not yet their obligations. On this ground of never yielding egos, Soseki attempts to find a truce, not temporary but permanent.

If Soseki the moralist undertakes such a merciless diagnosis of this domestic tension as a symptom of his heroes' malady, it is also the same Soseki who labors to seek some sort of satisfactory solu-tion, so that their tension may lead those involved to a higher spiritual plane. And Soseki's solution seems to lie in his philosophy of *sokuten kyoshi*, or "conform to heaven and forsake self." It is a religion rather than a philosophy in a more technical sense be-cause it is meant to be a workable means of salvation. At least in the Orient they are one and the same, a philosophical religion or a religious philosophy, or simply a way of life. Soseki suggests this as the only permanent solution to those suffering egoists, those sufferers of excessive egotism—at least in their particular world in which there is no god they can turn to for their souls' release. Yet it is no invention of Soseki; it is a solution Soseki proposed by returning to his own tradition; it is a solution characteristically Oriental, because Soseki now elevates Western individualism or its positive ego-assertion to Eastern individualism or its positive ego-negation. The suffering of Soseki heroes is by nature the suffering of excessive ego consciousness, the burden of self-consciousness. The best antidote to their modern malady is the traditional Oriental approach—its positive, not negative, ego-negation.[3]

It is thus on this way of *sokuten kyoshi* that Soseki finally founded a new ethos acceptable to his heroes. It has no real conflict with Soseki's stress on the primacy of moral individualism, since its moral basis is also the only human road to this state of salvation through a larger and universal self. Nor does it conflict with the fundamental spirit of all religions, since they all attempt to provide for a workable solution by insisting that man forsake his small shell of existence and adhere to something incomparably larger, in fact, the largest, namely God. It is something corresponding to what Christian mystics term one's total surrender to God. Whether personalistic or not, religion is perhaps the only permanent means by which man, while remaining human, can solve his existential problems on most satisfactory terms. All great founders of religions themselves returned to the human world to release their fellow men from the sufferings that stem from existence itself, and they also urged their disciples and lay followers not to forsake their earthly life, but to return to life, because salvation exists for the sake of life, not vice versa.

It has often been asked if Soseki personally attained this state. It is the kind of question that defies any clear-cut answer. In his letters written less than a month before his death Soseki wrote to a young Zen Buddhist: "As for me, I mean to go on my search for the way, in my own manner as far as I am capable. I realize there are so many things I'm not satisfied with. Every thing I do is false. I am ashamed." In another letter, written the following day: "Strange as it may sound, I am a fool who, at the age of fifty, has for the first time realized the need to seek the way." These, together with his own statement about *sokuten kyoshi*, may still fail to offer any satisfactory answer. But what is certain is that Soseki does not mince his words, is completely serious about the subject, that he feels the necessity of it, and even perceives its possibility. The point is that as he neared the end of his career he so often returned to this problem, suggesting that in this particular direction lay the possibility of salvation. Although what was to be in that unwritten portion of *Light and Darkness* is far from clear, this incompleteness, which to many critics is tantamount to Soseki's failure, does not detract from Soseki's stature as a moralist.

Rather, in diagnosing the tragic situation of modern Japanese intelligentsia, seeking in his ancient tradition the inspiration for an acceptable ethos, and thereby suggesting the way it comes out of isolation into a wide world, Soseki's art is also an art of hope, affirming the value of life, which tends to be lost in the frantic struggle between the old and the new. Indeed, it applies not only to Japanese intelligentsia at that particular period of history; it also speaks to modern intelligentsia, and finally to man generally who faces the same problem wherever he is. That is, Soseki is a writer of modern Japan; and by becoming a national writer in the fullest sense, he became a universal artist. He has a right to a place in the world's literature. It is Soseki who said near the end of his career: "What is ethical is artistic; what is truly artistic is always ethical." And this, Soseki proved by his own art.

Notes and References

The basic text for this study is the Iwanami edition of 1956–59, *Soseki Zenshu* (*The Complete Works of Soseki*), 34 vols., edited by Komiya Toyotaka. The editor's commentaries provided with each volume represent what we might call the "standard" opinion of the subject. The same editor's *Soseki no Geijutsu* (Tokyo, 1942) is a collection of his commentaries to the earlier 18-volume edition. Since all my references to the primary sources can easily be identified, the following notes are limited to the secondary materials.

Chapter One

For my discussion of Meiji literature here and elsewhere, I owe much to Homma Hisao, *Meiji Bungakushi*, 3 vols. (Tokyo, 1935–43); Ito Sei, *Kindai Nihon no Bungakushi* (Tokyo, 1958); Donald Keene, *Japanese Literature* (New York, 1955); John W. Morrison, *Modern Japanese Fiction* (Salt Lake City, 1955); and Okazaki Yoshie, *Japanese Literature in the Meiji Era*, tr. V. H. Viglielmo (Tokyo, 1955). And for Soseki's life, I am indebted to Ara Masato, *Hyoden: Natsume Soseki* (Tokyo, 1960); Komiya Toyotaka, *Natsume Soseki*, 3 vols. (Tokyo, 1953); Morita Sohei, *Natsume Soseki* (Tokyo, 1943) and *Zoku Natsume Soseki* (Tokyo, 1944); and Shiotani San, *Natsume Soseki Jiten* (Tokyo, 1956).

Chapter Two

1. Saito Takeshi, "English Literature in Japan: A Sketch," Nitobe Inazo *et al.*, *Western Influences in Modern Japan* (Chicago, 1931), p. 192.

2. Masamune Hakucho, *Sakkaro* I (Tokyo, 1957), p. 185.

3. Ara, p. 235.

4. Eto Jun, *Natsume Soseki* (Tokyo, 1960), pp. 58–59. For another negative view, see Yoshida Kenichi, *Tozai Bungakuron* (Tokyo, 1955), pp. 92–121.

5. As a stylistic motto *shaseibun* (sketch writing) was upheld by Masaoka Shiki as an effective means of revitalizing the tradition-ridden *haiku* and *waka*. Soseki, shifting emphasis to the author's men-

tal pose, defines it as "the attitude of an adult looking at a child," a sort of calm, sympathetic detachment toward the object. Although such an attitude is peculiar to the *haiku* tradition, Soseki discovers something of it in works by Austen, Gaskell, Dickens, Fielding, and Cervantes.

Chapter Three

1. Ara, pp. 126, 301–5.

Chapter Four

1. Shiotani, pp. 223–24.

2. It was precisely on this ground that a couple of years before, in *On Literature*, Soseki expressed some reservations about Charlotte Brontë's treatment of the love between Rochester and Jane Eyre, despite his admiration for the author's artistic power.

3. Ara, p. 133.

4. See Arai Kan's commentary on *The Gate* in *Meiji Taisho Bungaku Kenkyu*, No. 6 (November 1951), p. 86.

5. Cf. Masamune: "The scene describing his visit to a Zen temple in Kamakura is rather farcical" (p. 194). Sako Junichiro suggests that in describing the climax of this visit, especially Sosuke at the temple gate, Soseki may have had in mind the well-known passage in Matthew: "Ask, and it shall be given you; seek, and ye shall find; knock, and it shall be opened unto you: For every one that asketh receiveth; and he that seeketh findeth; and to him that knocketh it shall be opened" (*Kindai Nihon Bungako no Higeki* [Tokyo, 1957], pp. 41–42).

6. Arai, *Meiji Taisho Bungaku Kenkyu*, p. 87.

7. Ito Sei's comment on "Ten Nights' Dreams" as quoted in Ara, p. 303.

Chapter Five

1. Many critics agree with Komiya that the Shuzenji crisis marks a significant turning point in Soseki's career (*Soseki no Geijutsu*, pp. 329–43). But some dismiss this view as merely sentimental. Cf. Iyenaga Saburo: "We should not overstress the significance of the Shuzenji crisis, especially Soseki's momentary ecstasy, in his spiritual development" (*Nihon Shisoshi ni okeru Shukyoteki Shizenkan no Tenkai* [Tokyo, 1937], pp. 195–98). See Morita, *Zoku Natsume Soseki*, pp. 761–63, and Eto, pp. 115–24.

2. Matsumoto here is, obviously, referring to Soseki's own lecture of 1911, "The Enlightenment of Modern Japan."

3. Masamune, p. 196.

4. For the personal and literary significance of Soseki's interest in the detective, see Ara, pp. 306–19.

5. As regards the title of this novel opinion is still divided among Soseki students. Ordinarily if pronounced *kojin* as Soseki himself pronounced it, it would mean a wayfarer, a messenger, or a passer-by. If pronounced *gyojin*, it would, in keeping with Liehtzu, mean the living in contrast to *kijin*, the dead. No matter which way it is read, the title suggests the loneliness of man in his life journey.

6. For Morita's view that *Kojin* best represents Soseki's art, see *Zoku Natsume Soseki*, pp. 828–29. For a contrary view, that as a novel it is by no means well written, see Eto, p. 132. Cf. Edwin McClellan: "*Kōjin* may not be the most perfectly constructed of Soseki's novels. It is, nevertheless, a work of great significance, for it contains the most fully articulated statement of Soseki's main theme, man's isolation" ("An Introduction to Sōseki," *Harvard Journal of Asiatic Studies*, XXII [1959], 208).

7. Ara, p. 151.

8. In *Until After* Matsumoto, calling his nephew Ichizo's introversion the root of his tragedy, suggests that he seek whatever may absorb his mind. In *Kojin*, H is also delighted by Ichiro's self-forgetfulness while he is watching tiny crabs swarming around the roots of pampas grass. In a fragment of 1916 Soseki wrote: "In Tolstoy's *Anna Karenina* there is a scene in which Levin becomes unconscious of himself as he goes on mowing; as if his scythe assumed its own life, it swings of itself." Soseki here, apparently, refers to chapters iv and v, Part III. Especially illuminating is the following passage:

The longer Levin mowed, the oftener he felt the moments of unconsciousness in which it seemed not his hands that swung the scythe, but the scythe mowing of itself, a body full of life and consciousness of its own, and as though by magic, without thinking of it, the work turned out regular and well-finished of itself. These were the most blissful moments (Constance Garnett's translation).

One of Soseki's marginal notes in English on the Bible also reads: " 'Forget thyself' is the best thing we can attain in this world. Self-consciousness always destroys the charm of every object thought worth admiration."

9. While *Kojin* was appearing in the *Asahi,* a certain minister wrote to Soseki that he must be like Ichiro, and urged him to read the Bible. Soseki's reaction is not difficult to guess.

10. The Japanese word *kokoro,* which means "mind," "heart," etc., is really untranslatable; so are the other Japanese words, *sensei,* which means "teacher" or "master"; and *ojosan,* which means "miss," "young lady," or "honorable daughter."

11. V. H. Viglielmo believes that the *sensei*'s penitence is far from being genuine ("The Later Natsume Sōseki: His Art and Thought," unpublished Harvard thesis [1955], pp. 120–21).

Chapter Six

1. Even earlier, in his letter of November 1913, Soseki wrote: "On the spur of the moment I did say twice that I'd choose death over life, and when I said that, I wasn't either lying or joking. I really want all of you to shout *Banzai!* before my coffin when I die. Although I happen to believe that consciousness is all life has, I do not believe that that consciousness is the whole of my existence. I think I still exist even after death. I even believe that only in death can I return to my true and natural self."

2. Komiya, *Soseki no Geijutsu*, p. 267.

3. Masamune considers *Loitering* the most important of Soseki's novels in that it does serve as a commentary on the entire body of his works (p. 206).

4. Viglielmo, for instance, excludes both *Loitering* and *Light and Darkness* from his discussion of the later Soseki.

5. Kenzo's final comment singularly echoes Soseki's "still at work" as he refers to his own ailment. This remark by Kenzo should not be lumped together with Sosuke's fatalism, as suggested by his remark: "Um—but winter will soon be back."

6. Viglielmo, p. 6.

7. Ara, p. 181.

8. Shiotani, pp. 247–50.

9. Concerning this question of *sokuten kyoshi*, Matsuoka Yuzuru reports the conversation between Soseki and his disciples:

"Sir, what do you think of Tertullianus' famous dictum: 'I believe it because it is irrational'?"

"It is an interesting statement, but he didn't have to resort to such a twisted paradox as 'because it is irrational,' I think. He could have come out in a straightforward manner—like calling willows green and flowers red, that is, taking things as they are. This seems to be what we call belief. Suppose my daughter comes in to say good night, and I happen to notice she has lost one of her eyes—a matter of great alarm and concern to any parents since she is of marriageable age. They are bound to make a hell of a fuss about it. But now I think I could say 'Ah, so,' and take it quite calmly."

This was enough to shock us all. We said in unison.

"Sir, that would be too cruel. Don't you think?"

"Truths, you know, are invariably cruel things," Soseki said even more calmly and continued. "With sufficient discipline man could manage to attain this state, but our physical laws hinder the total realization of such spiritual enlightenment. While mentally we are confident we have overcome death, we may still hedge when we really face it. That's because of our human instinct."

"Then, would you say enlightenment is to overcome this instinct?" asked someone.

"No, I don't think so. Rather, it means to follow it and thereby learn to control it as we please. That's where we need discipline. Superficially this may seem to be an escapist attitude, but actually it is, I dare say, the highest possible attitude one can take in regard to life" (Quoted in Sako, pp. 110–12).

10. Masamune, pp. 201–2.

11. Ara, pp. 192–94; Masamune, p. 202.

12. One of Soseki's marginal comments in English on G. H. Lewes's *The Principles of Success in Literature* reads: "The influence of culture is only superficial. Test those who boast it, and you will find it only skin-deep. Down upon them all! What is noble in man is best shown in his nudity, and his powerfulness in nakedness. We are animals clad in men's skins which [are] thick enough to deceive ourselves and but thin enough to be mangled with the first out-burst of our inner spirits which are animality itself."

13. See Komiya's commentary on the novel, *Zenshu*, XV, 252.

14. Eto, pp. 186–87.

Chapter Seven

1. In his undergraduate essay, "Proposed Improvements on High School Education" (1892), Soseki also contends that education should be designed for the cultivation of individual character, not for the cause of a nation.

2. Nakamura Shinichiro as quoted in Eto, p. 205. Eto also notes the significance of Soseki's relationship with the younger generation (pp. 202–7).

3. For a study of this subject, see Sakamoto Hiroshi, "On *sokuten kyoshi*," *Meiji Taisho Bungaku Kenkyu*, No. 7 (June 1952), pp. 41–48. While most Soseki students take this problem seriously enough, Eto dismisses it as sheer myth (pp. 195–202). Rather novel in this regard is Viglielmo's contention that Soseki's final philosophy of *sokuten kyoshi* as a monument to his spiritual quest contains both Buddhist and Christian ideals (p. 27). Whatever it is, one thing is certain: that to Soseki *sokuten kyoshi* is an ideal at once artistic and religious, as suggested in his other motto, *wagashi shizen* (my model is nature). For a view of Soseki as "a great thinker"—in the tradition of Zen—see Iyenaga's chapter, "Natsume Soseki as a Thinker, and His Historical Significance" (pp. 149–221).

Selected Bibliography

PRIMARY SOURCES

1. In Japanese

The following list comprises only Soseki's major writings. The dates given here are those of their first book-form publication.

Wagahai wa Neko de Aru (*I Am a Cat*). 3 vols. Tokyo: Okura Shoten, 1905–7.

Yokyoshu (*Seven Stories*). Tokyo: Okura Shoten, 1906. A collection of seven pieces: "The Tower of London," "The Carlyle Museum," "The Phantom Shield," "The False Sound of the Lute," "One Night," "The Song of Evanescence," and "The Legacy of Love."

Uzurakago (*Three Stories*). Tokyo: Shunyodo, 1907. A collection of three stories: "Botchan," "The Grass Pillow," and "The 'Storm Day.' "

Bungakuron (*On Literature*). Tokyo: Okura Shoten, 1907.

Gubijinso (*The Poppy*). Tokyo: Shunyodo, 1908.

Kusa Awase. Tokyo: Shunyodo, 1908. A collection of "The Wintry Blast" and "Kofu" ("The Miner").

Bungaku Hyoron (*Eighteenth-Century English Literature*). Tokyo: Shunyodo, 1909.

Sanshiro. Tokyo: Shunyodo, 1909.

Sorekara (*And Then*). Tokyo: Shunyodo, 1910.

Shihen. Tokyo: Shunyodo, 1910. A collection of four pieces: "The Rice Bird," "Ten Nights' Dreams," "Spring Miscellanies," and "A Passage through Manchuria and Korea."

Mon (*The Gate*). Tokyo: Shunyodo, 1911.

Kirinukicho Yori. Tokyo: Shunyodo, 1911. This collection includes "Random Recollections."

Higan Sugi Made (*Until After the Spring Equinox*). Tokyo: Shunyodo, 1912.

Shakai to Jibun (*Society and I*). Tokyo: Jitsugyo no Nihonsha, 1913. A collection of six lectures: "Vocation and Avocation," "The Enlightenment of Modern Japan," "Substance and Form," "Literature and Morality," "The Novelist's Attitude," and "The Philosophical Basis of Literary Art."

Kojin. Tokyo: Okura Shoten, 1914.

Kokoro. Tokyo: Iwanami Shoten, 1914.

Garasudo no Naka (Within the Sash-Door). Tokyo: Iwanami Shoten, 1915.

Michikusa (Loitering). Tokyo: Iwanami Shoten, 1915.

Meian (Light and Darkness). Tokyo: Iwanami Shoten, 1917.

2. In Translation

Listed below are some of Soseki's prose writings available in European languages. For further information, the reader should consult Japan P.E.N. Club's *Japanese Literature in European Languages: A Bibliography.*

ANDO, KANICHI. *I Am a Cat.* Tokyo: Hattori Shoten, 1906.

GRIGORIEVA, M. P. *Barchuk.* Dairen: South Manchuria Railway Co., 1943. (Translation of "Botchan.")

HATA, SANKICHI, and SHIRAI, DOFU. *Ten Nights' Dreams and Our Cat's Grave.* Tokyo: Seito Shorin, 1934.

HORIGUCHI, DAIGAKU, and BONNEAU, GEORGES. *Kokoro: le pauvre cœur des hommes.* Paris: Inst. International de Coóperation Intellectuelle, 1939.

KARLINA, R. *Mal'chugan: povest'.* Moskva: Gos-lit-izdat, 1956. (Translation of "Botchan.")

KONRAD, N. I. *Serdtse: Roman.* Leningrad: Gos-lit-izdat, 1935.

MARTINIE, R. *La Porte.* Paris: Les Editions Rieder, 1927.

MATSUHARA, IWAO, and IGLEHART, E. T. *Within My Glass Doors.* Tokyo: Shinseido, 1928.

McCLELLAN, EDWIN. *Kokoro.* Chicago: Henry Regnery, 1957.

MORI, YASOTARO. *Botchan: Master Darling.* Tokyo: Seibundo, 1918.

OGATA, NAOTA. *Botchan.* Tokyo: Maruzen, 1923.

SASAKI, UMEJI. *Kusamakura and Buncho.* Tokyo: Iwanami Shoten, 1927. (Translation of "The Grass Pillow" and "The Rice Bird.")

SATO, INEKO. *Kokoro.* Tokyo: Kenkyusha, 1941.

SPANN, ALEXANDER. *Botchan: Ein Reiner Tor.* Osaka: Kyodo Shuppansha, 1925.

TURNEY, ALAN. *Three-Cornered World.* London: Owen, 1965. (Translation of "The Grass Pillow").

YU, BEONGCHEON. *The Wayfarer.* Detroit: Wayne State University Press, 1967. (Translation of *Kojin*).

SECONDARY SOURCES

To attempt a comprehensive bibliography of Soseki studies would in itself be a formidable task; moreover, it would be meaningless to the general reader not familiar with Japanese. Listed below are only those materials which I have found of special help in preparing the present study.

ARA, MASATO. *Hyoden: Natsume Soseki.* Tokyo: Jitsugyo no Nihonsha, 1960. A biographical and critical study of Soseki.

ETO, JUN. *Natsume Soseki.* "Million Books Series." Tokyo: Kodansha, 1960. A provocative critical assessment of Soseki's art.

————. "Natsume Sōseki: A Japanese Meiji Intellectual," *The American Scholar,* XXXIV, 4 (Autumn 1965), 603–19.

HOMMA, HISAO. *Meiji Bungakushi.* 3 vols. Tokyo: Tokyodo, 1935–43. A historical survey of Meiji literature.

ITO, SEI. *Kindai Nihon no Bungakushi.* Tokyo: Kobunsha, 1958. A brief but useful survey of modern Japanese literature.

IYENAGA, SABURO. *Nihon Shisoshi ni okeru Shukyoteki Shizenkan no Tenkai.* Tokyo: Sogensha, 1937. A collection of essays tracing the development of the religious view of nature in Japanese thought. The last chapter discusses the significance of Soseki's art and thought in this particular context.

KEENE, DONALD. *Japanese Literature: An Introduction for Western Readers.* New York: Grove Press, 1955. A critical introduction to Japanese literature, with concentration on poetry, drama, novel, and the significance of Western influence.

KOMIYA, TOYOTAKA. *Natsume Soseki.* 3 vols. Tokyo: Iwanami Shoten, 1953. A definitive biography of Soseki.

————. *Soseki no Geijutsu.* Tokyo: Iwanami Shoten, 1942. A collection of essays on all phases of Soseki's art, originally written for his 18-volume edition of Soseki.

————. *Soseki Torahiko Miekichi.* Tokyo: Kadokawa, 1959. A collection of essays on Soseki and his circle.

MASAMUNE, HAKUCHO. *Sakkaron I.* Tokyo, Shinchosha, 1957. A collection of critical essays on important writers of the Meiji period.

MATSUOKA, YUZURU. *Soseki: Hito to Sono Bungaku.* Tokyo, Chobunkaku, 1944. A critical biography.

McCLELLAN, EDWIN, "An Introduction to Sōseki," *Harvard Journal of Asiatic Studies,* XX (1959), 150–208. A balanced study of Soseki, exclusive of his last two works.

Meiji Taisho Bungaku Kenkyu. No. 6 (November 1951). This special Soseki issue contains discussions of many aspects of Soseki's art, with critical summaries of his major novels.

————. No. 7 (June 1952). This second Soseki issue deals with various Soseki problems.

MORITA, SOHEI. *Natsume Soseki.* Tokyo: Kocho Shorin, 1943. A critical biography with a highly personal approach.

————. *Zoku Natsume Soseki.* Tokyo: Yotokusha, 1944. A sequel to the above.

MORRISON, JOHN W. *Modern Japanese Fiction.* Salt Lake City: University of Utah Press, 1955. A general survey of the subject.

NATSUME, KYOKO. In collaboration with Matsuoka, Yuzuru. *Soseki no Omoide.* 2 vols. Tokyo: Kadokawa, 1960. Reminiscences of Soseki by his wife shedding new light on his personality.

NATSUME, SHINROKU. *Chichi Natsume Soseki.* Tokyo: Bungeishunjusha, 1956. An intimate portrait of Soseki by his second son.

NITOBE, INAZO *et al. Western Influences in Modern Japan.* Chicago: University of Chicago Press, 1931. A collection of essays assessing the significance of Western influence on modern Japanese culture.

OKAZAKI, YOSHIE. *Japanese Literature in the Meiji Era.* Translated and Adapted by V. H. Viglielmo. Tokyo: Obunsha, 1955. A comprehensive survey of Meiji literature.

REISCHAUER, EDWIN O. *Japan, Past and Present.* New York: A. A. Knopf, 1946. A lucid account of Japanese history.

SAKO, JUNICHIRO. *Kindai Nihon Bungaku no Higeki.* Tokyo: Gendai Bungeisha, 1957. A critical discussion of Natsume Soseki, Akutagawa Ryunosuke, and Arishima Takeo in the light of Japanese Christianity.

SANSOM, GEORGE. *The Western World and Japan.* Tokyo: Knopf, 1950.

SHIOTANI, SAN. *Natsume Soseki Jiten.* Tokyo: Sogensha, 1956. A very useful Soseki handbook.

VIGLIEMO, VALDO H. "The Later Natsume Sōseki: His Art and Thought." Unpublished Harvard dissertation (1955). A critical study of Soseki's later period.

YOSHIDA, KENICHI. *Tozai Bungakuron.* "One Hour Library." Tokyo: Shinchosha, 1955. An attempt to view modern Japanese literature in East-West perspective.

Index

Abe, Jiro, 53, 91
Abe, Nozei, 53, 91
Addison, Joseph, 35
Akutagawa, Ryunosuke, 171–72
Andreyev, L. N., 100
Aoyama, Seika, 20
Ara, Masato, 38
Aristotle, 29
Arnold, Matthew, 29
Asahi, newspaper, 78, 89, 90–91, 99, 104, 107, 128, 135, 139, 146, 164, 174
Augustine, St., 141
Austen, Jane, 151, 161, 180

Bergson, Henri, 144
Brontë, Charlotte, 180
Brooke, Stophord, 30
Buckle, Henry Thomas, 29
Buddhism, 24, 71, 94–95, 98, 122–23, 177
Bulwer-Lytton, Edward George, 18

Cervantes, Miguel de, 121, 180
Chao Chou, 146
Cowper, William, 48
Craig, W. J., 25–26

Dante, Alighieri, 120, 143
Defoe, Daniel, 35, 36–38
De Quincy, Thomas, 141
Dickens, Charles, 180
Disraeli, Benjamin, 18
Dostoevsky, Feodor, 20, 102, 120, 150–51, 158, 162

Eliot, T. S., 157

Elizabethan University Wits, the, 18–19
Eto, Jun, 38, 161
Eucken, Rudolf Christoph, 100, 105

Fielding, Henry, 180
Flaubert, Gustave, 20, 21
Fukuzawa, Yukichi, 18
Futabatei, Shimei, 19, 59, 174

Gaskell, Elizabeth, 180
Goethe, J. W. von, 20, 50, 141
Gogol, Nikolai, 158
Gorki, Maxim, 100

Hartmann, Karl Robert Eduard von, 20
Hawthorne, Nathaniel, 130
Hearn, Lafcadio, 29
Hoffmann, Ernst Theodor Wilhelm, 42
Hototogisu, magazine, 40, 72
Hugo, Victor, 18

Ibsen, Henrik, 52, 56, 100, 118
Ihara, Saikaku, 18, 20, 169
Ikebe, Sanzan, 107
Irving, Washington, 44
Iyenaga, Saburo, 180, 183
Izumi, Kyoka, 55

James, Henry, 151
Joyce, James, 74

Kenyusha school, the, 20
Kikuchi, Kan, 171–72
Komiya, Toyotaka, 53, 91, 97, 161

Kume, Masao, 171–72
Kunikida, Doppo, 20

Laotzu, 23, 173
Lawrence, D. H., 74
Lewes, G. H., 183
Li Po, 48
Liehtzu, 180
Lover, Samuel, 48

Malory, Sir Thomas, 45
Masamune, Hakucho, 20, 38, 112, 156–57, 180, 183
Masaoka, Shiki, 23, 24, 40, 173, 179
Matsune, Toyojo, 53
Matsuoka, Yuzuru, 182
Maupassant, Guy de, 20, 21
McClellan, Edwin, 181
Meiji, Emperor, 15–16, 124, 125, 126, 131–33, 165, 166
Meredith, George, 42, 63, 120, 151
Merejkowski, D. S., 74
Mill, J. S., 18
Mori, Arinori, 17
Mori, Ogai, 20
Morita, Sohei, 53, 91, 97, 107, 181
Murasaki, Lady, 169
Murdoch, James, 103
Mushakoji, Saneatsu, 91, 172

Nakae, Chomin, 18
Nakamura, Keiu, 18
Natsume, Soseki: *Asahi* literary columns, 90–91, 107, 171; *Asahi* offer, 57–59, 60, 64–65; Doctor of Letters degree, 103, 164; interest in dreams, 69–71; interest in haiku, 23, 24, 42–43, 45, 56, 100, 179–80; interest in the detective, 114, 115; philosophy of *jiko-hon-i*, 164, 167, 170; philosophy of *sokuten kyoshi*, 99, 123, 155–56, 176–78, 182–83; Shuzenji crisis, 99, 150, 163, 180; social consciousness, 43, 51–52, 75–76, 81–83, 84–85, 88–90, 103–4, 105, 133–34, 164–71; *Taiyo* popularity poll, 79, 103, 164; Thursday gatherings, 53, 147, 172; traits of heroes and heroines, 112–13, 118–19, 145–46, 152–54, 175–77; treatment of love, 153; use of the journey motif, 49–51, 109, 116, 159–60; use of the past, 97–98, 111–12, 142–45, 159–60; view of contemporary trends, 45, 46, 51, 60, 68–69, 104, 105; view of death, 137–38, 182; view of literature in East-West perspective, 29–34, 38, 48, 51, 100–1; view of love literature, 86–87, 180; view of Meiji literature, 55, 64, 168–70
WRITINGS OF:
And Then, 80–88, 91–92, 96, 98, 112, 113, 116, 128, 143, 145, 153, 158, 165
"Education and Literature," 103, 104, 107, 133
Eighteenth-Century English Literature, 29, 35–38
"The Enlightenment of Modern Japan," 104, 106, 107, 120, 121, 122, 165, 180
"An Evening Arrival in Kyoto," 78
The Gate, 91–98, 99, 112, 113, 123, 128, 145, 153, 158, 180
"The General Concept of Literature," 29–30
I Am a Cat, 39–44, 45, 46, 47, 48, 51, 52, 53, 54, 60, 140, 145, 152, 165
"Imitation and Independence," 134, 169
Kojin, 114–23, 124, 146, 152, 154, 165, 181
Kokoro, 123–34, 135, 145, 146, 153, 165, 181
Light and Darkness, 141, 146–62, 163, 178, 183
"Literature and Morality," 104–5, 107, 133
Loitering, 53–54, 138, 139–46, 150, 151, 152, 153, 154, 158, 183
The Miner, 64–69, 71, 72, 73, 74, 78, 89
"My Bicycle Diary," 39
"My Individualism," 135, 166–67

"New Year's Thoughts," 146, 167
"The Novelist's Attitude," 68–69, 72
"Official Exhibit and Art," 164
On Literature, 29, 31–34, 38, 39, 48, 60
"On the Ghost in *Macbeth,*" 38
A Passage through Manchuria and Korea, 88–90
"The Philosophical Basis of Literary Art," 59–60
The Poppy, 60–64, 69, 71, 72, 73, 74, 76–77, 78, 98, 112, 152, 155, 156, 157, 161
"Proposed Improvements on High School Education," 183
Random Recollections, 99–102, 135, 136, 137
"The Rice Bird," 72, 78
Sanshiro, 72–78, 80, 82–84, 88, 98, 113, 145, 152, 165
Seven Stories, 39, 42, 44–46, 69 ("The Carlyle Museum," 44; "The False Sound of the Lute," 44, 45; "The Legacy of Love," 44, 45; "One Night," 44, 45, 46, 48; "The Phantom Shield," 44–45, 48; "The Song of Evanescence," 44–45, 48; "The Tower of London," 44, 48, 53, 140)
Society and I, 165
Spring Miscellanies, 78–79, 135
"Substance and Form," 104, 105–6
"Ten Nights' Dreams," 69–71, 72, 78
Three Stories, 39, 46–52 ("Botchan," 46–48; "The Grass Pillow," 46, 48, 49–51, 56, 162; "The 'Storm Day,'" 46, 51, 52)
Until After the Spring Equinox, 107–14, 116, 117, 120, 122, 145, 150, 152, 156, 181
"Vocation and Avocation," 104, 105, 107
"The Wintry Blast," 51–52
Within the Sash-Door, 98, 135–39, 141

Nietzsche, Friedrich Wilhelm, 97, 120, 131, 162
Nogami, Toyoichiro, 53
Nogi, Maresuke, 126, 131–33

Ozaki, Koyo, 20

Perry, Commodore, Matthew C., 15
Pope, Alexander, 35–36, 42

Ribot, Théodule Armand, 32
Rousseau, J. J., 18, 122, 141
Russo-Japanese War, the, 17, 56–57, 73, 89, 165, 169, 170, 172
Ryudokai, the, 53

Saito, Takeshi, 38
Sakamoto, Setsucho, 53
Sako, Junichiro, 180
Schiller, Friedrich von, 20
Scott, Sir Walter, 18
Shakespeare, William, 50, 120, 121, 169
Shaw, G. B., 100
Shiga, Naoya, 172
Shimamura, Hogetsu, 20
Shimazaki, Toson, 20–21, 55
Shin Shosetsu, magazine, 170
Shirakaba group, the, 172
Smile, Samuel, 18
Steele, Sir Richard, 35
Sterne, Laurence, 24, 42
Stevenson, R. L., 37, 109
Strindberg, August, 119
Sudermann, Hermann, 74, 87–88
Suzuki, Miekichi, 53
Swift, Jonathan, 35, 36, 42

Takahama, Kyoshi, 40, 51
Takizawa, Bakin, 18, 169
T'ao Yüan-ming, 50
Tayama, Katai, 20, 21
Teikoku Bungaku, magazine, 46
Terada, Torahiko, 53
Tertullianus, Quintus Septimius Florens, 182
Thackeray, William Makepeace, 151
Tokuda, Shusei, 20
Tolstoy, Leo, 20, 29, 120, 181

Treitschke, Heinrich von, 167–68
Tsubouchi, Shoyo, 19, 20, 59
Tu Fu, 48
Turgenev, Ivan, 20, 77, 120

Viglielmo, V. H., 147, 182

Wang Wei, 50

Waseda Bungaku, magazine, 20
Whitman, Walt, 23, 173
World War I, 135, 167–68

Yamada, Bimyo, 19–20
Yomiuri, newspaper, 57, 90

Zola, Emile, 20, 21